MW00423621

REVELATION UNVEILED

Colombia para Cristo video introduction

Watch the *La Montaña* trailer, a film based on a true Stendal event

REVELATION UNVEILED

Understanding the Heart of Jesus In the Imminent Day of the Lord

Russell M. Stendal

Visit Russell's website: www.cpcsociety.ca

Revelation Unveiled – Russell M. Stendal

First edition published 2015

Cover Design: Amber Burger

Cover Photography: Angela Luchianiuc/Shutterstock

Editors: Part I: Sheila Wilkinson, Ruth Zetek. Part II: Bronwen Jorel, Heather Thomas

Printed in the United States of America

By Aneko Press – *Our Readers Matter*™

www.anekopress.com

Aneko Press, Life Sentence Publishing, and our logos are trademarks of

Life Sentence Publishing, Inc.
203 E. Birch Street
P.O. Box 652
Abbotsford, WI 54405

RELIGION / Biblical Studies / Prophecy

Paperback ISBN: 978-1-62245-289-7

Ebook ISBN: 978-1-62245-290-3

10 9 8 7 6 5 4 3 2

Available where books are sold.

Share this book on Facebook:

Contents

Part I

Understanding the Heart of Jesus In the Imminent Day of the Lord

Introduction to Part I

I began reading the Bible at a very early age because of an incident with a nursery story. My mother had decided to read *The Three Little Pigs* to me when I was a toddler. She thought, of course, that I would enjoy the cute little pigs. But being a dog lover, I felt sorry for the wolf. The last picture in the book haunted me. The wolf had gone down the chimney and landed in the pot of boiling water. Only the nose and eyes could be seen. For the next several days I quit talking and sat in a corner and stuttered, "Poor wolf! Poor wolf!"

After this, my mother only read Bible stories to me. I would make her read as many chapters as possible each night from *Hurlbut's Story of the Bible*. As soon as I learned to read, I was given a King James Bible, which I read from cover to cover several times each year. One of my favorite parts was Revelation, but I had to intensely study the rest of the Bible in order for it to make sense.

When I was about three, I would pretend to be a circuit-riding preacher and ride my rocking horse from town to town. I would give a message at each place, so the people could repent and believe the gospel and be saved. I did not want anyone to end up like that poor wolf!

At age four, I prayed that God would call my parents to be missionaries so I would not have to wait until I grew up to be one. By the time I was eight, our family was on the mission field. We arrived in Colombia on January 3, 1964.

My eighth grade school teacher at the missionary base in Colombia where I was raised was devoted to the study of Bible prophecy. Clifford Cartee was a humble, laid-back, southern gentleman who had been a US Army chaplain in World War II with the 17th Airborne Division. He retired with the rank of colonel and went to the mission field. Later, I found out that he had won a Silver Star on the battlefield for outstanding gallantry and intrepidity (very rare for a chaplain who did not even carry a firearm).

In spite of his Southern Baptist education and credentials, Mr. Cartee had serious doubts and questions about the prevailing evangelical view and doctrines regarding prophecy. He felt strongly that Christians should not fear the great tribulation. He taught me to read the Bible with an open mind and to seek the witness of the Holy Spirit. Mr. Cartee taught me not to take verses out of context and to compare passages without cherry-picking verses and jamming them together to support previous religious indoctrination.

At age thirteen, I could see that preconceived ideas and assumptions were affecting the writers of most of the books on Bible prophecy that I read at the interdenominational missionary base where my father was in charge of Bible translation teams working in forty-two languages. I devoured a huge selection of literature. Most of the confusion seemed to stem from the failure to define key terminology according to its use, trajectory, and meaning in the Scriptures.

My parents were electrified one day when I came home and told them that I no longer believed in the doctrine of the *secret* rapture. Their first, desperate reaction was to attempt to silence Mr. Cartee whom they thought must have brainwashed me. I was, however, given an opportunity to defend myself and spent long hours going over the key Scripture passages with my confused parents. It took six months to win the day.

From that time forward, God's blessing and anointing upon my parents' ministry increased in a noticeable way. I credit my parents and great mentors like Clifford Cartee with setting the basic foundation for much of the tremendous movement of God that is taking place in Colombia today.

Beginning with the intense persecution in 1980, and continuing over twenty-five years, more than a thousand foreign missionaries left the country or were recalled by their mission boards. Thousands of pastors fled or were killed. Hundreds of church buildings were abandoned or destroyed.

Mr. Cartee, now with the Lord, had taught me that great persecution and tribulation would give a golden opportunity for the gospel and that we should not fear losing our lives for the cause of Christ. We stayed in Colombia, and Mr. Cartee was right. The enemy onslaught was intense and was not over in just a few years. It continues, but the grace of God is even greater.

The book of Revelation describes not only the persecution that originates from Satan, but also announces the day when God will intervene and cleanse the earth. This is definitely something to look forward to if we are right with him.

More pastors and leaders have been tortured or killed in Colombia over the past several decades than in any other country upon the face of the earth. Over five hundred of my close friends and acquaintances have been killed here in Colombia. According to the United Nations, Colombia now has more than six million displaced persons, most of them Christians. This is surpassed only by Syria.

I have been taken hostage five times by guerrillas, three times by rogue paramilitary forces, and jailed twice by the government. Numerous attempts are continually being made upon my life. Yet my worst enemies are not the armed actors of the Colombian war (many of whom have come to the Lord), but rather the religious factions who fear that our literature and radio broadcasts will cause the people to escape from their heavy hand into the liberty of the Holy Spirit. Multiplied thousands are finding freedom, as one of the greatest revivals in history has been ignited in this land. This revival has been steadily building since 1932. Because it is not in the limelight and is in the midst of severe persecution, it has been difficult for anyone to contaminate it.

I see the present revival in Colombia (from which the spontaneous messages contained in this volume flow) as a continuation of what God has been doing over the centuries with the Reformation and the Great Awakening. A major distraction over the past century has greatly diminished the force and flow of revival in North America. This happens when theologians derive the meaning of the key words in Scripture from contemporary pagan usage and other sources instead of looking at God's introduction, development, and final usage of these words and key concepts throughout the Bible, starting with the narrative of the Hebrew Old Testament, then into the prophets, and then the transition into the Greek of the New Testament.

The Spanish edition of the *Jubilee Bible*, also known as *Reina Valera 2000* or *Version Antigua* (SEV), which I spent ten years editing and translating along with the English edition, is designed to help the average person understand the simplicity of the Scriptures. The *Jubilee Bible* is based on the translations and scholarship of the early Reformation that came forth under intense persecution. It is ideal for the leaders of the persecuted church who do not have a personal reference library. Millions of copies of this Spanish Bible are now in use. In the year 2000, the first year that we put the audio version on Internet servers, more than two million free copies were downloaded.

Within the limits of the Spanish (or English) language, a word is translated the same way throughout, doing away with the use of synonyms as much as possible. This allows the Bible to interpret itself. The key meanings of proper nouns and key terminology in this present work regarding the book of Revelation are derived from this Spanish Bible and the sources are listed on the flyleaf. (Please note that the Bible dictionary published in Spanish is much more extensive than the one published in the English *Jubilee Bible.*)

Before proceeding, it is important to take note of the last thing that Jesus did before his ascension:

Luke 24

45 Then he opened their understanding that they might understand the scriptures.

Ask the Lord Jesus to open your understanding and read the following pages with an open heart and an open mind.

Russell M. Stendal
April 27, 2015

Chapter 1

The Son of Man Appears

Revelation 1

1 *The Revelation of Jesus Christ, which God gave unto him, to show unto his slaves things which are convenient to do quickly, and he sent and signified it by his angel unto his slave John,*

The Apocalypse of Jesus Christ means the sudden revealing of Jesus Christ. John received this revelation by signs because its contents were impossible to express with normal language. The signs of this book must, therefore, be interpreted or decoded according to the way they have been previously described in the Bible.

Servants receive a salary but slaves have an owner. This revelation is to show believers (slaves of the Lord Jesus Christ) what they need to do. In order to see things from his point of view, the Lord must open our understanding as he did for his disciples. *Then he opened their understanding that they might understand the scriptures* (Luke 24:45).

This included John,

> *2 who bore witness of the word of God and of the testimony of Jesus Christ, and of all things that he saw.*
>
> *3 Blessed is he that reads and those that hear the words of this prophecy and keep those things which are written therein, for the time is at hand.*

The Holy Spirit can apply this book on several levels. One message is for each of us as individuals; other messages are to entire congregations or churches. Undoubtedly, a historical application permeates throughout church history. But the fullness of this revelation has to do with the imminent day of the Lord.

> 4 *John, to the seven congregations* [Gr. *ekklesia* – "called-out ones"] *which are in Asia: Grace be unto you and peace from him who is and who was and who is to come and from the seven Spirits which are before his throne*
>
> *5 and from Jesus, the Christ, who is the faithful witness and the first begotten of the dead and the prince of the kings of the earth. Unto him that loved us and washed us from our sins with his own blood*
>
> *6 and has made us kings and priests unto God and his Father; to him be glory and dominion for ever and ever. Amen.*
>
> *7 Behold, he comes with the clouds, and every eye shall see him and those also who pierced him; and all kindreds of the earth shall wail over him. Even so, Amen.*
>
> *8 I AM the Alpha and the Omega, beginning and end, saith the Lord, who is and who was and who is to come, the Almighty.*
>
> *9 I John, your brother and participant in the tribulation and in the kingdom and in the patience of Jesus*

> *Christ, was in the isle that is called Patmos for the word of God, and for the testimony of Jesus Christ.*

Patmos means "my death." The Word of God and the testimony of Jesus Christ will bring about the death of the old, natural man inside all of us.

> 10 *I was in the Spirit in the day of the Lord and heard behind me a great voice as of a trumpet,*

The day of the Lord is prophesied by all the prophets and is linked to the seventh millennium, the seventh prophetic day. This phrase occurs thirty-two times in Scripture, and this is the last usage (which means this is a key to comprehending the fulfillment of the day of the Lord).

> 11 *that said, I AM the Alpha and the Omega, the first and the last, and What thou seest, write in a book and send it unto the seven congregations which are in Asia: unto Ephesus and unto Smyrna and unto Pergamos and unto Thyatira and unto Sardis and unto Philadelphia and unto Laodicea.*

This book is dedicated to the congregations located in Asia (which means "east"). Abraham was called out of the east and journeyed to the west to the Promised Land. The wise men came from the east following the light of the star and found the Christ child.

> 12 *And I turned to see the voice that spoke with me. And being turned, I saw seven golden lampstands.*

If we were to make a lampstand according to the instructions given to Moses in Exodus, it would be made of one piece of hammered gold with sixty-six[1] intricate features – twenty-two knops, twenty-two flowers, and twenty-two bowls. The lampstand must be made of gold (symbol of the nature of God) and be fed with oil (symbol of the Holy Spirit) and be lit with the fire of the presence of Jesus Christ so the Holy Place (the realm of the

1 It is curious that there are sixty-six books in the Bible, and yet even with this many books, Scripture still says that the letter kills and only the Spirit gives life.

priests in Israel and the realm of the priesthood of all believers in the church) might have the light of God.

John saw the Lord Jesus revealed in the midst of seven lampstands. He had to turn in order to see him. We also may have to make a 180-degree change of direction if we are to see him in his glory.

> 13 *and in the midst of the seven lampstands one like unto the Son of man, clothed with a garment down to the feet and girt about the breasts with a golden girdle.*
>
> 14 *His head and his hairs were white like white wool, as the snow, and his eyes were as a flame of fire*
>
> 15 *and his feet like unto brilliant metal as if they burned in a furnace and his voice as the sound of many waters.*
>
> 16 *And he had in his right hand seven stars, and out of his mouth went a sharp twoedged sword, and his countenance was as the sun when it shines in its strength.*
>
> 17 *And when I saw him, I fell at his feet as dead. And he laid his right hand upon me, saying unto me, Fear not; I AM the first and the last,*
>
> 18 *and he that lives and was dead; and, behold, I am alive for evermore, Amen, and have the keys of Hades and of death.*
>
> 19 *Write the things which thou hast seen and the things which are and the things which must be after these.*

The book of Revelation is about things that John saw, things that were happening even as he was writing, and things that would happen after these other things. It covers the entire history of the Christian church with an emphasis on the end of the age. Some have applied the message of the seven letters to seven stages of church history, in which case we are now in the scenario depicted by Laodicea. There may be some truth to this. However, I am convinced that the complete fulfillment of this prophecy is in the day of the Lord, which is now upon us. Therefore, these letters are all pertinent for us today as Jesus Christ will soon return and fulfill all his promises of judgment and reward.

> 20 *The mystery of the seven stars which thou sawest in my right hand and the seven golden lampstands: The seven stars are the angels of the seven congregations* {Gr. ekklesia – called out ones}, *and the seven lampstands which thou sawest are the seven congregations* {Gr. ekklesia – called out ones}.

Seven angels refer to all the angels of all the congregations. *Seven lampstands* indicates all the lampstands, all the congregations that exist upon the earth. *Seven* indicates that there is completion and nothing is lacking.

One of the first things we can deduce here is that there is not one church or congregation; there are many, and they are defined by locality and not by denominational affiliation.

From the references in the New Testament to congregations in houses (e.g., Philemon 2), we see that the believers were meeting in many sites across a given city or place, yet this verse mentions one special angel per locality. Jesus said that wherever two or three are gathered together in his name, he would be there (Matthew 18:20). His presence is symbolized by the lampstand, and he may maintain or withdraw his presence (or light) from any given congregation.

Although there are many different congregations (or churches), there is only one body of Christ. The body of Christ is universal (Ephesians 4:4). It contains people who have died and gone to be with the Lord as well as those who are alive and remain now, everyone who has responded to the gospel and is joined to Christ. We often create a problem when we use the term *local body of Christ*, because sooner or later someone wants to be the head of the local body and begins to displace Christ. Make no mistake: There is only one body, and the body has only one head. Each member of the body must have a direct connection to the head as well as ligaments and bonds to the other members.

Jesus says there is a mystery surrounding the seven stars and seven lampstands. A mystery is something that we will never understand unless God reveals it. Human intellectual curiosity will never discover the reality of Jesus and how he is manifest in his people unless God reveals it. This revelation of his plans will only be given to his close friends (John 15:12-17) who keep his commandment to love one another.

Therefore, a mystery exists regarding the seven angels that he has in his right hand. The right hand is a symbol of power and authority. Each angel of each congregation of each locality operates directly under his power and authority. He places someone in authority who answers directly to him. The letters that follow are not addressed directly to each local congregation; they are addressed to the angel of each congregation. Note that the letters are not addressed to a committee either.

In the Bible, the angel of the Lord is a messenger sent with power and authority to represent the Lord. *Malachi* means "my angel" (or "messenger"). The Scriptures refer to angels that are celestial beings like cherubim and seraphim, but the word *angel* can also be applied to humans like us. Some Scriptures even seem to imply that each of us may have a celestial counterpart (Matthew 18:10; Acts 12:15). The relationship between us and the guardian angels that God delegates remains shrouded in mystery, at least in part, because we are each to have a direct relationship with God, and God has not yet chosen to allow us to give orders to his angels.

Let us pray

Heavenly Father,

Please open our understanding that we might understand the Scriptures. May we receive the revelation of Jesus Christ. Amen.

Chapter 2

Letters to Ephesus, Smyrna, Pergamos, and Thyatira

Revelation 2

1 *Unto the angel of the congregation of Ephesus write; These things, saith he that holds the seven stars in his right hand, who walks in the midst of the seven golden lampstands:*

2 *I know thy works and thy labour and thy patience and how thou canst not bear those who are evil; and thou hast tried those who say they are apostles and are not and hast found them liars,*

3 *and hast suffered, and doth suffer and for my name's sake hast laboured and hast not fainted.*

4 *Nevertheless I have against thee that thou hast left thy first love, charity.*

Charity is not the natural love of man; it is the supernatural love of God. Charity is love that redeems and is born of sacrifice when we repent and turn from our own lives that we might live his life.

It seems they were doing fine in Ephesus except that they had left that which is most important. They were no longer flowing in the love that only comes from the nature of God.

> 5 *Remember, therefore, from where thou art fallen and repent and do the first works, or else I will come unto thee quickly and will remove thy lampstand out of its place, except thou repent.*

What are the *first works*? They are the works of God. What are the Ephesians involved in now? The works of man. We can do nothing in and of ourselves that could possibly save us or anyone else. Only the work of Jesus Christ can save us. As he was dying on the cross, he declared, *It is finished, and he bowed his head and gave the Spirit* (John 19:30). Now he desires to apply the great victory that he won on the cross to us. He desires to work in us and through us by the Holy Spirit. He desires to completely transform our hearts so we flow in charity, in the love of God. It is only by the Spirit that we can put to death the deeds of the flesh and live (Romans 8:13).

To remove their lampstand out of its place is not to remove an individual or two who are deficient or causing trouble. Jesus is threatening to come and completely remove his light from the entire place. Even the glowing report of all their work and patience and discernment and what they had suffered for the cause of Christ was not enough to offset the terrible fact that they were no longer flowing in the love of God. Paul wrote that without charity, their good works were nothing (1 Corinthians 13:3). Peter wrote that charity covers a multitude of sins (1 Peter 4:8).

Throughout the long history of the church, how many congregations have been like Ephesus? What about today?

> 6 *But this thou hast, that thou hatest the deeds of the Nicolaitans, which I also hate.*

Nico means "to conquer," and *laitan* or *laity* means "the people."

God hates the deeds of those who would subjugate the people of God under a ruling class or clergy interposed between the people and God. True God-ordained leadership would join the people directly to the Lord.

> 7 *He that has an ear let him hear what the Spirit saith unto the congregations; To him that overcomes I will give to eat of the tree of life, which is in the midst of the paradise of God.*

Even though this letter is addressed to the angel of the congregation of Ephesus, it pertains to all the congregations of those whom God has called out of the world and out of the religion of man. This is a letter that the Holy Spirit may apply whenever and to whomever he desires (2 Timothy 3:16). This message is increasingly urgent as we enter the day of the Lord.

This verse delivers an important promise to those who overcome: They will be allowed to return to the presence of God and partake of the very life of God. This is the opportunity that Adam and Eve lost in the garden.

The only way to overcome is to remain in Jesus Christ and continue to flow in his agape love (charity). I wonder what happens to those who are out on their own and do not overcome? Are they not allowed into the Paradise of God? Are they denied access to the Tree of Life? What is their eternal condition?

> 8 *And unto the angel of the congregation of Smyrna write: These things, saith the first and the last, who was dead, and is alive:*

Smyrna means "myrrh," and this is a symbol of the way of the cross. Jesus is the first man to overcome sin and death, and he is also the last. No one will ever be able to say that they are the second or the third. Our only path to victory is in him. If we follow him, he will take us on the way of the cross. This means death to our old man and to our old nature. However, if we suffer with Christ we will also reign with him (Romans 8:17).

> 9 *I know thy works and tribulation and poverty, (but thou art rich), and I know the blasphemy of those who say they are Jews and are not, but are the synagogue of Satan.*
>
> 10 *Fear none of those things which thou shalt suffer; behold, the devil shall cast some of you into prison, that ye may be tried; and ye shall have tribulation ten days; be thou faithful unto death, and I will give thee the crown of life.*
>
> 11 *He that has an ear let him hear what the Spirit saith unto the congregations; He that overcomes shall not be hurt by the second death.*

The second death is linked to hell and the lake of fire (Revelation 20:14). The consequences of not being an overcomer are unthinkable. Every true member of the body of Christ is an overcomer, because he has already won the victory. He does, however, require that we abide in him, if we are to be fruitful and remain in victory, for apart from him we can do nothing (John 15:1-8).

> 12 *And to the angel of the congregation in Pergamos write; These things, saith he, who has the sharp sword with two edges:*

Pergamos means "a high place" and was the center of paganism at the time John was writing this. The pagan high priest was called the Pontifus Maximus, a title which was later transferred to Rome.

> 13 *I know thy works and where thou dwellest, even where Satan's throne is, and thou holdest fast my name and hast not denied my faith, even in those days in which Antipas was my faithful witness [or martyr], who was slain among you, where Satan dwellest.*

Antipas means "like a father." The Devil tried to stamp out the work of God by going after the person God used to start or father the work. Paul and Peter and many others were martyred in the face of the Enemy's onslaught. In the early church, however, they said that the blood of the martyrs is the seed of the church, because every time Satan killed someone like Antipas, the Lord greatly multiplied the Christians.

> 14 *But I have a few things against thee because thou hast there those that hold the doctrine of Balaam, who taught Balac to cast a stumblingblock before the sons of Israel, to eat things sacrificed unto idols and to commit fornication.*
>
> 15 *So hast thou also those that hold the doctrine of the Nicolaitans, which I hate.*
>
> 16 *Repent, or else I will come unto thee quickly and will fight against them with the sword of my mouth.*
>
> 17 *He that has an ear let him hear what the Spirit saith unto the congregations; To him that overcomes I will give to eat of the hidden manna and will give him a small white stone and in the stone a new name written, which no one knows except the one that receives it.*

This is a much different situation than in Ephesus where they had left their first love, and therefore the character of God was replaced with a farce. Jesus threatened to completely remove his lampstand unless they returned to their first works (his works). In Pergamos, Jesus also gives a repent-or-else message, but it is directed only against those who are causing the problems. He is not considering pulling the plug on the whole shebang.

Ephesus (meaning "permitted") is a place where the people have freedom to follow God, and the Devil persuades them to meander away from the love and character of God. Therefore, this church is dynamically going on in a flurry of apparently well-meaning activity that results in the glorification of man instead of God. Jesus will have none of it.

Pergamos, on the other hand, is a case of God doing something right in the Enemy camp. If the Enemy can infiltrate God's people, God can also infiltrate the Enemy's people. Jesus is not going to abandon a beachhead like this. He will arrive with the two-edged sword of his Word and fight those who are attempting to subvert his congregation.

The Enemy is attempting to contaminate the Christians at Pergamos with idolatry, fornication, and human control, all of which are being formalized as doctrine.

Overcomers at Pergamos are promised the *hidden manna,* which is found only within the ark of the covenant in the Holy of Holies. This is an incorruptible word (or provision) that is linked to the very life of Christ. It is hidden under the seat of reconciliation of the ark upon which the blood of our redemption is applied. The white stone with a new name indicates a complete change of nature.

> 18 *And unto the angel of the congregation in Thyatira write; These things, saith the Son of God, who has his eyes like unto a flame of fire and his feet like unto brilliant metal:*

Thyatira means "the aroma of persecution or of tribulation." Some will come out of great tribulation having washed their robes and having made them white in the blood of the Lamb (Revelation 7:14). Others deny the Lord when they get just a little whiff of the aroma of persecution.

> 19 *I have known thy works and charity and service and faith and thy patience and thy works and the last to be more than the first.*

> 20 *Notwithstanding I have a few things against thee*

> *because thou sufferest that woman Jezebel (who calls herself a prophetess) to teach and to seduce my slaves to commit fornication, and to eat things sacrificed unto idols.*

Jezebel means "she does not cohabit" (with her husband). Pagan worship includes sexual immorality. In the church, when God's people do not cohabit with their true husband, Jesus Christ, they are open to be seduced by other spirits that are supernatural but not holy. The ensuing offspring are spiritual bastards who claim to have the church (Jezebel) as their mother, but God is not their father. Jesus says that when he comes, he will kill her children.

> 21 *And I have given her time to repent of her fornication, and she repented not.*
>
> 22 *Behold, I will cast her into a bed and those that commit adultery with her into great tribulation unless they repent of their deeds.*
>
> 23 *And I will kill her children with death, and all the congregations shall know that I AM he that searches the kidneys and hearts, and I will give unto each one of you according to your works.*

Please note that salvation is by grace through faith by *his* work (Ephesians 2:8-10), but we are all going to be judged according to *our* works (Revelation 20:12). Jesus said that we shall know them by their fruit (Matthew 7:15-20). It is of supreme importance that the fruit of the Holy Spirit be found in us. If evidence of his work is not found in us, we may not pass the judgment. Faith without works is dead (James 2:14-26). This is not referring to our own self-works; it is referring to his overcoming, victorious work in and through us as we are moved by the Spirit.

> 24 *But unto you I say and unto the rest in Thyatira, as many as do not have this doctrine and who have*

not known the depths of Satan (as they say); I will put upon you no other burden

25 *But that which ye have already hold fast until I come.*

26 *And he that overcomes and keeps my works unto the end, to him will I give power over the Gentiles;*

27 *and he shall rule them with a rod of iron; as the vessels of a potter they shall be broken to shivers, even as I received of my Father.*

28 *And I will give him the morning star.*

29 *He that has an ear let him hear what the Spirit saith unto the congregations.*

The congregation at Thyatira seems to perfectly sum up the parable of the wheat and the tares. Two basic types of people are depicted here: those who are told to hold fast until Jesus comes, and those who will be destroyed when Jesus comes (Matthew 13:36-43). Jesus says that he will put those in the church who commit adultery along with "Jezebel" into great tribulation. Those who commit spiritual fornication and adultery with religious spirits masquerading as angels of light will never have a clean personal life.

The overcomer here is equated with the person who keeps the works of Jesus unto the end (Jude 24).

Let us pray

Heavenly Father,

We ask that we may live this message, that we may overcome and keep the works of Jesus, that we may enter into the fullness of your promises. Amen.

Chapter 3

Letters to Sardis, Philadelphia, and Laodicea

Revelation 3

> 1 *And unto the angel of the congregation in Sardis write; These things, saith he that has the seven Spirits of God, and the seven stars: I know thy works, that thou hast a name that thou livest and art dead.*

S*ardis* means "those who are red." *Adam* means "red." Sardis seems like a lively crowd, but most of them are still dead in trespasses and sin in the life of Adam and are not alive in the life of Christ.

> 2 *Be watchful, and strengthen the things which remain, that are ready to die; for I have not found thy works perfect before God.*

The works of the natural man will never be perfect. The works of Christ are always perfect, and he loves to do his work in and through us.

> 3 *Remember, therefore, of that which thou hast*

> *received and heard and hold to it and repent. If therefore thou shalt not watch, I will come to thee as a thief, and thou shalt not know what hour I will come upon thee.*

Those who are in Jesus Christ and are doing his works (who love one another as he has loved us) are considered his friends. Jesus said that he shares the intimate details of his plans with his friends (John 15:15). His friends, who are in the light, will have a heads-up regarding the time and the season of his return, even though the day and the hour is known only to the Father (Matthew 24:36). Those who remain in Adam, in the dark, pretending to "do church," will be taken unawares when Jesus returns as a thief in the night (1 Thessalonians 5:1-10).

They do not even stop for a moment to consider what the consequences will be if their secret-rapture hypothesis does not pan out according to their expectations, and if their hearts are not pure and clean before the Lord. The only requirement to be used by the Lord is to have a pure heart and to be wearing the fine linen of the garments, which is the righteousness of the saints (Revelation 19:8), for *The steps of a good man are ordered by the LORD* (Psalm 37:23).

> 4 *Yet thou hast a few persons in Sardis who have not defiled their garments, and they shall walk with me in white, for they are worthy.*

The white robes of fine linen depict the righteousness of the saints. The robes must be washed in the blood of the Lamb (the life is in the blood). This is our covering so that we are not found naked at his appearing (Revelation 7:14; 16:15).

> 5 *He that overcomes shall likewise be clothed in white raiment, and I will not blot out his name out of the book of life, but I will confess his name before my Father and before his angels.*

> 6 *He that has an ear let him hear what the Spirit saith unto the congregations.*

Scripture is clear: If we deny the Lord before men, he will deny us before his Father (Matthew 10:33). Jesus Christ will never be blotted out of the Book of Life, and the only way that we can overcome is if his life is in us (2 Timothy 2:11-13).

There are at least eight Scriptures that mention names or even entire groups being blotted out of God's book. It would behoove us all to be aware of them. Here is the first one:

Exodus 17

> 14 *And the LORD said unto Moses, Write this for a memorial in the book and tell Joshua that I must utterly blot out the remembrance of Amalek from under heaven.*

Amalek, meaning "strangers," is a symbol of the natural, Adamic man that God has sworn to destroy. Salvation is only in the new man in Christ.

When King Saul disobeyed the direct order from God and did not stamp out the Amalekites (1 Samuel 15), God eventually withdrew his Spirit from Saul, and most of Israel became like Sardis. The consequences of Saul's failure turned up centuries later in the days of Queen Esther when the evil Haman, an Agagite (descendant of Agag, king of the Amalekites), almost succeeded in exterminating all of the Jews in the entire world.

The only ones who will be covered when Jesus returns are those who have not defiled their "garments" with the stain and stench of the works of man. The overcomers will be found in Christ, as streams of living water flow out of their innermost being, to bless those around them with the love of God (John 7:38).

Revelation 3

> 7 *And to the angel of the congregation in Philadelphia write; These things, saith he that is Holy and True, he who has the key of David, who opens and no one shuts and shuts, and no one opens;*

Philadelphia means "brotherly love." Jesus only gave us one new commandment: We are to love one another (John 13:34-35). This is the congregation where Jesus' commandment is being consistently fulfilled. As we fulfill Jesus' command and as the doors begin to open for us that no one can shut, we realize more and more how little strength we have and how much we need the unlimited fullness of God in order to adequately proceed.

> 8 *I know thy works; behold, I have set before thee an open door, and no one can shut it, for thou hast a little strength and hast kept my word and hast not denied my name.*

David was a man after God's own heart. The key of David is linked to the sure mercies of David (Isaiah 22:22; 55:3). Here is where God grants mercy and favor and open doors that no one can shut. His grace will then follow through.

> 9 *Behold, I give of the synagogue of Satan, who say they are Jews and are not, but do lie; behold, I will constrain them to come and worship before thy feet and to know that I have loved thee.*

When Jesus visited what Scripture calls *their synagogues* (Mark 1:23, 39), invariably they were filled with demons. Satan clearly made the synagogues a prime target. This is also true of many churches. God says that when a man's ways please the Lord, he makes even his enemies to be at peace with him (Proverbs 16:7). I have experienced this many times as my adversaries in many realms have experienced great deliverance.

> 10 *Because thou hast kept the word of my patience, I also will keep thee from the hour of temptation, which shall come upon all the entire world, to try those that dwell upon the earth.*

Friends, if we patiently focus on pleasing the Lord and unselfishly fulfilling his commandment to us that we love one another in the power of the Holy Spirit, then he will spare us from the coming events that will devastate large sectors of Israel and the church. We will not need to invent escapist theology or attempt to move to some seemingly "safe" physical place of refuge. If we are pleasing the Lord, all we have to do is hold fast to what we have so he may find us faithful at our assigned post when he returns. Those of the congregation or church of Philadelphia are prime candidates to receive the seal of God in their foreheads (Revelation 7:3).

> 11 *Behold, I come quickly; hold fast that which thou hast, that no one take thy crown.*

> 12 *He that overcomes I will make a pillar in the temple of my God, and he shall go out no more, and I will write upon him the name of my God, and the name of the city of my God which is the new Jerusalem, which comes down out of heaven from and with my God, and I will write upon him my new name.*

> 13 *He that has an ear let him hear what the Spirit saith unto the congregations.*

Solomon's temple had two pillars (1 Kings 7:18-22). One was named *Jachin* ("the LORD establishes") and the other *Boaz* ("only in him is there strength"). There are two hundred pomegranates (symbol of the fruit of righteousness in the body of Christ) related to each pillar, and upon the top of the pillars was lily work (lily is a symbol of Christ). If we are to be made a pillar in the new temple built without hands of living stones, we must not only understand the message but we must also live it and bear the fruit of righteousness in the life of Christ. This is why he writes all the names having to do with the nature of God and the fruitfulness of his new creation upon us.

> 14 *And unto the angel of the congregation of the Laodiceans write; Behold he who saith, Amen, the faithful and true witness, the beginning of the creation of God:*

Laodicea means "righteousness of the people or self-righteousness." Note that the salutation is different from the previous letters. Jesus says that this is the church of the Laodiceans. This seems to be their church instead of his church!

> 15 *I know thy works, that thou art neither cold nor hot; I would that thou wert cold or hot.*
>
> 16 *So then because thou art lukewarm and neither cold nor hot, I will spue thee out of my mouth.*
>
> 17 *Because thou sayest, I am rich and increased with goods and have need of nothing and knowest not that thou art wretched and miserable and poor and blind and naked,*
>
> 18 *I counsel thee to buy of me gold refined in the fire, that thou may be made rich; and clothed in white raiment, so that the shame of thy nakedness not be uncovered; and anoint thine eyes with eyesalve, that thou may see.*
>
> 19 *As many as I love, I rebuke and chasten; be zealous therefore, and repent.*
>
> 20 *Behold, I stand at the door and call; if anyone*

hears my voice and opens the door, I will come into him and will sup with him, and he with me.

Jesus is outside the door of the church of the Laodiceans, calling to see if anyone will open the door and let him back inside their lives. The only way out of the self-righteousness of the Laodiceans is for them to, one by one, repent and submit to the chastening of the Lord. Jesus' rebuke and offer to correct them is a sign of his love for them.

21 *To him that overcomes will I grant to sit with me in my throne, even as I also overcame and have sat down with my Father in his throne.*

22 *He that has an ear let him hear what the Spirit saith unto the congregations.*

What must we overcome if we desire to reign and rule with Jesus Christ? If we accept the correction and discipline of the Lord, he will deliver us from all our lukewarm self-righteousness, so we may overcome the flesh, the world, and the Devil in his righteousness.

Let us pray

Heavenly Father,

May you find in us a pure heart and the fine linen of righteousness. As you open doors, may we recognize your strength and overcome whatever causes us to be lukewarm. In the name of Jesus we pray. Amen.

Chapter 4

The Throne of God

Revelation 4

1 *After these things I looked, and, behold, an open door in heaven, and the first voice which I heard, was like a trumpet that spoke with me, saying, Come up here, and I will show thee the things that need to be done after these.*

Scripture states that what we bind on earth shall be bound in heaven and whatever we loose on earth shall be loosed in heaven (Matthew 18:18).

When God's people heed the urgent message of Jesus to his congregations on the earth, we get access, which causes repercussions in the heavenly realm.

2 *And immediately I was in the spirit, and, behold, a throne was set in heaven, and there was one seated upon the throne.*

Jesus desires for us to meet his Father and to have access to the throne of the Father (John 15:16).

3 *And he that was seated was like a jasper and a*

> *sardine stone to look upon; and there was a rainbow round about the throne, in sight like unto an emerald.*

Jesus had already said, *To him that overcomes will I grant to sit with me in my throne, even as I also overcame and have sat down with my Father in his throne* (Revelation 3:21).

Jesus is one with his Father, and here he that was seated is described as two precious stones (jasper and sardine or ruby). The jasper was the last stone on the last row of the twelve precious stones on the pectoral on the High Priest. The ruby is the first stone on the first row. The wall around the city of God is made of jasper, because he is our protection. The light of the city of God has the clarity of God and is also compared to a jasper stone shining like crystal (Revelation 21:11).

A round rainbow is called a glory, and this one has as its predominant color a deep emerald green, which is a symbol of righteousness, justice, and resurrection life.

> 4 *And round about the throne were twenty-four thrones, and upon the thrones I saw twenty-four elders sitting, clothed in white raiment; and they had on their heads crowns of gold.*

The number twenty-four (used seven times in Revelation) is linked to the peace offering (Numbers 7:88), which is voluntary for those who have dealt with sin and guilt and therefore are blameless. Paul encourages us to present our bodies as a living sacrifice (Romans 12:1). To deal with sin and guilt is mandatory. To become a living sacrifice (peace offering) is voluntary. Elders are those who have come to maturity in Christ. The immature will not be allowed to reign and rule. The word for *maturity* is the same word also translated as *perfection.*

> 5 *And out of the throne proceeded lightnings and thunderings and voices; and there were seven lamps*

> *of fire burning before the throne, which are the seven Spirits of God.*

Lightnings and thunderings are evidence of the presence and the voice of God (Exodus 20:1-18).

Paul wrote that the outpouring of the Spirit that began at Pentecost was just the earnest or down payment on the fullness of the inheritance (Ephesians 1:13-14). The seven lamps of fire, which are seven Spirits of God, represent the fullness of our inheritance in Christ. This is the fullness of the glory and clarity of the light of God in the Holy of Holies. This is an unlimited realm beyond Pentecost, beyond the experience of the church, from which we will reign and rule with Christ.

> 6 *And before the throne there was a sea of glass like unto crystal, and in the midst of the throne and round about the throne were four animals full of eyes in front and behind.*

The sea of humanity is unable to affect the peace and rest of the presence of God. Those who reign and rule with Christ can walk upon this sea with ease. The throne of God is also surrounded with special creatures called cherubim. Here they are called animals because they have biological aspects and may operate with different faces (Ezekiel 1). In Genesis chapter 1, creatures were created for all three realms: the sea, the land, and the heavens.

> 7 *And the first animal was like a lion and the second animal like a calf, and the third animal had a face as a man, and the fourth animal was like a flying eagle.*

> 8 *And the four animals had each of them six wings about him, and they were full of eyes within, and they did not cease day or night, saying, Holy, holy,*

holy, the Lord God Almighty, who was and is and is to come.

This is similar to the description of the cherubim by Ezekiel where each had four faces instead of one face like us (Ezekiel 1). The cherubim seen by Ezekiel had four wings (a heavenly number), and the cherubim seen by John had six wings (a number associated with man and the animals of the earth).

9 *And when those animals give glory and honour and praise to the one that is seated on the throne, who lives for ever and ever,*

10 *the twenty-four elders fall down before him that is seated on the throne and worship him that lives for ever and ever and cast their crowns before the throne, saying,*

11 *Thou art worthy, O Lord, to receive glory and honour and virtue; for thou hast created all things, and by thy will they have their being and were created.*

Those who come to maturity in Christ (as elders) know that it is the Lord who is worthy to receive glory and honor and virtue, because he accomplished our redemption. His work and not ours has brought us to maturity as we have yielded to him.

Let us pray

Heavenly Father,

We thank you for making access to your throne possible through our redemption as we become a living sacrifice, for only you are worthy. Amen.

Chapter 5

The Book with Seven Seals

Revelation 5

1 *And I saw in the right hand of him that was seated on the throne a book written within and on the backside, sealed with seven seals.*

The book in the right hand of him that is seated on the throne is nothing less than the Scriptures. According to the prophet Isaiah, the Scriptures have been sealed so that the natural man cannot understand them.

Isaiah 29

11 *And every vision is unto you as the words of a book that is sealed, which if it were delivered to one that knows how to read, saying, Read this, I pray thee: he shall say, I cannot; for it is sealed.*

Each key term or symbol used in the book of Revelation has a trajectory through the rest of the Bible. When a book is mentioned in Scripture, and even when someone in Scripture makes the statement, *For it is written*, it is invariably referring to the written Word of God. There is a third dimension to the

Scriptures that cannot be unsealed or understood by the natural man or by those who are spiritually immature. No one, except for those who have come to maturity in Christ, has been able to look upon it, and the only way we can come to maturity is in him. He is the only one that is worthy.

Revelation 5

> 2 *And I saw a strong angel preaching with a loud voice, Who is worthy to open the book and to loose its seals?*
>
> 3 *And no one was able not in heaven nor in the earth neither under the earth to open the book neither to look upon it.*

In all their cunning, the Devil and his fallen angels have absolutely no idea what is in this book. Yes, they are aware of the historical facts (the first dimension), and they know something about the spiritual truth that is linked to the second dimension (the Holy Place, the realm of the priesthood of all believers of the church), but they know next to nothing about God's prophecies and plans regarding the Holy of Holies (the third dimension). Neither does anyone else in heaven nor in the earth nor under the earth know, unless it is unsealed to them. John was in the Spirit on the day of the Lord when he received this revelation. It has had partial application throughout the age of the church. But now, as we enter into the reality of the day of the Lord, the fullness of this revelation will suddenly happen at every level. This is the Apocalypse or sudden revealing of Jesus Christ.

> 4 *And I wept much because no one was found worthy to open the book nor to read it neither to look upon it.*
>
> 5 *And one of the elders said unto me, Weep not: behold, the Lion of the tribe of Juda, the Root of David, who has overcome to open the book and to loose its seven seals.*

This revelation is indelibly linked to the Lamb who was slain. It is revealed to those who have lost their own lives, so that the life of Christ might come forth in them (Mark 8:35).

> 6 *And I saw, and, behold, in the midst of the throne and of the four animals and in the midst of the elders, stood a Lamb as it had been slain, having seven horns and seven eyes, which are the seven Spirits of God sent forth into all the earth.*

The *seven Spirits of God* are the fullness of the Spirit, which will be sent forth into all the earth. *The earth* is a symbol of Israel and the church. *Seven horns* are a symbol of the fullness of the power of God. *Seven eyes* indicate that he perceives everything.

> 7 *And he came and took the book out of the right hand of him that was seated upon the throne.*

> 8 *And when he had taken the book, the four animals and the twenty-four elders fell on their faces before the Lamb, each one of them having harps, and golden vials full of incense, which are the prayers of the saints.*

There have been lots of prayers over the past two millennia asking for Jesus to return and straighten everything out. These prayers are about to be answered. The *harps* have to do with the song of Moses (Revelation 15:2-3) and the psalms of David.

> 9 *And they sang a new song, saying, Thou art worthy to take the book and to open its seals, for thou wast slain and hast redeemed us unto God by thy blood, out of every kindred and tongue and people and nation*

> 10 *and hast made us unto our God kings and priests, and we shall reign on the earth.*

The new song may only be learned by the redeemed (Revelation 14:3).

This appears to take place at or near the end of the age of the church and at the beginning of the age of the kingdom, which begins with the day of the Lord. This is in keeping with the time frame designated when John declares that he is in the Spirit on the day of the Lord (Revelation 1:10) as he receives this revelation. The day of the Lord pertains to the seventh prophetic day, the seventh millennium.

> 11 *And I beheld, and I heard the voice of many angels round about the throne and of the animals and of the elders; and the number of them was ten thousand times ten thousand, and thousands of thousands;*

Ten thousand is a symbol of a military unit that is under perfect discipline and control. *Ten thousand times ten thousand* is the perfection and power of all the heavenly hosts of the armies of God under the command of Jesus Christ.

One thousand is symbolic of perfection, and *thousands of thousands* signify the sum and the results of walking in the perfection of Christ.

Daniel saw a similar scene of the throne of God and reported these same numbers (Daniel 7:9-14). He saw dominion over everything being given to one like unto a Son of man, and judgment by fire on the kingdoms of this world.

> 12 *saying with a loud voice, Worthy is the Lamb that was slain to take power and riches and wisdom and strength and honour and glory and blessing.*

This is the setting in heaven prior to the second coming of Jesus. Peter said the following regarding the return of Jesus: *whom it is certainly necessary that the heaven must receive until the times of restitution of all things, which God has spoken by the mouth of all his holy prophets since the age began* (Acts 3:21).

Therefore, the unsealing of the book that Jesus receives from the right hand of the Father is absolutely essential for the restitution of all things that will happen at Jesus' return. Events in heaven and upon the earth are linked until the veil that separates the two realms is removed (Isaiah 51:6; 2 Peter 3:10; Revelation 6:14). God plans to once again join the two realms. When this happens, the earth will be cleansed of all that is unclean.

> 13 *And I heard every creature which is in heaven and upon the earth and under the earth and such as are upon the sea and all that are in it, saying, Blessing and honour and glory and power, be unto him that is seated upon the throne, and unto the Lamb for ever and ever.*
>
> 14 *And the four animals said, Amen. And the twenty-four elders fell on their faces and worshipped him that lives for ever and ever.*

This scene ends with heaven in perfect order; no accuser of the brethren is holding forth, and every creature is blessing and praising God. Many of the scenes in Revelation seem to overlap as each vision John has continues until it reaches the appropriate conclusion.

Let us pray

> *Heavenly Father,*
>
> *We desire to be not just hearers of the Word; we want to be doers of the Word. We want to become what you desire for us to be; we want to come to maturity in Christ so we might abide in the fullness of your presence.*
>
> *We ask this in the name of our Lord Jesus Christ. Amen.*

Chapter 6

Opening the Seals

Revelation 6

1 *And I saw when the Lamb had opened the first seal, and I heard the first of the four animals, saying as with a voice of thunder, Come and see.*

2 *And I saw and, behold, a white horse; and he that was seated upon him had a bow, and a crown was given unto him, and he went forth victorious, that he might also overcome.*

With the opening of each seal come immediate results. The first four events on display are each announced by a different cherubim. White horses are associated with the armies of heaven and holiness (Revelation 19:11, 14). This ministry has been sent forth from the very presence of God with a crown of authority. Habakkuk 3:3-15 and Joel 2:4 present an interesting parallel.

The day of the Lord begins with a serious message being sent to the angel of each congregation upon the earth. Then the focus is upon the heavenly throne room, and the subsequent effects of each seal or trumpet or vial that follow are immediate.

The opening of this first seal is similar to when *Jehu* (meaning "the LORD is he") was anointed; he lost no time in riding forth with his bow. Soon he had killed the apostate kings of Judah and Israel and had caused Jezebel to be cast down. All this took place in the space of about an hour. Then he went after all the worshippers of Baal who were among the people of God (2 Kings 9 and 10).

> 3 *And when he had opened the second seal, I heard the second animal, which said, Come and see.*
>
> 4 *And another horse went forth that was red, and unto him that was seated thereon was given power to take away the peace of the earth and that they should kill one another; and there was given unto him a great sword.*

Jesus warned the congregation at Pergamos that if those who were holding to the doctrine of Balaam and to the doctrine of the Nicolaitans did not repent, he would come and fight against them with the sword of his mouth (Revelation 2:16).

The earth is presently the realm of religion. If we are truly born again from above, the heavenly Jerusalem is our mother, and our spiritual citizenship is not of this earth. Those who use the things of God for personal gain and to obtain the things of this world are those who *dwell in the earth*. They will face serious trouble as the day of the Lord progresses. When the Lord commissions a ministry directly from his throne and sends the "horses" forth to apply the two-edged sword of his truth, *the peace of the earth* will vanish.

When Jesus came the first time he said, *Think not that I have come to introduce peace into the land [into the earth]; I came not to introduce peace, but a sword* (Matthew 10:34). This is what happened when Jesus arrived with the sword of the truth two thousand years ago and entered the religious land of the Jews.

The events leading to the second coming will continue this conflict on a worldwide scale.

> 5 *And when he had opened the third seal, I heard the third animal, which said, Come and see. And I saw and, behold, a black horse, and he that was seated upon him had a yoke in his hand.*
>
> 6 *And I heard a voice in the midst of the four animals, which said, A choenix of wheat for a denarius and three choenix of barley for a denarius; and see thou hurt not the oil and the wine.*

A black horse is symbolic of the ways of God, which look black to the natural man. This is the way of the cross. Zechariah describes a chariot with black horses that went forth to the north country; this is the cold land of adversity, but Scripture also states that God lives on the sides of the north (Zechariah 6:6; Psalm 48:2). Jesus wants us to take his yoke upon us, so we can go his way into adversity with his help, because he will be in the yoke pulling with us. Therefore, he says that his yoke is easy and his burden is light (Matthew 11:30).

The voice in the midst of the cherubim is the voice of God. The Feast of Passover is at the winter wheat harvest, and Jesus is typed as the first of the firstfruits which are offered to God. If we enter at the narrow gate (Jesus is the narrow gate), he will apply his blood to us, and we will enter into his service. A denarius is a day's wage, and we receive one measure of "wheat" (the bread provision of God for us). Jesus is our Passover Lamb, and Scripture states that man shall not live by bread alone but by every word that proceeds from the mouth of God (Matthew 4:4).

The feast of Pentecost comes next and is at the time of the barley harvest. In Pentecost we are given three measures of barley for the same denarius (the same wage), because as God brings us into fruitfulness and blessing, he will give us more than we need to see what we will do with the excess.

The Feast of Tabernacles is at the time of the grape and olive harvest. It is unlimited but comes with a stern warning. Do not hurt the oil (the anointing) and the wine (the life of Christ that is flowing by the Spirit). Those who hurt the oil and the wine will be disqualified from the fullness of the inheritance.

> 7 *And when he had opened the fourth seal, I heard the voice of the fourth animal, which said, Come and see.*
>
> 8 *And I looked and, behold, a green horse, and he that was seated upon him was named Death, and Hades followed with him. And power was given unto him over the fourth part of the earth, to kill with sword and with hunger and with death and with the beasts of the earth.*

Jesus has the keys to death and to Hades (Revelation 1:18). In Zechariah 6, the horses representing death were grisled and bay (Zechariah 6:3). Death was terrible, and even the patriarchs like Abraham were being held by death in Hades prior to Jesus' work of redemption on the cross (Luke 16:19-23). Jesus took captivity captive and ascended on high (Ephesians 4:8). Now he uses death as a tool to finish off the old man, the old nature. Death is now mounted on a green horse. Green is the color of righteousness and resurrection life.

When Cain offered the work of his hands in the form of grain to God, his offering (or present) was rejected (Genesis 4:5). The only way that the work of our hands will be acceptable unto God is if we are under a covenant with God that involves a blood sacrifice. Abel knew this. Under the law of Moses, a daily sacrifice of a lamb was to be offered evening and morning. Each lamb had to be offered with one-tenth of an ephah of flour mingled with the fourth part of a hin of beaten oil and the fourth part of a hin of wine. The flour (grain) that represents the work of our hands had to be mingled with oil (anointing), and a drink offering of wine (new life) was also made. The amount of oil and wine depended on the type and circumstances of the sacrifice.

The term *the fourth part* is used only fourteen times in Scripture, with the first being in Exodus 29:40, and the last being in this passage in Revelation 6. *The fourth part* always symbolizes the part of the harvest of oil and wine of all Israel that belongs to the Lord. He was the Lamb that was sacrificed for the sins of the entire world. In the case of the earth (Israel and the church), as we enter the great Feast of Tabernacles at the end of the age of the church and the beginning of the age of the kingdom, Jesus will also harvest his special part, because he has been given power over any and all means used by the Enemy.

> 9 *And when he had opened the fifth seal, I saw under the altar the souls of those that had been slain because of the word of God and for the testimony which they held.*
>
> 10 *And they cried with a loud voice, saying, How long, O Lord, holy and true, dost thou not judge and avenge our blood on those that dwell in the earth?*

The vision has now shifted back to heaven, to the heavenly altar of the Holy of Holies. The souls of those slain for the Word of God and for their testimony are no longer being held in Hades (as was the case prior to the death and resurrection of Jesus). They are under the heavenly altar; they are under the blood of Jesus Christ. They are protected in his life. And, they are not happy with the religious people who *dwell in the earth*, those who are misrepresenting the Lord and doing dastardly deeds in his name.

> 11 *And white robes were given unto each one of them; and it was said unto them, that they should rest yet for a little while until their fellow servants and their brethren, that should be killed as they were, should be fulfilled.*

Before we go any further, there is something of extreme importance that must be explained. The apostle John, who received this revelation, is a *witness* (Revelation 1:2), and *witness* is the same word as *martyr* in the Greek. Yet he is the only one of the original apostles who, according to church tradition, did not die a violent death. John, however, risked his life continually for the Lord. Therefore, in God's book, John is a martyr. And Scripture calls him a martyr even before he physically dies of old age.

On the other hand, Paul makes the case in 1 Corinthians 13:3 that even if someone were to give their body to be burned, if they do not have the love of God within, their death will profit them nothing.

The *fellow servants and brethren, that shall be killed as they were* definitely include the witnesses mentioned in Revelation 11. This Scripture in Revelation 6:11 will be fulfilled, and God will judge and avenge at that time. In Hebrew, the word *redeemer* is the exact same word as the term *avenger of blood*, which is used eighteen times in Scripture.

> 12 *And I saw when he had opened the sixth seal, and, behold, there was a great earthquake; and the sun became black as sackcloth of hair, and the moon became as blood;*

A great earthquake indicates a huge shakeup in Israel and the church, as God is busy harvesting those who are willing to lay down their own lives for him and for the cause of the gospel. The sun is a symbol of the system of this world (which is in serious trouble). The moon, the symbol of the light or of the witness of the church and Israel, has become as blood due to the consequences of the previous seals. This moon has been reflecting the light and glory of the sun of this world, and as the sun goes black, the moon turns to blood (these conditions are described in 2 Thessalonians 2:3 and Matthew 24:12).

> 13 *and the stars of heaven fell upon the earth, even as a fig tree casts her figs, when she is shaken of a mighty wind.*
>
> 14 *And the heaven departed as a scroll when it is rolled together; and every mountain and island were moved out of their places.*

This *heaven departed* is a firmament separating the natural and the spiritual realms (Genesis 1:6-8). It is similar to the veil between the Holy Place and the Holy of Holies in the temple. In the Old Testament, the people thought that if they saw the angel of the Lord, they would die. They knew that man in his unregenerate state could not survive in the presence of God. A parallel passage in Isaiah 51:6 says the heavens will vanish like smoke. *The earth* is always singular in Scripture, but many times the word *heavens* is plural. Paul received a special revelation in the third heaven (2 Corinthians 12:2).

The mountains and islands in verse 14 represent religious strongholds and private kingdoms that are about to be severely shaken as the day of the Lord commences.

> 15 *And the kings of the earth and the princes and the rich and the captains and the strong and every slave and every free man hid themselves in the caves and among the rocks of the mountains*
>
> 16 *and said to the mountains and to the rocks, Fall*

on us and hide us from the face of him that is seated upon the throne and from the wrath of the Lamb;

17 *for the great day of his wrath is come, and who shall be able to stand before him?*

All the dwellers of this earth will encounter much trouble when they suddenly find themselves exposed to the direct presence of God and the Lamb (Jesus). None of their human coverings will suffice on that day.

Anyone born from above who is a citizen in good standing of the heavenly Jerusalem that is the mother of us all (Galatians 4:26) will be in no danger at all. In fact, we are told to rejoice (Revelation 12:12).

Let us pray

Heavenly Father,

In the midst of this serious message, may we recognize the dangers of the religiocity of men; may we rejoice with all who have a citizenship in heaven, and may we be found to be faithful witnesses until the end. We pray in the name of our Lord Jesus Christ. Amen.

Chapter 7

Sealing Twelve Thousand of Each Tribe

Revelation 7

1 *And after these things I saw four angels standing upon the four corners of the earth, holding back the four winds of the earth that no wind should blow upon the earth nor upon the sea nor upon any tree.*

2 *And I saw another angel ascending from the rising of the sun, having the seal of the living God: and he cried out with a loud voice to the four angels, to whom it was given to hurt the land and the sea,*

3 *saying, Hurt not the land neither the sea nor the trees until we have sealed the slaves of our God in their foreheads.*

The heavens are open; those who dwell upon the earth are scrambling for cover; and judgment is about to fall, when an angel makes an important announcement: Those who belong to God are to be sealed in their foreheads.

God has never destroyed the righteous along with the wicked.

In every previous example of judgment, God has sealed and protected the righteous. In the day of Jehu, they even made one last inspection among the worshippers of Baal to make sure that no servants of the Lord were in the house of Baal by mistake before the order was given to destroy it (2 Kings 10:23). God instructed Ezekiel to set a mark on the forehead of those who sigh and cry out because of all the abominations in the midst of Jerusalem. Those with the mark of God were spared when everyone else in the city of religion was slaughtered (Ezekiel 9).

The judgments are about to hurt the land (symbolic of Israel and the church), the sea (lost humanity), and the trees, *for the tree of the field is man's life* (Deuteronomy 20:19-20).

> 4 *And I heard the number of those that were sealed: and there were sealed a hundred and forty-four thousand of all the tribes of the sons of Israel.*

This is a symbolic number: twelve times twelve times one thousand. God began the nation of Israel with the twelve sons of Jacob, which became the twelve tribes. Jesus began the church with twelve apostles. One thousand is a number that represents perfection. Therefore, one hundred and forty-four thousand means the perfect number of those who are sons of Israel (sons of God). In Christ there is no division between Jew and Gentile (Romans 10:12), for there is no salvation outside of Christ.

> 5 *Of the tribe of Juda were sealed twelve thousand. Of the tribe of Reuben were sealed twelve thousand. Of the tribe of Gad were sealed twelve thousand.*
>
> 6 *Of the tribe of Aser were sealed twelve thousand. Of the tribe of Naphtali were sealed twelve thousand. Of the tribe of Manasses were sealed twelve thousand.*
>
> 7 *Of the tribe of Simeon were sealed twelve*

thousand. Of the tribe of Levi were sealed twelve thousand. Of the tribe of Issachar were sealed twelve thousand.

8 *Of the tribe of Zebulon were sealed twelve thousand. Of the tribe of Joseph were sealed twelve thousand. Of the tribe of Benjamin were sealed twelve thousand.*

This is not the list of the tribes of natural Israel. Ephraim (meaning "double ash heap") and Dan ("judgment") are missing, while Levi ("unity") and Joseph ("let God add") have been included. Israel is the name of God, which he placed upon Jacob, who fought with the angel of the Lord all night and was converted at Peniel ("the face of God"). Then Jacob was given God's name, Israel (Genesis 32:24-32). The change in name indicates a potential change in nature (or conversion).

Now the scene shifts from the earth back into the heavens.

9 *After this I saw, and behold, a great multitude, which no man could number, of all nations and kindreds and peoples and tongues stood before the throne and before the Lamb clothed with long white robes and palms in their hands*

10 *and cried with a loud voice, saying, Salvation unto him who is seated upon the throne of our God and unto the Lamb.*

11 *And all the angels stood round about the throne and about the elders and the four animals; and they fell upon their faces before the throne and worshipped God,*

12 *saying, Amen: The blessing and the glory and the wisdom and the thanksgiving and the honour and*

> *the power and the might, be unto our God for ever and ever. Amen.*

The sight of the vast multitude of redeemed humanity clothed in white robes with palm branches in their hands and celebrating what appears to be a giant, heavenly Feast of Tabernacles has a tremendous effect on all the angels, causing them to fall on their faces and worship God.

> 13 *And one of the elders responded and asked me, Who are these who are arrayed in long white robes? and where did they come from?*
>
> 14 *And I said unto him, lord, thou knowest. And he said unto me, These are those who came out of great tribulation and have washed their long robes, and made them white in the blood of the Lamb.*

The word *tribulation* is used fifty-five times in Scripture. All God's people are told to expect trials and tribulations. This is the opportunity for us to wash our robes in the blood of the Lamb, for the life is in the blood, and we shall be saved by his life (Leviticus 17:11; Romans 5:10). This multitude of people who came out of great tribulation are standing before the throne in white robes even before the seven trumpets of the judgments of God upon the church and upon Israel have sounded, and before the seven vials of the judgments of God upon the world have been poured out.

> 15 *Therefore, they are before the throne of God and serve him day and night in his temple, and he that is seated on the throne shall dwell among them.*
>
> 16 *They shall hunger no more neither thirst anymore; neither shall the sun be thrust upon them nor any other heat.*

The religious and the secular world shall no longer be able to persecute them.

> 17 *For the Lamb which is in the midst of the throne shall govern them and shall lead them unto living fountains of waters, and God shall wipe away all tears from their eyes.*

Let us pray

Heavenly Father,

As we see your righteous judgment about to fall, we thank you that you never destroy the righteous with the wicked. May we stand firm in this time; may we be your witnesses before the lost. In Jesus' name we pray. Amen.

Chapter 8

Opening of the Seventh Seal

Revelation 8

1 *And when he had opened the seventh seal, there was silence in heaven about the space of half an hour.*

As with the letters to the seven churches, some aspects of the message of the seals have been in effect since John wrote this down and even have application at the personal level. Jesus sends the rider with the bow on the white horse of holiness to shoot the arrows of his truth deep into our being. The red horse and the sword will take away our peace and bring us under conviction, so the blood of Jesus might be applied to us, and our hearts might be circumcised.

The black horse is to teach us the ways of the Lord, so we may come under his yoke and experience the three obligatory feasts of the Lord. Jesus is our Passover Lamb, and his blood must be applied to the doorposts of our life. We must be immersed into the Holy Spirit at Pentecost, so the fire of God will purify our hearts. We must learn to be careful not to hurt the "oil" and the "wine." Those who play games with the anointing or use the gifts and talents of God for personal gain will be disqualified from the fullness of the inheritance in the Feast of Tabernacles.

I can see how the effects of the opening of the first five seals have been going on for quite some time throughout church history. On a certain level, the letters that originally went to seven real churches have also described and ministered to certain segments of the time line of the church age.

The real day of the Lord, however, is a different matter. This is when the fullness of the Spirit will be poured out on those who have been called and chosen and are faithful. The fullness of all of the Scriptures (promises and warnings) will be unsealed and applied. When the last two seals are opened, events take place that have never, ever even come close to happening before. Our enemies will be blindsided. In fact, as the reality of what is about to happen next sinks in, silence falls upon heaven for half an hour.

> 2 *And I saw the seven angels which stood before God, and to them were given seven trumpets.*

We know that the trumpet represents the message of the direct voice of God. In Revelation 1, the voice of the Lord sounds like a trumpet. The case has also been made for different trumpets of the message of God, sounding at key intervals throughout the church age. What is about to happen next is different, like the situation that Joshua faced at Jericho. Every day for six days the people had marched around the city blowing a trumpet, while they themselves were silent. On the seventh day, however, the rules changed. They did not just blow the seventh trumpet. They blew all seven trumpets; the people shouted; and the foundations of Jericho were destroyed. Only one family was saved from Jericho (Joshua 6:17), and among the Israelites, as a result of greed among the people of God, one family was lost (Joshua 7:24-25).

The family of Jesus Christ will be saved wherever they are, and the family of Adam will perish. The day of the Lord will sort this out.

We are now entering this day of the Lord – the seventh prophetic day since Adam was expelled from the garden, the seventh millennium. On this day, all seven trumpets will sound, and the enemy defenses of the city of religion will completely collapse like Jericho. *Jericho* means "she has her own moon." This is similar to the meaning of *Laodicea* ("righteousness of the people or self-righteousness") and to the message given to the church of the Laodiceans.

> 3 *And another angel came and stood at the altar, having a golden censer; and there was given unto him much incense of the prayers of all the saints, that he should offer upon the golden altar which was before the throne.*
>
> 4 *And the smoke of the incense of the prayers of the saints, ascended up before God out of the angel's hand.*
>
> 5 *And the angel took the censer and filled it with fire of the altar and cast it into the earth; and there were voices and thunderings and lightnings and an earthquake.*

Thunderings and lightnings and trumpets are associated with the throne and with the presence of God (Exodus 20:18-19). The trumpets will sound in the midst of an outpouring of the fullness of God upon his sealed people. This is a very exciting time to be alive if you have the seal of God upon your forehead. The church has been operating in the realm of the Holy Place, of the priesthood of all believers, in the realm of Pentecost with the earnest or down payment of the Spirit (2 Corinthians 1:21-22).

Now that the veil has been removed, all the rules change, because the realm of the Holy of Holies operates on an entirely different basis. This is the message of the seven trumpets.

> 6 *And the seven angels who had the seven trumpets prepared themselves to sound their trumpets.*

Note that all seven angels are preparing at once. This makes me think that when the trumpets begin to sound, they will all sound in close succession as they did on the seventh day at Jericho. Scripture implies that the trumpet needs to make a sound that is clear and certain (1 Corinthians 14:8), that will strike fear into the hearts of the Enemy, and announce liberty to those who belong to the Lord.

The trumpet is also linked to the Day of Reconciliation and the year of liberty, which is a special Jubilee (Ezekiel 46:16-17) in which gifts given by the prince to his sons shall be theirs perpetually. Gifts given to servants shall only be theirs until the year of liberty when these gifts return to the prince. Many have received gifts, talents, and ministries. But if they are hirelings who serve the Lord for personal gain or are servants to the flesh, the world, or the Devil, and have never submitted to God, when God's trumpets sound, all their gifts will return to the prince in the year of liberty.

It is most likely that 1967 was the 69th Jubilee since the writing of the book of Leviticus circa 1483 BC. If this is the case, 2017 will be the 70th Jubilee. I expect that it will be a very special year. The fact that we are currently in the midst of four blood moons alternating between Passover and Tabernacles, with the fourth to occur on September 28, 2015, is also very significant. The fall season of 2015 will be the beginning of the 49th year since 1967. The Jewish New Year is on the first day of the seventh month. In this case it is on September 13, which is the New Moon. Four blood moons means that heavenly judgment is about to commence upon the religious realm of Israel and the church. In prophetic language this is the realm of the earth (Note that this also entails blessing and reward for those who are clean and righteous). Those who believe this judgment will begin in the secular realm (the sea) are mistaken. The sea will be affected, however, as the great mountain of religiosity throws itself into the sea as the second trumpet sounds.

The golden altar is in the Holy of Holies. It is in the direct presence of God. This represents the prayers of the saints who have clean hearts and have access to the throne room in the life of Jesus Christ as members of his body. Even though many, many prayers have been prayed over the centuries without seeming to have immediate results, they have not been forgotten. The *incense* of all the prayers has been accumulating, and none of it will be lost or forgotten.

Let us pray

Heavenly Father,

We ask that the days might be shortened so that your kingdom will come quickly; that the number will soon be complete; that we may be found among those who dwell in the heavens and not among the dwellers of the earth; that our hearts will not be fixed upon the things of this world when everything begins to be shaken. We ask this in the name of our Lord Jesus Christ. Amen.

Chapter 9

Preparing for the Trumpets

We must understand that this Apocalypse is the revealing of Jesus Christ. John's vision is from the perspective of the day of the Lord from God's point of view, not from our point of view. In our natural state, we cannot perceive the direct presence of God. We cannot access the throne of God in our own life, but we do have spiritual access through the life of the Lord Jesus by the Holy Spirit.

Jesus can place us before the throne of God as he did with John. Many people claim to know the Lord, but they do not perceive the throne of God or have a revelation of Jesus as he is for many reasons. The revelation of the Lord is not automatic but comes when he grants it. We cannot come to this revelation by believing facts, by religious discipline, or by complying with rites or rituals. Our capacity to see into the spiritual realm involves the status of our hearts. The pure in heart shall see God (Matthew 5:8), and we will only obtain and maintain a pure heart if we allow God complete authority to work in our lives and to discipline us as his sons.

Many can pray and say that they belong to the Lord; they can be participating in much religious activity, but according to the book of Revelation, if they are only dwellers of the earth and not dwellers of the heavens they will soon find themselves in serious trouble. Many do not dwell in the presence of the Lord. It is possible to walk here upon the earth yet have our real citizenship in heaven. If this is the case, we will love him and follow his commandments with all our heart. We will not be seeking after the things of this world, even though they may still be necessary and useful for the work that the Lord shows us to do. For if we seek the kingdom of God and his righteousness, all these earthly things will be added unto us according to the wisdom of God (Matthew 6:33).

Scripture states in Revelation 7:3 that the servants of God will be sealed – after the seven seals are opened. The first use of the word *seal* in Scripture is when the names of the tribes of Israel are engraved upon two onyx stones (with engravings like that of a seal) and are tied, one on each shoulder of the high priest (Exodus 28:9-12). Jesus is our High Priest of the order of Melchisedec (King of Righteousness), and he will carry those who are sealed upon his shoulders (Isaiah 9:6-7) into the Holy of Holies to participate in the government of his kingdom.

Many are concerned with the mark of the beast (Revelation 13:16-17), which is the manner of acting and thinking of the natural man. This mark is obligatory upon the hand and forehead of those who worship the beast and desire to buy and sell in the world system. The seal of God is the Spirit of God, the mind of Christ; he motivates us to act and think according to the desires of the new man in Christ, for he will write his law in our souls and on our hearts (Jeremiah 31:33). Those who have the seal of God will not have the mark of the beast.

It is in the new man in Christ that we have access to the Holy of Holies which is beyond the veil of our flesh that impedes the natural man from perceiving the direct presence of God (2 Corinthians 3:13-18). The natural man is excluded from the Holy of Holies upon pain of death (Genesis 3:24). He is not allowed to alter or to contaminate anything.

We can be praying and asking for many things for a long time without seeing our prayers answered. The corruption in the world around us may bother us; the decadence that we see in the church or in our country may trouble us; or we may be praying and interceding for individuals who are trapped in such difficult circumstances that sometimes our prayers seem ineffective. Some of us have an intense desire to have a clean, pure heart even when the actual state of our heart leaves something to be desired. God takes all of this into account. These prayers are stored up until the right moment arrives, and a powerful answer comes from the throne.

God has been quietly working in many of our lives over many years, but a time will come when he will overthrow the system of this world. At that time a message will go forth for those who can hear in the spiritual realm (even though they may not yet have clear vision in this realm), and they will be able to understand. The trumpets of God will be of great encouragement and will help them choose to risk their lives for the Lord and for the gospel, even while the powerful blasts of the trumpets strike fear into the hearts of the Enemy. The clear sound of the trumpets calls God's people into the heat of the battle where they will find liberty to do the will of God.

In the past, as the church has been contaminated by man, the sound of the trumpet has been uncertain (1 Corinthians 14:8). This will not be the case at this time. When the heavens are rolled up like a scroll, and the veil is lifted, the spiritual realm will have a head-on collision with the natural realm in which much of the church is operating. All those dwelling upon the earth will become suddenly aware of the One sitting upon the throne and of the wrath of the Lamb.

Any who claim to represent or belong to God upon the earth and are not citizens of heaven will panic. The true citizens of the heavenly Jerusalem will shine with the clarity and glory of God. This will give those who are sitting on the fence a last chance to rally to the sound of the trumpet and join us wholeheartedly, on fire for God. Otherwise, the Lord will spue those who are lukewarm out of his mouth, so they cannot continue to give a twisted, distorted example to the lost.

When the thunderings and lightnings and earthquakes that accompany the trumpets hit, they will shake the false peace of everyone who is not right with God. Job was a righteous man who could hear the voice of God, but he could not see into God's realm until everything he held dear was shaken or removed. At first, he thought that God was being unreasonable with him by allowing such terrible tribulation to come upon him. After Job's eyes were opened, however, God accepted him, and he was even able to pray and intercede for his three religious friends (Job 42:9-10).

God will soon shake everything that can be shaken so we can inherit a kingdom that will never be moved (Hebrews 12:25-29). The Apocalypse will be a terrible disaster to anyone who is trusting in anything other than Jesus Christ. People trusting in their own works, in their pet doctrines, in worldly wealth, or in the "covering" of anointed human leadership will be dismayed when Jesus Christ is revealed from heaven. Those who have a heart for God and for the people of God will rejoice. Those who are lost and out in the cold will notice when God's house, his people, is put in order, and they will have a wonderful opportunity to come in from the cold.

The revealing of Jesus Christ will bring great joy to the people of God, because he will break the vicious cycle of never-ending injustice upon the earth. This will continue into a new heavens and a new earth in which dwell righteousness. Nothing that is unclean will be allowed.

Let us pray

Heavenly Father,

We thank you for the promise of a clear sound of trumpets that brings encouragement as we do your will. We thank you for the promise to break the vicious cycle of injustice on the earth, and we thank you for the promise of new heavens and a new earth. In the name of our Lord Jesus Christ, Amen.

Chapter 10

The Trumpets Begin to Blow

Revelation 8

7 The first angel sounded the trumpet, and there followed hail and fire mingled with blood, and they were cast upon the land; and the third part of the trees was burnt up, and all the green grass was burnt up.

Isaiah prophesied that the hail would sweep away the refuge of lies (Isaiah 28:17).

Hail and fire were one of the plagues of Egypt. Until now the message that has gone forth during the age of Pentecost has been that of the early rain and the latter rain, which have to do with the agricultural cycle leading to the harvest (James 5:7-8). Hail and fire mingled with blood is different. All the green grass is burnt up. Those who feed on the milk (or grass) of the Word and fatten their flesh (using the provision of God to get the things of this world) will suddenly face a severe famine, not of bread but of hearing the words of the Lord (Amos 8:11). The possibility of fattening their flesh (like cattle) on the lush, green grass of the Word is now eliminated by the intensity of the word that will go forth as the first trumpet is blown.

As that first trumpet sounds, the third part of the trees is burned up. Three basic realms are mentioned in Scripture relating to the tabernacle: the outer court, the inner court or Holy Place, and the Holy of Holies. They correspond to the realms of the sea and the land and the heavens. They also correspond to three ages: The age of the law (of the Jews) went on for fifteen hundred years; the age of grace (of the church) is ending after two thousand years; and the age of the kingdom is projected one thousand years into the future (Revelation 20:4).

If trees represent the life and sustenance of man, then they may grow in any of the three realms. If the third part is consumed, in which of these realms are all the trees burned up? The lukewarm who are in the Holy Place are the ones in immediate danger when the veil is removed. Note that when the Scripture refers to the third part, it is not just 33-⅓ percent of the total. It could also mean one of three possibilities (or that one out of three possible realms is affected).

The trumpet was made of a ram's horn. Two perfect rams had to be sacrificed to anoint a new high priest (Exodus 29:1). Aaron and his sons had to present *two tenth deals of flour mingled with the third part of a hin of oil.* The drink offering was to be the third part of a hin of wine (Numbers 15:6-7). The use of the words *the third part* in the Old Testament is linked to the sacrifice of a ram and, therefore, to the substitutionary sacrifice of Jesus Christ (Genesis 22:13-14), which is the key to our access into the realm of the Holy of Holies.

Three is the number associated with fruitfulness. When a person or even an entire congregation or nation is not producing healthy spiritual fruit, this is a very bad sign, the first of the three signs. Of course, a case is mentioned in Scripture where someone can be saved even if all their works are burnt up in the fire of judgment.

A second sign, however, is if the person or group is being chastised or disciplined by the Lord, because he always disciplines his true sons whom he loves. If good fruit is not evident and the correction of the Lord is absent or is not being taken seriously, that person or entity has two strikes against them.

The third strike is when, in addition to the first two signs, evidence exists that evil fruit is being produced (for the tares have been planted by the Evil One and are poisonous when they approach maturity). If this is the case, as the evil fruit reaches maturity, a point of no return will be reached before the cancer can fully metastasize. At this point God will lift his hand of protection, and the person, group, or nation will be cut off and will no longer be allowed to represent the Lord. If they continue their evil works, they will eventually be destroyed.

King Saul in the Old Testament and Judas in the New Testament are examples of those who went past the point of no return. One of the most tragic stories in the Bible is that of Jonathan, who was unable to break the soul tie with his father, King Saul, and died at his father's side in the battle when he could have been the right-hand man of King David in David's kingdom.

I thank God for all the godly mentors I have had. One mentor, however, was different. I had a close relationship for many years with an extremely gifted evangelist who could fill stadiums all across the country. Sadly, all three of the above signs happened to him one by one. When it was clear that his personal life was a horrible disaster and he refused to desist and repent, the Lord gave me a very clear word: I needed to separate myself from this man who had been a longtime friend. Otherwise, like Jonathan, I would also have been subject to the judgment that was about to fall upon him. Cutting that tie was one of the most difficult things I have ever done. The last I heard of him, he was locked up in a high security mental institution because he had attempted to harm members of his own family. He was obviously demon possessed by this time.

Those who go down this road often attempt to drown out

the guilt and the conviction of their conscience with alcohol, drugs, or even prescription psychological medicine. Any attempt to anesthetize the conscience makes it harder for the Holy Spirit to bring them to repentance. Once the point of no return is reached, God will allow what had been unthinkable before. He will lift his hand and allow them to be overrun by the Enemy, as the insatiable appetites of the old nature spike.

King Saul received an evil spirit sent from God (1 Samuel 16:14). Satan entered into Judas at the Last Supper when Jesus himself served him the sop (the bread dipped in wine). During the day of the Lord, God sends an angel to unlock the bottomless pit of the insatiable appetites and desires of the natural man, and the hordes of locusts begin to swarm. Even at this late date, however, a recovery is still possible. Paul mentioned a case where he turned someone over to the Devil for the destruction of his flesh, so he might be saved in the end (1 Corinthians 5:5).

Here is another way to look at this:

Mark 4

26 *He also said, So is the kingdom of God, as if a man should cast seed into the ground*

27 *and should sleep and rise night and day, and the seed should spring forth and grow up, he knows not how.*

28 *For the earth brings forth fruit of herself: first the blade, then the ear, after that the full grain in the ear.*

29 *But when the fruit is brought forth, immediately he puts in the sickle because the harvest is come.*

Scripture clearly states that at the time of the harvest, the tares are gathered and burned first and then the wheat is gathered and stored in the barn (Matthew 13:30). The maturity of the fruit triggers the harvest. The tares are gathered and burned, and Jesus returns for a bride without spot or wrinkle.

On the Day of Reconciliation (Atonement), the only day each year that the Levitical high priest was allowed to enter the Holy of Holies behind the veil, Scripture declares that anyone among the people of God who has not come to repentance and refuses to afflict his soul will be cut off from the people of God. Anyone who is found doing his own work (instead of God's work) will be destroyed (Leviticus 23:27-32). This is why Jesus sent such a strong warning to the congregation at Ephesus.

The Day of Reconciliation is a prerequisite to the celebration of the fullness of the harvest at the Feast of Tabernacles. At this time, the tares are burned up. This is when the wicked are removed from among the righteous (Matthew 13:49). The fulfillment of the Day of Reconciliation is the next major event on God's prophetic calendar and coincides with Revelation 6:14 and 11:19.

Revelation 8

> 8 *And the second angel sounded the trumpet, and as it were a great mountain burning with fire was cast into the sea; and the third part of the sea became blood;*
>
> 9 *and the third part of the creatures which were in the sea, and had life, died; and the third part of the ships were destroyed.*

Notice that all these judgments are flagged with the statement *the third part*. This is because the judgment begins from the house of the Lord. We are the priesthood of all believers, and the place in the temple that is reserved for the ministry of the priests is the Holy Place. But this is also where Jesus told us to watch for the abomination of desolation (Matthew 24:15; Mark 13:14). Only the high priest can move to a higher realm, into the mountains of God, into the Holy of Holies.

Jesus is our High Priest, and we are to be part of him as the body of Christ. In order to sanctify a new priest, two rams had to be offered with a present of grain, which represents the work of our hands (Exodus 29:1; Leviticus 8:2; 23:18). The flour was to be mingled with the third part of a hin of oil, and a drink offering of the third part of a hin of wine was to be poured out before the Lord (Numbers 15:6-7). If the oil (anointing of the Spirit) and the wine (life of Christ) are deficient or absent, the work of our hands will not be acceptable; we will not be received (Revelation 6:6). If Jesus removes his presence (removes his lampstand) from this realm because man has allowed an unclean abomination, then *the third part* of everything will be affected, including whatever outreach was going on in the realm of the sea (in the world or sea of lost humanity).

Notice that the first trumpet affected the land. Then the effects of the second trumpet start on the land and cause serious repercussions in the sea and with the *ships* dedicated to outreach and commerce in the sea.

It was when Jesus cleaned the buyers and sellers out of the temple for the second time that his ministry was rejected (Matthew 21:12-17). As he left Jerusalem with his disciples, Jesus was disappointed because there was no fruit on a fig tree that he saw beside the road as he was going up to the Mount of Olives. Jesus cursed the fig tree and said it would never bear fruit again, and it withered away. The fig tree is a symbol of the people of God under law. The olive tree is a symbol of the people of God under grace.

Matthew 21

20 *And when the disciples saw it, they marvelled, saying, How soon is the fig tree withered away!*

21 *Jesus answered and said unto them, Verily I say unto you, If ye have faith and doubt not, ye shall not only do this to the fig tree, but also if ye shall say unto this mountain, Be thou removed, and be thou cast into the sea, it shall be done.*

Mark 11

> 23 *For verily I say unto you that whosoever shall say unto this mountain, Remove thyself and cast thyself into the sea, and shall not doubt in his heart but shall believe that what he says shall be done whatsoever he says shall be done unto him.*

This was not just any mountain. Jesus was standing at the foot of the Mount of Olives when he said, *if ye shall say unto this mountain*. The Mount of Olives has become the symbol of religion where religious people refuse the grace of God. The garden of Gethsemane is located there. This is where the lynch mob arrested Jesus. Even today, the Mount of Olives is cluttered with graves and gravestones because religious people think that this will qualify them for resurrection when Jesus returns.

The message of the second trumpet blast will cause this mountain of religious hypocrisy to be removed. It will cast itself into the sea, as the fire of the righteous judgment of the true presence of him who is seated upon the heavenly throne and the wrath of the Lamb scorches it. Remember that this is happening in response to the faith of the saints. When this burning mountain hits the sea, the consequences will be devastating. All the proselytizing by those promoting a gospel that has not been commissioned from the throne of God will go up in smoke (Matthew 23:15).

Another view, however, is that religious hypocrisy is blocking the way to salvation for many who are in the world, out in the sea of lost humanity (Matthew 23:13). The only way for any person to live in the sea is to be on a ship. The ships of religion are what keep the people alive. The ships keep the people from drowning. The religion of man attempts to help all of its proselytes save their own lives.

In God's view, this is all backwards, for he who saves his life shall lose it and he who loses his life for the sake of the Lord and for the gospel shall find it (Mark 8:35). Jonah had to learn this lesson the hard way and afterward became a very successful preacher. In order for us to prosper in the new life of Jesus, the old man, the old nature must die. When the mountain of religious hypocrisy casts itself into the sea, and the "ships" start sinking, and the third part of those creatures who are living in the sea die, God might be giving some of them one last opportunity to be saved. In God's kingdom, the way to eternal life is through death to the old man.

I am not sure if the third part of those who dwell in the sea will be saved or lost (in the end, each one must make his own decision), but I am sure that when vials are poured out, no one will survive in the realm of the sea or in the realm of the land. The only secure place will be with the dwellers of the heavens (Ephesians 2:5-6; Revelation 12:12).

Remember that the heart of God in all of this is to see how many will be saved. God is not willing that any should perish (2 Peter 3:9). The trumpets are the response from the throne of God to the prayers of his people. Even though all of us should desire the conversion and salvation of our enemies, many will perish because they refuse to repent.

Let us pray

Heavenly Father,

Help us to recognize chastisement and discipline as a sign of your love for us; then help us to respond that we might grow into what you would have for us. May we not fall into the trap of religious hypocrisy such that we cause others to perish. We pray in the name of our Lord Jesus Christ. Amen.

Chapter 11

Wormwood and Religiosity

Revelation 8

10 *And the third angel sounded the trumpet, and a great star fell from heaven, burning as a lit torch, and it fell upon the third part of the rivers and upon the fountains of waters;*

11 *and the name of the star is called Wormwood; and the third part of the waters became wormwood; and many men died of the waters because they were made bitter.*

The mountain of religious hypocrisy throws itself into the sea, but when the Devil falls from heaven, he affects the earth and falls upon the third part of the waters. The third part of the waters represent the Holy Place that is corrupt as a consequence of the abomination of desolation. The waters flow from the innermost being of the priesthood of all believers. Some of those in this area, however, are tares (sons of the Evil One) that have been planted among the wheat (sons of God); when they come to maturity, poison flows out of them.

The first use of the word *wormwood* occurs as Moses was

giving final instructions to the people who would inherit the Promised Land.

Deuteronomy 29

> 18 *Peradventure there shall be among you man, woman, or family, or tribe, whose heart turns away today from the LORD our God to go and serve the gods of those Gentiles; peradventure there shall be among you a root that bears poison and wormwood;*
>
> 19 *and it shall be, when that one hears the words of this curse, that he blesses himself in his heart, saying, I shall have peace, though I walk in the imagination of my heart, to add drunkenness to thirst.*
>
> 20 *The LORD will not forgive him, but then the anger of the LORD and his jealousy shall smoke against that man, and all the curses that are written in this book shall lie upon him, and the LORD shall blot out his name from under heaven.*

Jeremiah 23

> 11 *For both prophet and priest are feigned; even in my house I have found their wickedness, said the LORD.*
>
> 12 *Therefore their way shall be unto them as slippery ways in the darkness; they shall be driven on and fall therein; for I will bring evil upon them, even the year of their visitation, saith the LORD.*
>
> 13 *And I have seen folly in the prophets of Samaria; they prophesied in Baal and caused my people Israel to err.*

Baal is the god of the prosperity of this world, the worship of the sun of this world. God is going to bring the consequences of this down around the ears of all those who have perpetrated and participated in this worship; for in spite all the pretty words of the false prophets, the consequences are wormwood.

> 14 *I have also seen a horrible thing in the prophets of Jerusalem: they committed adultery and walked by lies; they strengthened also the hands of evildoers, that no one is converted from his malice; they are all of them unto me as Sodom and the inhabitants thereof as Gomorrah.*
>
> 15 *Therefore, thus hath the LORD of the hosts said against those prophets: Behold I will cause them to eat wormwood and make them drink the waters of gall, for from the prophets of Jerusalem is hypocrisy gone forth upon all the land.*
>
> 16 *Thus hath the LORD of the hosts said, Hearken not unto the words of the prophets that prophesy unto you: they make you vain: they speak a vision of their own heart, and not out of the mouth of the LORD.*
>
> 17 *They say boldly unto those that stir me to anger, The LORD hath said, Ye shall have peace; and they say unto anyone that walks after the imagination of his own heart, No evil shall come upon you.*
>
> 18 *For who has stood in the secret of the LORD and has seen and heard his word? Who has payed attention to his word and heard it?*
>
> 19 *Behold, that the whirlwind of the LORD shall go forth with fury, and the whirlwind which is ready shall fall grievously upon the head of the wicked.*
>
> 20 *The anger of the LORD shall not return until he has executed and until he has performed the thoughts*

of his heart: in the last of the days ye shall understand it with understanding.

We are in the last of the days, the day of the Lord, and even the smooth-talking false prophets that abound in the church today will soon seek to hide themselves from the One seated upon the throne and from the wrath of the Lamb.

21 *I did not send those prophets, yet they ran; I did not speak to them, yet they prophesied.*

22 *But if they had stood in my secret, they would also have caused my people to hear my words, and they would have caused them to return from their evil way and from the evil of their doings.*

23 *Am I a God of the near only, said the LORD, and not a God of the far?*

This prophecy of Jeremiah and many others throughout Scripture apply to us today.

False prophets are committing spiritual adultery with demons that are passing themselves off as angels of light. These stars will fall on the day of the Lord, and their duped followers in the church will reap the consequences as the "waters" become bitter with the corruption of wormwood.

We will do well to heed the message of the second trumpet that reveals the consequences of listening to the false prophets that abound around us. The word that comes from the Devil and his demons who have been passing themselves off as stars, as angels of light, will soon be revealed for the bitter poison that it really is.

Revelation 8

11 *and many men died of the waters because they were made bitter.*

Those who attempt to use their supernatural gifts, ministries, and talents from God to satisfy the desires of the flesh will find the waters to be extremely bitter in the end.

> 12 *And the fourth angel sounded the trumpet, and the third part of the sun was smitten and the third part of the moon and the third part of the stars, in such a manner that the third part of them was darkened, and the third part of the day did not shine, and the night likewise.*

The fourth trumpet affects the heavens. For the heavens and the earth shall be shaken. This trumpet presents much difficulty for those who insist upon their own literal interpretation of the signs and symbols of this book. However, when properly interpreted and decoded, we will be able to understand what judgments will literally happen.

The use of the phrase *the third part* signals that this relates to the Holy Place, the realm of the church. In the profaned Holy Place, Jesus told us to watch for the abomination of desolation that the effects of this fourth trumpet register (Daniel 12:11; Matthew 24:15; Mark 13:14). The Holy Place is the first place to be judged when the veil is removed; the fire of God, coming from behind where the veil had been, devastates the private kingdoms of man that have been built in his name. If the Holy Place is the third part of the total picture, then as it is judged, the third part of the sun is smitten along with the third part of the moon and stars so that the third part of the day and night do not shine.

This means that the Holy Place has gone totally dark, because God has removed his presence and given men the consequences of the abomination that they have so carefully cultivated.

Jesus said, *Immediately after the tribulation of those days shall the sun be darkened, and the moon shall not give her light, and the stars shall fall from the heaven, and the powers of the heavens shall be shaken* (Matthew 24:29).

With the fourth trumpet, the shaking of the powers of the heavens is well underway.

> 13 *And I saw and heard an angel flying through the midst of heaven, saying with a loud voice, Woe, woe, woe to the inhabiters of the earth by reason of the other voices of the trumpet of the three angels, who are yet to sound their trumpets!*

The inhabitants of the earth may find themselves in much trouble as the message and sound of the trumpets unfold. They will fall into one of three categories: hot, cold, or lukewarm. Those who are hot correspond to the citizens of the heavenly Jerusalem; they are sealed and told to rejoice as God cleans house (Revelation 12:12). Those who are cold correspond to those who dwell in the sea, and the trumpets only indirectly affect them when the mountain of religiosity is lit on fire and throws itself into the sea (Mark 11:23). Those who are lukewarm and inhabit the earth are in a real crunch. By the time the remaining three trumpets are blown, God is going to make sure that being lukewarm is no longer an option for anyone.

Let us pray

> *Heavenly Father,*
>
> *We give you thanks for this revelation, and we ask that we may be stimulated and moved to yield to your dealings with any part of our being, so we might be part of the bride without spot or wrinkle or any such thing that you are preparing for your Son, Jesus Christ. Amen.*

Chapter 12

The Fifth Trumpet

Revelation 9

1 *And the fifth angel sounded the trumpet, and I saw a star fall from heaven unto the earth; and to him was given the key of the bottomless pit.*

In Scripture, the *pit* is indelibly linked to death and Hades (*Sheol* in Hebrew), and we know that Jesus has the key to it. In Genesis 3:14, God told the Devil: *upon thy belly shalt thou go, and dust shalt thou eat all the days of thy life*. The realm of the belly is a bottomless pit of the insatiable desires of the unregenerate. No matter how much dust the Devil and his demons eat, they are never satisfied and always want more and more. Adam was made from the dust of the earth and is now a symbol of unregenerate man.

2 Peter 2

4 *For if God did not forgive the angels that sinned, but cast them down into the deepest abyss* [Gr. Tartarus] *and delivered them into chains of darkness, to be reserved unto judgment;*

Jude

> 6 *And the angels who did not keep their first estate but left their own habitation, he has reserved in eternal chains under darkness unto the judgment of the great day.*

God has chained these angels in the realm of the belly, the realm of insatiable desires, the realm of the dark, bottomless pit. He can also send someone with the key to open the bottomless pit and sic them on whomever he chooses, just as he sent the Babylonians and Romans against Jerusalem when God's people refused to hear his voice and desist from their abominations. Right now the West fears radical Islam, but what if God is the one who is lifting his hand of protection and letting them and other enemies loose?

Revelation 9

> 2 *And he opened the bottomless pit, and there arose smoke out of the pit as the smoke of a great furnace; and the sun and the air were darkened by reason of the smoke of the pit.*

The words *smoke of a great furnace* were first used in Scripture to describe the judgment of Sodom (Genesis 19:28). The second use describes the presence of God upon Mount Sinai amidst thunderings and lightnings and tremendous trumpet blasts, when the children of Israel stood back in terror, because they knew that the presence of God would destroy the carnal, natural man (Exodus 19:16-19).

Locusts were the eighth plague of Egypt (right after the hail); darkness was the ninth plague (Exodus 10:12-23). In the land of Goshen, however, the sons of Israel had light in their dwellings.

> 3 *And there came out of the smoke locusts upon the*

earth and unto them was given power, as the scorpions of the earth have power.

Note that this judgment is taking place upon the earth (the religious realm of the church and Israel).

God has a history of using locusts to judge his people, and the locusts respond to his commands. Scorpions are listed along with snakes as agents of the Devil. Jesus said, *Behold, I give unto you power to tread on serpents and scorpions and over all the power of the enemy, and nothing shall by any means hurt you* (Luke 10:19).

What is the power of the locusts that is like the scorpions of the earth?

The "locusts" can produce a lot of pain, because they will destroy the basis for the false hope of the dwellers of the earth. They will cause a huge (spiritual) famine in the land that will affect all those who do not have the seal of God in their forehead, those who are not separated in holiness unto the Lord (Exodus 39:30-31; Leviticus 8:9).

There is, however, a solution. This is what God told King Solomon:

2 Chronicles 7

13 *If I shut up the heavens that there be no rain or if I command the locusts to devour the land or if I send pestilence among my people;*

14 *if my people, upon whom my name is invoked, shall humble themselves and pray and seek my face and turn from their wicked ways, then I will hear from the heavens and will forgive their sin and will heal their land.*

In the church we encourage individuals to deal with sin, but we often forget that corporate sin requires corporate repentance.

Revelation 9

4 And it was commanded them that they should not hurt the grass of the earth neither any green thing neither any tree, but only those men who do not have the seal of God in their foreheads.

This judgment is not taking place in the literal, biological realm of green, growing plants. This takes place in the Holy Place, the realm of the earth. It will not affect anyone who has been born again into the life of Jesus Christ and has the seal of God in their forehead.

This is the judgment of God to remove the tares from among the wheat at harvest time. This is when the wicked are removed from among the righteous (Matthew 13:40-43). The spiritual famine that is the result of the sting of the locusts will bring the operations of those who are running huge religious feed-lots (where sheep and cattle are being fattened on a word that is laced with noxious additives) to a screeching halt (Joel 1).

As the day of the Lord develops, a huge change will occur. In the history of the church, the Devil and his associates have persecuted those who are on fire for God. Now everyone who belongs to God has been sealed, and God uses the Enemy to judge those who are lukewarm in the earth (in the church).

5 And to them it was given that they should not kill them, but that they should torment them five months; and their torment was as the torment of a scorpion when he strikes a man.

Scorpion stings do not normally kill people, but someone who has been stung by a scorpion will remember it for a very long time. Anyone in the earth who does not have the seal of God in their forehead is fair game. The first time that a period of five months is mentioned in Scripture is when the waters prevailed upon the earth one hundred and fifty days (thirty times five) when Noah and his family and the animals were in the ark (Genesis 7:24). Even though Noah and his family were saved, they had to have felt quite a sting as they rode out the five months of judgment in the ark, realizing that their earthly home and goods and possessions had been lost. God is hoping that many will be saved when they feel the unforgettable scorpion sting of being severed from the earthly treasure that they have been trusting in. This will give them the opportunity to seek God with all their hearts. This must have been going on in the ark with Noah's family in the midst of the most terrible storm recorded in history.

> 6 *And in those days men shall seek death and shall not find it and shall desire to die, and death shall flee from them.*

Proverbs 21:6 says, *The getting of treasures by a lying tongue is a vanity tossed to and fro of those that seek death.* Those who have stored up deceitful treasures on earth are those who seek death, and they will not find it. God causes the locusts to sting them, hoping that they will repent (Joel 2). This trumpet could have a devastating effect on the economy wherever there is corruption.

> 7 *And the appearance of the locusts was like unto horses prepared unto battle; and on their heads were as it were crowns like gold, and their faces were as the faces of men.*

Crowns like gold means that God has authorized this. If God has authorized demons to move our enemies, then anyone on earth who does not have the seal of God in their forehead could be torn to pieces.

> 8 *And they had hair as the hair of women, and their teeth were as the teeth of lions.*

Scripture states that a woman's hair is a glory to her, for her hair is given her for a covering (1 Corinthians 11:15). These locusts appear to be operating under a "covering" of legalistic law, and the reference to women implies that groups or congregations organize them. Lions snatch and tear their prey to pieces. (Ironically, this is where the Hebrew root of the word *rapture* comes from.) Joel 1:6 is part of a parallel passage.

> 9 *And they had breastplates, as it were breastplates of iron; and the sound of their wings was as the sound of chariots of many horses running to battle.*

Breastplates of iron means that the law protects them because they are bringing about the effects of the curse written in the Word of God (Deuteronomy 29:23). *Wings* means that they operate in a spiritual realm. The chariots and many horses are linked in Scripture to the legalistic, heavy-handed machinery of the kingdoms of man, starting with Pharaoh in Egypt.

> 10 *And they had tails like unto scorpions, and there were stings in their tails; and their power was to hurt men five months.*
>
> 11 *And they had a king over them, who is the angel of the bottomless pit, whose name in Hebrew tongue is Abaddon, and in Greek, Apollyon meaning destroyer.*

The first use of this word *destroyer* is linked to the Passover.

Exodus 12

> 23 *For the LORD will pass through smiting the Egyptians, and when he sees the blood upon the lintel and on the two side posts, the LORD will pass over that door and will not allow the destroyer to come in unto your houses to smite you.*

God, however, reevaluates the Passover at harvest time (Deuteronomy 26:2-3). People are required to place their fruit in a basket and present it before God. If God does not like the fruit, the consequences are serious:

Amos 8

> 2 *And he said, Amos, what seest thou? And I said, A basket of summer fruit. Then said the LORD unto me, The end is come upon my people of Israel; I will not again pass over them any more.*
>
> 3 *And the cantors of the temple shall howl in that day, said the Lord GOD; there shall be many dead bodies in every place; they shall cast them forth with silence.*

God can cancel the Passover and unleash the destroyer, if he does not approve of the fruit. The letter to Ephesus is a serious warning shot across the bow of those who claim to be the people of God, yet have walked away from their first love and are not producing the fruit of the Spirit.

God says that he is the one who sends the destroyer (Jeremiah 22:7). These locusts destroy all the spiritual mixture and garbage of the rotten fruit that religion has been feeding on. This is dealt with in the book of Joel (see Afterword).

Those who have been providing, feeding on, and living off the doctrines of men and demons are "stung" as they lose their income and livelihood and begin to feel the effects of spiritual famine. The kingdoms of man within the walls of religion are now in the same position as Pharaoh at the end of the darkness of the ninth plague. The economy and sustenance of Egypt was devastated, and Pharaoh still refused to let God's people go. The modern-day religious and secular pharaohs do not want to release God's people into freedom either.

> 12 *The first woe is past; and, behold, there come two more woes after these things.*

Near the beginning of Jesus' earthly ministry he proclaimed the Beatitudes of Matthew 5 and near the end of this ministry, the woes of Matthew 23. Within thirty-seven years, Jesus' woes all came true, and the religious kingdoms of the scribes, Pharisees, and priests had all been destroyed in Jerusalem, the city of religion. The trumpets of God described in Revelation will affect the entire world.

Let us pray

Heavenly Father,

We thank you for giving us this clear warning of your judgment on this earth. We thank you too for giving us every opportunity to seek you and deal with the sin in our lives. We thank you for providing for complete redemption through your Son Jesus Christ in whose name we pray. Amen.

Chapter 13

The Sixth Trumpet

Revelation 9

13 *And the sixth angel sounded the trumpet, and I heard a voice from the four horns of the golden altar which is before the presence of God,*

The golden altar of incense (symbol of prayer) is in the Holy of Holies before the throne of God. Four horns indicate heavenly power. The sixth trumpet is a direct result of the effective prayer and intercession of the clean people of God.

14 *saying to the sixth angel who had the trumpet, Loose the four angels who are bound in the great river Euphrates.*

Euphrates means "abundant and fertile" and this river is the northern border of the Promised Land, which is a symbol of our inheritance in Christ. But, as in the time of Joshua and Caleb, it has been overrun with enemies and abominations.

15 *And the four angels were loosed, who were prepared unto the hour and day and month and year, to slay the third part of men.*

The use of the phrase *the third part* again flags this as relating to the priesthood of all believers in the Holy Place, the realm of the church. This judgment will fall at a precise, predetermined time that is calculated down to the hour.

> 16 *And the number of the army of the horsemen were two hundred million: and I heard the number of them.*

When Israel was first mustered under King Saul (before his apostasy) to fight against Amalek (symbol of the natural man that God ordered destroyed), there were two hundred thousand men (1 Samuel 15:4). Two hundred thousand times one thousand is two hundred million. This is a symbolic number that describes the army of God walking in perfection. Two hundred is linked to the fruit of righteousness or justice (1 Kings 7:20).

> 17 *And thus I saw the horses in the vision, and those that sat on them, having breastplates of fire and of jacinth and brimstone; and the heads of the horses were as the heads of lions; and out of their mouths issued fire and smoke and brimstone.*

Fire is associated with the angels and ministers of God (Psalm 104:3-4; Hebrews 1:7). Jacinth is the eleventh foundation stone of the New Jerusalem (Revelation 21:20), and eleven is a number that is linked to Christ. Jesus told a parable of some workers who were hired at the eleventh hour and sent into the harvest (Matthew 20:6-7). These eleventh-hour workers may appear to be a motley crew, but they are fearless warriors. Many of David's mighty men were Philistines he picked up during the almost five months that he spent in their country. In fact, the Philistines were the ones who killed King Saul and opened the way for David to be made king of Judah and then king over all of Israel.

The first usage of the word *brimstone* in Scripture is when

God rained brimstone down upon Sodom (Genesis 19:24). Isaiah compares brimstone to the breath of the Lord (Isaiah 30:33). Brimstone is mentioned twenty times in Scripture and is always linked to the righteous judgments of God.

Our modern world has been conditioned to associate the effects of fire and brimstone with the Devil, but Scripture portrays fire and smoke and brimstone as proceeding from God.

> 18 *By these three plagues was the third part of men killed, by the fire and by the smoke and by the brimstone, which issued out of their mouths.*

Note that this is similar to the company of the two witnesses of Revelation 11.

The third part of men refers to anyone in the Holy Place, the church, or the land of Israel who does not have the seal of God in their forehead.

> 19 *For their power is in their mouth and in their tails; for their tails were like unto serpents that have heads, and with them they do hurt.*

> 20 *And the rest of the men who were not killed by these plagues did not repent of the works of their hands, that they should not worship demons and the images of gold and of silver and of brass and of stone and of wood, which neither can see nor hear nor walk.*

The rest of the men who were not killed are those who inhabit the sea of lost humanity and are not among the hypocrites that the judgments of God have been cleaning out of Israel and the church for the purpose of restoration (Romans 11).

> 21 *And they did not repent of their murders nor of their witchcraft nor of their fornication nor of their thefts.*

In order to judge the world, in order to judge the realm of the sea, God must have a pure, clean people that he can put on display. Jesus is coming back for a bride without spot or wrinkle or any such thing. The trumpets of God on the day of the Lord will make sure the wicked, who are described as spots or blemishes, are *removed* from among the righteous (2 Peter 2:13; Jude 12).

Let us pray

Heavenly Father,

Thank you for listening to the effective, fervent prayer of your people. Thank you for allowing us to intercede on behalf of those who still need you. And thank you for continuing to work with us to mold us into the people you want. In the name of our Lord Jesus Christ, Amen.

Chapter 14

The Little Book

Revelation 10

1 *And I saw another mighty angel come down from heaven, clothed with a cloud; and a rainbow was upon his head, and his face was as the sun, and his feet as pillars of fire:*

This is similar to the description of the glorified Jesus Christ in the first chapter of Revelation. Jesus Christ is now being revealed from heaven and is joined to his body, his bride. *Clothed with a cloud* means that the entire body has the heavenly nature of God. The rainbow upon his head means the covenant is fulfilled, and Jesus, the head of the body of Christ, has full authority to judge everyone and everything. He is the Sun of Righteousness, and his feet, his people who are alive and remain upon the earth, are as pillars of fire. They have been refined in the fire, but the wicked will be ashes under the feet of the righteous (Malachi 4:1-3).

2 *And he had in his hand a little open book, and he set his right foot upon the sea and his left foot upon the land.*

God's plans and purposes as recorded in Scripture have been unsealed and are being implemented in fullness. *His right foot upon the sea* means that he is taking direct authority over the Gentiles as part of his inheritance. *His left foot upon the land* shows his authority over Israel and the church.

> 3 *And cried out with a loud voice as when a lion roars; and when he had cried out, seven thunders uttered their voices.*

Here is a link to the army of two hundred million where the heads of their horses were as the heads of lions. Joel saw the same army and wrote: *the LORD shall utter his voice before his army* (see Afterword, Joel 2:11). This angel of the sixth trumpet is the same as the army of the sixth trumpet (Revelation 9:16-19). This is the gospel with the fullness of the power and authority of God. Thunder (the sound of God's voice) is always associated with lightning, which is a sign of the direct presence of God.

> 4 *And when the seven thunders had uttered their voices, I was about to write, and I heard a voice from heaven, saying unto me, Seal up those things which the seven thunders have spoken and do not write them.*

The message of the seven thunders, which was sealed when John wrote this book, just as certain aspects of the book of Daniel were sealed, is about to come forth because now is the time of fulfillment (Daniel 12:9).

> 5 *And the angel whom I saw standing upon the sea and upon the land lifted up his hand to heaven.*

> 6 *and swore by him that lives for ever and ever, who created the heaven and the things that are therein, and the earth, and the things that are therein, and*

the sea and the things which are therein, that there should be time no longer;

This does not mean the end of hours, minutes, and seconds; it means that the end of the age has come and everything will be judged. We are at the time of the harvest, and all the fruit will now be evaluated. Jesus said we shall know them by their fruit (Matthew 7).

7 *but in the day of the voice of the seventh angel when he shall begin to sound the trumpet, the mystery of God shall be finished, as he did evangelize unto his slaves the prophets.*

The seventh trumpet is the last trumpet (1 Corinthians 15:52).

8 *And the voice which I heard from heaven spoke unto me again and said, Go and take the little book which is open in the hand of the angel who stands upon the sea and upon the land.*

9 *And I went unto the angel and said unto him, Give me the little book. And he said unto me, Take it, and eat it up; and it shall make thy belly bitter, but it shall be in thy mouth sweet as honey.*

The prophet Ezekiel was told to eat a similar book (Ezekiel 3:1-4) as a prerequisite to ministering to the house of Israel. Honey is a symbol for the Word of God, and it will purge the old man and cleanse our appetites. We must be purged of the carnal appetites of the belly as a prerequisite for ministry. For this to happen, we must eat the entire book when God gives the order. Ezekiel and John were not allowed to pick and choose their favorite Scripture portions; they were ordered to eat the entire book.

10 *And I took the little book from the angel's hand and ate it up; and it was in my mouth sweet as*

> *honey: and as soon as I had eaten it, my belly was bitter.*
>
> 11 *And he said unto me, Thou must prophesy again as to many peoples and nations and tongues and kings.*

This means that John will prophesy again and the vision will come from yet a different angle, as God deals with many peoples, nations, tongues, and kings. This is the realm of the sea.

Chapter 10 comes to a conclusion after the wicked have been removed from among the righteous, and the power and authority of God is restored upon the land and the sea with the revealing of a glorious Jesus Christ perfectly joined to his body. The heavens are now joined to the earth by the body of Christ.

Let us pray

> *Heavenly Father,*
>
> *May we be patient as we wait for these things to come about in your time, but we also desire to be ready to immediately follow your orders as your great army comes together between heaven and earth. As we see this day approach, may we lift up our heads, knowing that the fullness of our redemption is near. We ask this in the name of the Lord Jesus. Amen.*

Chapter 15

Two Witnesses

Please notice and remember that the next fourteen verses are also within the context of the sixth trumpet, which goes all the way from Revelation 9:13 to 11:14. All of this is part of the second woe unto the inhabitants of the earth.

Revelation 11

> 1 *And there was given me a reed like unto a rod, and he said unto me, Rise and measure the temple of God and the altar and those that worship therein.*

The *measure* is the rod of God's justice. We are *the temple of God. The altar* is the gospel that is being preached, and the worshippers are those who have received the gospel and surrendered their lives to God.

> 2 *But leave out the court which is within the temple and measure it not, for it is given unto the Gentiles, and the holy city shall they tread under foot forty-two months.*

The outer court is where the altar is located and is to be measured. The court that is within the temple is the Holy Place and is not to be measured. This is where the abomination of desolation has been located (Daniel 12:11; Matthew 24:15; Mark 13:14). Forty-two is a number associated with the Levites, when they were given forty-two cities (in addition to the six cities of refuge) in the Promised Land for the purpose of teaching the way of the Lord to the tribes of Israel (Numbers 35:6). This effort of the Levitical priesthood totally failed in Israel, and it has also failed in large sectors of the church, which is supposed to be the priesthood of all believers (1 Peter 2:5, 9).

Forty-two, therefore, is a symbol of what needs to be restored to the people of God. Forty-two is the correction factor and is linked to the inner court of the Holy Place (the church). The main thing that has been lacking is the presence of God. The trumpets of Revelation are about restoring that direct presence by removing the veil and cleaning out the abominations of man (Revelation 6:14-17).

> 3 *And I will give my two witnesses, and they shall prophesy a thousand two hundred and sixty days, clothed in sackcloth.*

Sackcloth is a symbol of grief, mourning, and repentance. This word is used forty-eight times in Scripture, and this is the last occurrence.

One thousand two hundred and sixty days is forty-two times thirty or forty-two months (if we assume a thirty-day month). This is also a symbolic number of the correction factor (forty-two) multiplied by thirty which means maturity or perfection. Therefore, this ministry continues until the Holy Place, the place of priestly ministry (prophetically the realm of the earth), has been corrected and the people of God have been brought to maturity. This is an essential prerequisite for God's people to receive the fullness of the inheritance in Christ.

> 4 *These are the two olive trees and the two lampstands standing before the God of the earth.*

Zechariah saw a very similar vision. Two olive trees are a symbol of the people of God under grace.

Zechariah 4

> 1 *And the angel that talked with me came again and waked me, as a man that is wakened out of his sleep.*

If we are to understand this Scripture, the Lord must awaken us out of our spiritual lethargy and open the eyes of our understanding.

> 2 *and said unto me, What seest thou? And I said, I have looked and behold a lampstand all of gold, with a bowl upon the top of it, and its seven lamps upon the lampstand, and seven pipes for the lamps, which are upon the top thereof:*
>
> 3 *and two olive trees over it, one upon the right hand side of the bowl and the other upon the left hand side thereof.*
>
> 4 *So I answered and spoke to the angel that talked with me, saying, What is this, my lord?*
>
> 5 *Then the angel that talked with me answered and said unto me, Dost thou not know what this is? And I said, No, my lord.*
>
> 6 *Then he answered and spoke unto me, saying, This is the word of the LORD unto Zerubbabel, saying, Not by might, nor by power, but by my Spirit, said the LORD of the hosts.*

Zerubbabel means "a new shoot or branch out of Babylon." *Babylon* means "confusion." Even today, God is restoring a remnant out of the confusion of man that has taken the people of God captive. This time it will be done by the fullness of the Spirit of God.

> 12 *And I spoke the second time and said unto him, What are these two olive branches which through the two golden pipes empty the golden oil out of themselves?*

The prophet was having a hard time understanding this. The Levitical priesthood had to spend much time and effort preparing the oil, filling the lamps, trimming the wicks, etc. This is producing the light for the Holy Place (the light for the realm of the priesthood of all born-again believers) by the grace of God without any human effort.

> 13 *And he answered me and said, Dost thou not know what these are? And I said, No, my lord.*

> 14 *Then he said, These two sons of oil are those that stand by the Lord of the whole earth.*

The *sons of oil* are the sons of God. They are all those who stand by the Lord of the whole earth (Israel and the church). The number *two* speaks of a body: two olive trees, two golden pipes, two sons of oil. Initially, this body was one witness when Jesus Christ came the first time.

Zechariah saw two olive trees and one lampstand. Jesus showed John that the lampstand represents his presence and light in each congregation. John saw Jesus revealed in the midst of seven lampstands – in the midst of all the congregations of his people. However, in the first two chapters of Revelation only one lampstand (one witness) is shown per congregation, like the vision of Zechariah. Now John sees two lampstands that represent two witnesses.

Zechariah saw the lampstand of Jesus Christ as one witness. The two lampstands, which are a symbol of the light of Jesus through the body of Christ (the bride of Christ joined to Jesus, the Head), cannot be fully perceived until the body has come to maturity and received the fullness of the Spirit instead of the down payment or earnest that was poured out on the day of Pentecost upon the early church. (This is the vision of Revelation 10.)

These witnesses are portrayed in the book of Esther. At first, Mordecai sat at the king's gate, dressed in sackcloth, after hearing that Haman has sentenced all of God's people to be destroyed. Esther, the second witness, is not revealed as a Jew until after she decides to risk her life and enter the forbidden throne room of the king. Esther declares herself at the second banquet, and Haman is finished. Every matter of life or death requires at least two witnesses (Numbers 35:30; Deuteronomy 17:6).

Some may be confused in thinking that since the people of God are now under grace (symbolized by the two olive trees), the Old Testament law does not apply. It is true that those who are led by the Spirit are not under the law (Galatians 5:18), but Haman (representing the Devil and his sons) is not being led by the Spirit. The full brunt of all the consequences of disobedience under the law will fall upon the tares (the sons of the Evil One) that have been planted by the Enemy in and among the wheat.

At the end of the book of Revelation, these same two witnesses continue:

Revelation 22

17 *And the Spirit and the bride say, Come. And let him that hears say, Come. And let him that is thirsty come; and whosoever will, let him take of the water of life freely.*

This has been developing throughout the long history of the people of God, but now it will come to brilliant fullness as the body of Christ shines while connected to an unlimited source of anointing (Matthew 13:43).

Revelation 11

5 *And if anyone desires to hurt them, fire proceeds*

out of their mouth and devours their enemies; and if anyone desires to hurt them, he must in this manner be killed.

6 These have power to shut the heaven, that it not rain in the days of their prophecy and have power over the waters to turn them to blood and to smite the earth with all plagues, as often as they will.

Compare the above to Revelation 9:17-19 and 10:3. Essentially the same thing is viewed from three different angles within the context of the sixth trumpet.

When the body of Christ begins to operate in the fullness of the Spirit, a direct confrontation will occur with powers of darkness similar to when Moses confronted Pharaoh or when Jesus confronted the religious leaders of his day.

7 And when they shall have finished their testimony, the beast that ascends out of the bottomless pit shall make war against them and shall overcome them and kill them.

Please note that the only way out for those of us who are alive and remain is by death (1 Thessalonians 4:13-17). However, two options by death are available. We can die as a result of obedience to God or as a result of disobedience. A big difference exists between the death of the righteous and the death of the wicked.

Hebrews 9

27 And as it is appointed unto men to die once, and after this the judgment;

This Scripture and others like it poke holes in the secret-rapture theory that has become dogmatic doctrine in many places.

Some people attempt to make the case that Enoch and Elijah did not die and, therefore, must be the two witnesses. According to Scripture, Enoch clearly died (Hebrews 11:13). He did not, however, see death (Hebrews 11:5) because he was not locked up in Hades by death, as was the case with almost everyone prior to the work of redemption done by Jesus Christ. Enoch died a death of obedience and went straight into the presence of the Lord. This was also the case with Moses and Elijah. Moses was told by God to go up to the mountain and die. He promptly did so at the age of one hundred and twenty. And Elijah miraculously walked through the waters of the Jordan, a symbol of death.

The portrayal of this in the book of Esther is intriguing. Haman made plans to have all the Jews killed on a certain day, because he was upset that Mordecai refused to worship him. Haman did not just want to kill Mordecai; he wanted to wipe out the entire race. Mordecai dressed in sackcloth at the king's gate from the moment he heard the news. After Haman's decree went forth, sealed with the signet ring of the king, every Jew in the 127 provinces of the kingdom had to decide whether or not to continue to bear witness that they were part of God's people. They knew that anyone identified as a Jew would most certainly be killed. Total annihilation is still the Enemy's plan. It was not enough to attempt to kill the Lord Jesus. Today, the Enemy desires to wipe out the entire race of the body of Christ.

In the case of Esther and Mordecai and their people, the Enemy's plan failed at the last minute, and the tables unexpectedly turned. Haman was immediately hanged on his own gallows. All the Jews, most in sackcloth, considered themselves dead, but were suddenly given the power to defend themselves at the proper time. When the time came, the enemies of the Jews either desisted or were killed. Many became Jews.

Joel's army (really the Lord's army) has body armor that is unique. Their breastplates (body armor) are *of fire and of jacinth and brimstone* (Revelation 9:17). Jacinth represents the righteousness of Christ (standard armor for a Christian), but the fire and brimstone mean that anyone who even attempts to touch them will be killed. This is the same as with the two witnesses (Revelation 9:18; 10:3; 11:5). Joel goes so far as to say, *and even falling upon the sword, they shall not be wounded* (see Afterword, Joel 2:8).

There is still a mystery regarding all of this that will not be fully revealed until the seventh trumpet sounds (Revelation 10:7).

> 8 *And their dead bodies shall lie in the streets of the great city, which spiritually is called Sodom and Egypt, where also our Lord was crucified.*
>
> 9 *And those of the peoples and kindreds and tongues and Gentiles shall see their dead bodies three days and a half and shall not suffer their dead bodies to be put in graves.*

The city of religion has done this with countless martyrs over the past three thousand five hundred years (three-and-one-half prophetic days). They have put religious relics and even the bones and body parts of those killed by religion on display all over the world. Instead of burying the martyrs, they make images of them and cause them to be seen as objects of worship to the peoples and kindreds and tongues and Gentiles.

> 10 *And those that dwell upon the earth shall rejoice over them and make merry and shall send gifts one to another because these two prophets tormented those that dwelt on the earth.*

They even make holidays on the saints' days and rejoice over them and make merry and send gifts. Those who *dwell upon the earth* really make merry at Christmas and send gifts to one another even though most leave out the story of Jesus' death and resurrection. Prohibiting manger scenes is now common practice.

In the book of Esther, God unexpectedly turned everything around. Instead of certain death, God's people were allowed to defend themselves. What Haman intended to do to Mordecai was inverted, and Haman was hanged on his own gallows that he had made for Mordecai. What happened to Haman and his followers is what is about to happen to Satan and his followers. Key elements to God's plan are wrapped up in mystery that will not be fully revealed until the seventh trumpet sounds. The fact that we are seeing all of this so much more clearly now indicates that the day of the Lord is upon us.

By decree of Queen Esther, the feast of Purim was inaugurated, and God's people were directed to celebrate on the fourteenth and fifteenth days of Adar (the twelfth month). This was a good day of banquets and joy and of sending portions to one another and gifts to the poor (Esther 9:22).

> 11 *And after three days and a half, the Spirit of life from God entered into them, and they stood upon their feet; and great fear fell upon those who saw them.*

Soon a first resurrection will occur. The martyrs who have been killed throughout history will be bodily resurrected and ascend to the throne of God where they will be commissioned to reign and rule with Christ for a thousand years, which means unto perfection (Revelation 20:4).

What are we waiting for? How long will this take?

Here is the explanation given earlier:

Revelation 6

> 9 *And when he had opened the fifth seal, I saw under the altar the souls of those that had been slain because of the word of God and for the testimony which they held:*

The souls are under the heavenly altar, but at the time of the seventh trumpet they will be bodily resurrected and transformed. They will bodily ascend to the throne of God just as Jesus did in his ascension.

> 10 *And they cried with a loud voice, saying, How long, O Lord, holy and true, dost thou not judge and avenge our blood on those that dwell in the earth?*
>
> 11 *And white robes were given unto each one of them; and it was said unto them, that they should rest yet for a little while until their fellow servants and their brethren, that should be killed as they were, should be fulfilled.*

The first resurrection will take place after the last martyr is killed. Scripture is clear that our last enemy is death (1 Corinthians 15:26). We have the ability to conquer death because Jesus already did so. If we are dead in Christ to our own life, to sin, and to the world, we will go down in God's book as martyrs, no matter what the circumstances are regarding our physical death. We have no way out of here, however, without the actual, literal death of the old man and his old nature, *for flesh and blood cannot inherit the kingdom of God* (1 Corinthians 15:50).

1 Thessalonians 4

> 15 *For this, we say unto you by the word of the Lord, that we who are alive and remain unto the coming of the Lord shall not precede those who are asleep.*
>
> 16 *For the Lord himself shall descend from heaven with a shout, with the voice of the archangel, and with the trumpet of God; and the dead in Christ shall rise first;*

This is in keeping with Revelation 11:11-12 and pins the physical return of the Lord to the voice of the trumpet. Which trumpet? The sixth trumpet is a prime candidate because the Lord is at the head of his army and is joined to the fullness of his body. Then, with the seventh trumpet, the first resurrection takes place. Instead of two realms represented by the Holy Place and the Holy of Holies, the Holy of Holies has been expanded, forming only one realm. The heavens have been joined to the earth by the mature (perfect), overcoming body of Christ. This is depicted in the temple that Ezekiel saw (Ezekiel 40-47).

> 17 *then we who are alive and remain shall be caught up together with them in the clouds, to meet the Lord in the air, and so shall we ever be with the Lord.*

The word translated *caught up* (Gr. *harpazo*) comes from Hebrew trajectory that means to be snatched or torn away in the same sense that a lion tears apart its prey (see Appendix B). It means being ripped or torn right out of our earthly existence in the flesh. The only possible way to make it is to be safe and secure in the overcoming life of Jesus Christ.

In the battle of Jericho, Rahab was not miraculously translated out before the city fell. No, she and her household were the only ones left standing after everything else came down. She was ripped or torn (raptured) right out of all the corruption of Jericho immediately after the sound of the seven trumpets and the shout of God's people on the seventh-day march of the army of God. She was still in the city with a scarlet thread hanging out of the window of her house over the city wall when the foundations and all the rest of the walls of Jericho came down flat. Then the army of God snatched her out and utterly destroyed everyone and everything in the rest of the city and burned it with fire (Joshua 6).

It behooves us to understand that well before the city of Jericho went down, Joshua (meaning "Jesus") was already on the ground inside the Promised Land with his army. Similar to what is described in Revelation 6:14-17, Rahab told the spies that *I know that the LORD has given you this land because the fear of you has fallen upon us and all the inhabitants of the land faint because of you* (Joshua 2:9).

Rahab received the spies that God had sent, and Scripture

states that love covers a multitude of sins (1 Peter 4:8; James 5:19-20). God also says that anyone who receives a righteous man because he is a righteous man shall receive the reward of a righteous man (Matthew 10:39-42). God does not destroy the righteous along with the wicked (Genesis 18:23-33).

Rahab means "violence" in the sense of being "seized by violence." It is curious that *Webster's Unabridged Dictionary* lists this as being the number-one definition for our English word *rapture* (a definition which they say is now obsolete).

Revelation 11

> 12 *And they heard a great voice from heaven saying unto them, Come up here. And they ascended up to heaven in a cloud; and their enemies beheld them.*
>
> 13 *And in the same hour there was a great earthquake, and the tenth part of the city fell, and in the earthquake were slain the names of seven thousand men; and the others were frightened and gave glory to the God of heaven.*

By law, *the tenth part* belongs to the Lord. Therefore, he can capture it (like Rahab) out of the city of religion. To be an effective witness for God, our own name (nature) must be killed, so God can give us a new name (a new nature). *Seven thousand* is the perfect number of those who will come forth in the nature of God. If we follow the story of Rahab, she married Salmon (meaning "covering"), one of the spies who helped save her, and actually became part of the genealogy of King David and Jesus Christ (Matthew 1:5).

Another Scriptural precedent states: *And I will cause seven thousand to remain in Israel, all the knees which have not bowed unto Baal, and every mouth which has not kissed him* (1 Kings 19:18). In 1 Kings 20:15, these were the valiant men that went forth in the name of the Lord and delivered Israel.

Revelation 11

14 *The second woe is past; and, behold, the third woe comes quickly.*

15 *And the seventh angel sounded the trumpet, and there were great voices in the heaven, saying, The kingdoms of this world are reduced unto our Lord and to his Christ; and he shall reign for ever and ever.* This is a parallel passage with Daniel 2:34-35, 44.

The seventh trumpet is the last trumpet, the marker for the first resurrection.

1 Corinthians 15

52 *in a moment, in the twinkling of an eye, at the last trumpet, for the trumpet shall sound, and the dead shall be raised without corruption, and we shall be changed.*

Revelation 11

16 *And the twenty-four elders, who sat before God on their thrones, fell upon their faces and worshipped God,*

17 *saying, We give thee thanks, O Lord God Almighty, who art and wast, and art to come because thou hast taken to thee thy great power and hast reigned.*

18 *And the Gentiles were angry, and thy wrath is come, and the time of the dead, that they should be judged, and that thou should give the reward unto thy slaves the prophets and to the saints and those that fear thy name, to the small and to the great, and should destroy those who destroy the earth.*

> 19 *And the temple of God was opened in heaven,*
> *and the ark of his testament was seen in his temple:*
> *and there were lightnings and voices and thunder-*
> *ings and earthquakes and great hail.*

When the temple of God is opened in heaven and we can see the *ark of his testament*, we will know that the Day of Reconciliation, the Day of Atonement, has fully arrived (1 Corinthians 13:12).

Let us pray

Heavenly Father,

We ask that this word might enter into the very depths of our being like the book that Ezekiel and John were required to eat. Even though this tastes like honey, let it purge the depths of our belly and deliver us from the bottomless pit of the insatiable desires of the unregenerate.

May we completely lose our desire and appetite for the things of this world. May we wisely invest our time and resources in your kingdom.

We ask this in the name of our Lord Jesus Christ. Amen.

Part II

God´s Ultimate Plan

Introduction to Part II

Revelation is a book that revolves around the number seven. It first appears in Scripture describing the seventh day of creation when God finished his work and then rested (Genesis 2:2).

Not very long after God rested, Adam and Eve disobeyed God, and the deception, rebellion, and betrayal of the serpent surfaced. This dragon is revealed as Satan the accuser or the Devil (Revelation 12:9).

In his plan of redemption, the Lord Jesus began his ministry upon the earth with seven beatitudes. The prayer he taught his disciples also has seven lines that correlate with these beatitudes and the seven beatitudes embedded in the book of Revelation.[2]

The book of Revelation also has seven declarations of the holy name of God (I AM) throughout the book. Almost everything in Revelation comes in sevens. There are seven letters to seven churches that were apparently sent to seven literal congregations. In a larger sense, seven also refers to all the congregations from the first century forward throughout the age.

Revelation also mentions a scroll, or book, sealed with seven seals that can only be opened by the Lamb that was slain. These seals are opened one by one. The use of seven seals also means

2 See *God's Plan for Spiritual Battle*, Russell Stendal, Aneko Press

that the scroll was completely sealed. These seals have not yet been completely opened, but the time is very near.

Seven trumpets sound and have to do with a message from God being announced. The mystery of God shall be finished when the seventh trumpet sounds. This is when the kingdoms of this world come tumbling down, and God's kingdom rises over them. The seventh trumpet serves as the marker for the first resurrection and has not yet sounded. Even though different messages or trumpets from God have sounded at various times throughout the Church Age. I think all seven trumpets will sound in very close succession at the time of the end, just like the seven trumpets that were blown on the seventh day march around Jericho before the walls came down (Joshua 6:15-16).

Revelation contains a series of visions from God's perspective. They all have different facets, or angles, but possess many details that coincide. Themes, signs, and symbols that originate and develop throughout the Scriptures converge in Revelation.

After the seventh trumpet, Revelation goes on to mention seven vials of the wrath of God that will be poured out by seven angels. These vials are linked to the prayers of the saints that have accumulated over history. They are also a response to the evil fruit of the inhabitants of the earth and of the sea. Things come to a conclusion when all the fruit is mature at the time of the harvest. There can be good fruit or evil fruit, but both are harvested. Everyone and everything is revealed for what it is, and the status of the fruit determines the judgment and consequences.

Much of Revelation is a vision from heaven that John saw from the perspective of the throne of God. It contains signs and symbols, because it deals with things that are not easy for us to perceive or understand unless the Lord opens our understanding (Luke 24:45).

Many scenes in Revelation overlap and display the same

events and time frame from different perspectives. The following verse is an inflection point.

Revelation 10

> 11 *And he said unto me, Thou must prophesy again as to many peoples and nations and tongues and kings.*

Now consider the opening verses of the next chapter.

Revelation 11

> 1 *And there was given me a reed like unto a rod, and he said unto me, Rise and measure the temple of God and the altar and those that worship therein.*
>
> 2 *But leave out the court which is within the temple and measure it not, for it is given unto the Gentiles, and the holy city shall they tread down forty-two months.*

In the physical realm, we can measure the dimensions of things such as buildings or count a number of items. We also use the term "measure up," which refers to the intangible. But how can we ever measure up to what God requires of us? Jesus tells us that *where there are two or three gathered in my name, there am I in the midst of them* (Matthew 18:20). This doesn't happen when we come together in *our* name or in some name we've invented. We must come together in *his* name and *his* nature, assembled by him to listen to what he says and do what he desires. This is the only way we can measure up to what God looks for in his people, for we are the temple of God (1 Corinthians 3:16; 2 Corinthians 6:16).

The precursor is Ezekiel's vision of when he measured the temple. The presence of God didn't return to the new temple described by Ezekiel until everything measured up to God's design. This new temple was much larger inside than outside and clearly represents the people of God at the end of this age. *So he measured the court, one hundred cubits long and one hundred cubits broad, foursquare; and the altar that was before the house* (Ezekiel 40:47).

Numbers carry profound meanings throughout Revelation. For instance, one hundred is symbolic of the plan of God and squaring the number signifies the results or consequences. God's plan is to have a people, or temple, that measure up to the righteousness of Christ.

The word *foursquare* is mentioned in two other Scriptures, one of which is Exodus 27:1. *Thou shalt also make an altar of cedar wood, five cubits long and five cubits broad; the altar shall be foursquare, and its height shall be three cubits.* Five is a number that has to do with the grace of God. And the number three has to do with fruitfulness. This altar represents the gospel, which has to do with the consequences of God's grace being brought forth in the fruitfulness of redemption.

Foursquare occurs again in the later part of the book of Revelation. *And the city lies foursquare, and the length is as large as the breadth; and he measured the city with the reed, twelve thousand furlongs; and the length and breadth and the height of it are equal* (Revelation 21:16). Twelve has to do with divine order, and twelve thousand is the perfection of divine order. The holy city has no temple, *for the Lord God Almighty is her temple, and the Lamb* (Revelation 21:22). This city depicts the perfection of divine order in three-dimensional form. It illustrates how God's people walk in righteousness in the heavenly realm and upon the earth. The two realms converge in the holy city.

The New Testament makes it clear that we are the temple of God. As individuals he resides in our being, but corporately he desires a clean people in which we are all individual living stones. Jesus will return with and for a clean people and will use them to edify a clean temple of living stones. Therefore, the people of God must be measured.

This does not describe a replica of Solomon's temple here upon the earth, by the way. It speaks of the true temple of God, much of which is now in heaven with our Lord Jesus Christ.

When Moses built the tabernacle in the wilderness, it served as a copy of the true temple of God that was revealed unto him from heaven (Exodus 25:9).

When David received the plans for Solomon's temple, almost all the materials were precious and would cost an astronomical amount today. But Scripture declares that David received the plans as he contemplated the beauty of the Lord (Psalm 27:4). In reality, the true temple has to do with Christ. The Lord Jesus is the head of a greater body of Christ comprised of many members. He is the chief cornerstone of the structure.

The Scriptures introduce a tabernacle in the book of Exodus and then a glorious temple in Chronicles. But if we continue through to the end of the book of Revelation, there is no material temple in the city of God, because he will be present with all of his saints in the holy city that descends from heaven to earth (Revelation 21:22).

The final situation is a new creation in which there is no temple, because God dwells permanently with his people. There is no need for the sun because he is the light, and there is no night in his presence. The gates of the city are open during the eternal day, and nothing that is unclean, works an abomination, or tells a lie will be allowed to enter the glorious city of his light. Only those who are written in the Lamb's book of life will be allowed to live in the new creation.

Therefore, when John writes here of measuring the temple, this means that the Lord is going to measure us. He provides the standard of measurement as the head cornerstone that the builders of the religion of men upon earth rejected.

There is, however, one part of the temple that is not to be measured. As we saw earlier, Revelation 11:2 gives instruction to *leave out the court which is within the temple and measure it not, for it is given unto the Gentiles, and the holy city shall they tread down forty-two months.*

As far as I'm aware, aside from the Jubilee Bible, which is the source used throughout this book, all other English translations cite this verse as referring to the court or courtyard *outside* the temple. But that's not what the Greek really says. It's also not how the early Reformation Bibles translated this verse. The area that is not to be measured is the court *within* the temple. It refers to the Holy Place. It isn't measured, because the abomination of desolation contaminates it. The Holy Place corresponds to the ministry of the priests, now represented by the priesthood of all believers. The Holy Place is where the lampstand was located in the tabernacle and where the ten lampstands were located in the temple of Solomon. It's the location of the table of showbread in the tabernacle and the ten tables in the temple. This is where the priests tended the golden altar of incense, located in the Holy of Holies, by reaching their hands through the protective veil.

This book of Revelation begins in the Holy Place because the Lord is walking among the lampstands. The lampstands represent the presence of the Lord in the different congregations. The Lord is the light and the bread of life. He desires for us, his people, to become the light, salt, and nourishment that he is.

After the letters to the congregations, or churches, there is an open door in heaven, and Jesus' good friend, John, goes up through it (Revelation 4:1). This is Jesus' ultimate plan for all of his friends. Jesus desires for all of us to have a direct relationship with his heavenly Father. He wants us to come before the throne of the Father and ask what we will in the name of the Son, so that our petitions may be answered.

Other Scriptures state or imply that if our prayers are not answered, it's because we ask amiss or do not know God the Father. It is possible to live here upon the earth while our real citizenship is in the heavenly realm of God, where we have entrance through our Lord Jesus. This is in contrast to those who do not prepare their hearts, like the priests who didn't take due care of the clean things of God and didn't practice or teach the difference between the precious and the vile. Therefore, they couldn't enter the presence of God even though they were allowed to continue to minister outside (Ezekiel 44:10-16).

Ezekiel speaks of an entire race of priests that won't be allowed to enter into the presence of God. They may minister on the outside, but they cannot stand in the presence of God. The only priests allowed in God's presence belong to one family and are known as the sons of Zadok (righteousness).

The Lord Jesus, however, is king and high priest of another order – one that is not descended from Levi. He's from the order of Melchisedec (in Hebrew Melchi-zadoc), meaning *king of righteousness*. He doesn't come from a Levitical background, and isn't interested in ceremonies, rites, and rituals. He desires to lead us into reality.

The ministry of the Lord Jesus centers on us walking with him in communion with God the Father by the indwelling presence of the Holy Spirit, along with those who walk in communion with them. It is very important to keep this in mind.

Some say or teach that the fullness of the presence of God is only found in great meetings where mighty leaders perform miracles, officiate, and distribute the anointing to the whole world. Many have visited one place or another where this is purported to be taking place. It's extremely important that we take heed of what Jesus told the Samaritan woman at the well. *The woman said unto him, Lord, I perceive that thou art a prophet. Our fathers worshipped in this mountain, and ye say that in Jerusalem is the place where it is necessary to worship. Jesus said unto her, Woman, believe me, the hour comes when neither in this mountain nor in Jerusalem shall ye worship the Father. Ye worship what ye know not; we worship what we know, for saving health is of the Jews. But the hour comes, and now is, when the true worshippers shall worship the Father in spirit and in truth, for the Father seeks such to worship him. God is a Spirit and those that worship him must worship him in spirit and in truth* (John 4:19-24).

It's clear, then, that unless we are prompted and led by the Holy Spirit, blind attendance at a routine meeting at a certain physical place will not, in and of itself, ensure that our worship is acceptable to God. True worship in Spirit and in truth is a lifestyle. God desires that everything that we do or say be pleasing to him, 24/7. Our worship will please God if we have clean hands and a pure heart (Psalm 24:3-6).

The belief that our worship can only be acceptable to God if it's carried out in a certain place or under the auspices of a certain leader isn't the only area in which we can be led into error. Consider Matthew 24:23-24. *Then if any man shall say unto you, Behold, here is the Christ* (here is the anointing), *or there, believe it not. For there shall arise false Christs* (false anointed) *and false prophets and shall show great signs and wonders in such a matter that they shall deceive, if possible, the very elect.*

The only man who will never be deceived is Jesus, who is also God. If he is our head, then we will not be deceived. At the beginning of this book of Revelation, John said, *And I turned to see the voice that spoke with me* (Revelation 1:12). *And when I saw him, I fell at his feet as dead* (Revelation 1:17).

Brethren, there is danger if we aren't able to *see* into the spiritual realm – if we don't have spiritual discernment from the Lord. The capability for such vision is linked to the status of our hearts. Jesus said: *Blessed are the pure in heart for they shall see God* (Matthew 5:8). The Greek is exclusive and means that *only* the pure in heart shall see God. Those who are not pure in heart, who cannot see or discern in the spiritual realm in a way that allows them to perceive God, may perceive something else and be mistaken and deceived. If we are to discern (see) God, it is necessary for God to do a work in our heart and replace our heart with his.

Let's return to John's vision.

Revelation 11

> 1b *Rise and measure the temple of God and the altar and those that worship therein*
>
> 2a *But leave out the court which is within the temple.*

Those were the instructions given to John. It's obvious that this court or Holy Place (typed as the earth) would not measure up, because what the Lord is interested in is the Holy of Holies (typed as the heavens). He's also not interested in beginning his judgment with those of the outer court (typed as the sea), because, before judging them, he must first place his clean people on display. The altar represents the gospel, the conditions under which we may come to God, and is extremely important. God wants to make sure that man has not tinkered with any of the measurements of the altar, that is, any of the conditions of the gospel being presented. The altar was located in the outer court of the temple near the brazen sea (2 Chronicles 4:1-5).

Before entering the Holy Place, the priests washed themselves with water, which is a symbol of the Word. Through the prophet Isaiah, God promised that the glory of the Lord would cover the earth as the waters cover the sea. When prophetic language in the Bible describes the realm of the sea, it refers to those lost members of humanity who do not know God. There is also the realm of the earth (the Holy Place), which should be the people of God (the priesthood of all believers). However, many in this realm are focused on the things of this world here below and use the name of God to get what they selfishly want. In this way they pervert their God-given gifts and ministries. This is what causes the abomination of desolation in the Holy Place.

Beyond the realm of the sea and the realm of the earth, there is the realm of heaven and of the throne of God, which is symbolized by the ark of the covenant under the wings of the cherubim. Some readers may be surprised to know that this realm, too, has had unclean intrusions in the form of Satan and his fallen angels. Satan is also known as the accuser of the brethren. There are several instances in Scripture that make mention of unclean spirits operating in the heavenly realm of the throne of God. For example, Job said that *there was a day when the sons of God came to present themselves before the LORD, and Satan came also among them* (Job 1:6). On one occasion, God sent an evil spirit to trouble King Saul (1 Samuel 16:14). Another time, God sent a lying spirit to deceive all the prophets of King Ahab (1 Kings 22:22). And in Zechariah, we learn that Satan was standing by to resist Joshua, the high priest, until his filthy garments were changed (Zechariah 3:1-7).

This type of thing, well documented in Scripture, will eventually lead to war in heaven and the creation of new heavens and a new earth where only righteousness dwells.

Revelation 11

> 3 *And I will give my two witnesses, and they shall prophesy a thousand two hundred and sixty days, clothed in sackcloth.*

In Scripture, sackcloth is synonymous with repentance.

John the Baptist baptized people in water prior to the ministry of the Lord Jesus at his first coming. Scripture implies that, spiritually, he baptized them into repentance (Matthew 3).

John was a man on a mission. Even though he was the son of a high priest, he didn't come in beautiful clothes. With no need for the finery of this world, he dressed with a leather girdle and a cloak of camel's hair and came in the spirit and power of Elijah (Luke 1:17). Many of his hearers awaited the first coming of the Lord Jesus according to Scripture, and they became disillusioned because they didn't understand that the messiah was to come twice. They didn't understand that the purpose of his first coming was to die in order to save us. Because of this, he would ascend and reign at the right hand of the Father until the new covenant became a reality in the lives of countless faithful witnesses throughout the past two millennia, including us. Then a second coming would fulfill the rest of the prophecies.

Like John, in our modern day, we encounter many who have been deceived and think that the second coming will not take place, or who expect events linked to the second coming that contradict scripture. Deception has been running rampant.

The Scripture which describes the ministry of the two witnesses is very clear (Revelation 11:3). This ministry will last for 1,260 days. There is a historical explanation of this in which some came to think that this ministry would last 1,260 *years,* since curiously, the Spanish Inquisition lasted exactly 1,260 years. There's also a more recent interpretation in which Hitler is said to have spent approximately 1,260 days exterminating the witness of Jews and Christians.

Such theories may be intriguing, but we know that there is no private interpretation of prophecy and true interpretation must be by the Spirit of God. Of course God may interpret Scripture on as many different levels as he desires. But even though we realize that the Holy Spirit may apply Bible prophecy to as many individuals, peoples, and situations as he desires throughout history, we are also aware that we are coming to the end of the age and to a grand finale.

Peter puts this into context. *We have also the most sure word of the prophets, unto which ye do well that ye take heed, as unto a light that shines in a dark place, until the day dawns and the morning star arises in your hearts, understanding this first, that no prophecy of the scriptures is of any private interpretation. For the prophecy did not come in times past by the will of man, but the holy men of God spoke being inspired by the Holy Spirit* (2 Peter 1:19-21).

Therefore, today we diligently seek the fullness of the interpretation of these prophecies. What will happen between the end of the day of man, the end of the age of the church, and the day of the Lord that is dawning?

We know that the day of the Lord is at the door, and that, as a prelude, the Lord will have a ministry that clearly declares the truth. The Lord didn't end the age of the law without sending John the Baptist to bring warning for six months, followed by Jesus' ministry for three and a half years. Even after Jesus' rejection by the Jews, God continued to minister through the apostles with great power and authority for what appears to have been another three and a half years. Until he decided to pour out the Holy Spirit upon the house of Cornelius the Gentile and raise up Paul as an apostle to the Gentiles. God continued to extend his grace to the Jews for another thirty years, from AD 37 to AD 67, until the siege of Jerusalem and the complete destruction of the city, the temple, and all the rebellious Jews by AD 70. This Roman siege of Jerusalem lasted approximately three and a half years, and the scenario seems to have a great deal in common with the end of the age of the church (Matthew 24; Mark 13; Luke 21). The book of Revelation is believed to have been written well after the destruction of Jerusalem in approximately AD 90.

The entire process, from the birth of Jesus to the destruction of the temple, took approximately seventy years. That was the end of the age of the law. Now the age of grace, the age of the church, is also ending, and the process may be very different from what many expect. We find the real division of history in the events which lead up to and surround the second coming of the Lord Jesus. Now is the time when unfulfilled prophecies scattered through virtually every book in the Bible will come to pass in fullness. Now is when the meek shall inherit the earth (Matthew 5:5).

Chapter 16

The New Creation is Brought Forth Out of the Old

Revelation 12

1a *And there appeared a great sign in the heaven:*

Notice this sign is *in the heaven*, not in the earth. In other words, this sign is from God's perspective.

1b *a woman clothed with the sun, and the moon under her feet, and upon her head a crown of twelve stars.*

Who is this woman?

That question has been asked for many years.

This sign appeared in heaven and the woman is *clothed with the sun*, the sun being a type of the world and the world system. Israel under law and portions of the church, on the other hand, are linked to the moon in Scripture. As the moon reflects the light of the sun, so Israel and the church should reflect the light of the grace and glory of God. Sadly, the light that the "moon" has reflected much of the time, as it has waxed and waned throughout world and church history, has been the light of the world and its system.

The sun and moon are part of the natural creation, and the Lord made the natural creation for a purpose. First came the separation of the waters and the creation of all green living plants that we know as life on earth. Then came the sun, moon, and stars, which were all created on the fourth day (Genesis 1:6-19).

God's plan had a purpose and a balance. He created the greater light to rule over the day and the lesser light to rule the night (Genesis 1:16). However, Scripture also implies that the first creation was subjected to vanity (Romans 8:20). The purpose God had for the first creation was frustrated by the fall and came under the curse. Instead of the Sun of righteousness, we have had the god of this age for the past six thousand years (Malachi 4:2; 2 Corinthians 4:4). Spiritually, it has been night for a very long time.

The wickedness of mankind has been a grief to the Lord. *And GOD saw that the wickedness of man was great in the earth and that every imagination of the thoughts of his heart was only evil continually. And the LORD repented of having made man on the earth, and it grieved him at his heart. And the LORD said, I will destroy man whom I have created from the face of the earth, both man and beast and the animals and the fowls of the air; for I repent of having made them. But Noah found grace in the eyes of the LORD* (Genesis 6:5-8).

Instead of destroying us, in his mercy, the Lord chose to use the old, natural creation that was frustrated as a seedbed to bring forth a new creation. Jesus Christ, now a freeborn son, is the first of the firstfruits of the new creation, which is the body of Christ (James 1:18). Noah and those saved in the ark were a prophetic example of God's redeeming work.

1b *and upon her head a crown of twelve stars.*

Twelve is a number that has to do with government, meaning either divine order or the god of this age.

Here in Latin America, where I currently live, there are numerous statues and paintings of Mary that attempt to depict this passage. However, in many of the statues or artwork I've seen, there are thirteen stars instead of twelve. It's interesting that the artists would confuse this detail, because thirteen can mean rebellion or the kingdom.

> 2 *and she being with child cried out, travailing in birth, and pained to be delivered.*

Pain in childbirth came as a result of the fall along with the promise that the seed of the woman would bruise the head of the serpent (Genesis 3:16).

Here is a mystery: This woman is of the old creation and is still under the effects of the curse which includes travail in childbirth (Genesis 3:16). Therefore, she cannot be considered the bride of Christ, because the bride is of the new creation. We have a promise that there will be a woman who will not experience travail during childbirth (Isaiah 66:7). When John wrote this in about 90 AD, our Lord Jesus had already been born, lived, died, had been resurrected, and ascended into heaven. However, what many do not understand is that Jesus was the first of many brethren who together make up the overcoming body of Christ that will rule the Gentiles with a rod of iron, as portrayed in the next three verses in Revelation.

> 3 *And there appeared another sign in the heaven; and, behold, a great red dragon, having seven heads and ten horns, and seven crowns upon his heads.*

> 4 *And his tail drew the third part of the stars of heaven and cast them to the earth; and the dragon stood before the woman who was ready to be delivered, to devour her child as soon as it was born.*

> 5 *And she brought forth a man child, who was to rule all the Gentiles with a rod of iron; and her child was caught up to God and to his throne.*

The Devil attempted to *devour,* or destroy, baby Jesus, and so it has been with all who are born again (Matthew 2:13-18).

In the letter to the congregation at Thyatira, we find a clue as to the identity of this *man child* who appears in verse 5. The word used in the original Greek refers to a son who is born free, and not born into slavery. The translation into English as *man child* is a bit clumsy but serves to mark a distinction between this child and a "normal" child who is born as a slave to the flesh, the world, and the Devil. The members of this man child, the body of Christ with Jesus as their head, are citizens of heaven. They are dwellers of the heavens even as they walk here upon the earth (1 Corinthians 15:48-49; Ephesians 1:3 and 2:6; Hebrews 12:22).

The words of Revelation 12:5 echo those of Revelation 2:26-27, which state: *And he that overcomes and keeps my works unto the end, to him will I give power over the Gentiles; and he shall rule them with a rod of iron; as the vessels of a potter they shall be broken to shivers, even as I received of my father.*

What Jesus Christ receives from his father is clarified in Psalm 2:7-9, in terms that foreshadow these verses in the Book of Revelation. *I will declare the decree; the LORD hath said unto me, Thou art my Son; this day I have begotten thee. Ask of me, and I shall give thee the Gentiles for thine inheritance and unto the uttermost parts of the earth for thy possession. Thou shalt break them with a rod of iron; thou shalt dash them in pieces like a potter's vessel.*

The corporate son of this woman, the overcoming body of Christ with Jesus as the head, does not dwell upon the earth but rather is caught up to the throne of God and is a dweller of the heavens. A new creation (corporate man) is brought forth from an old creation (people or a woman). This is why Scripture states that the woman who was deceived in the rebellion shall be saved through child bearing (1 Timothy 2:15). The woman of Revelation 12:1 is linked to Eve, because Eve was called *the mother of all living* (Genesis 3:20). It is also important to remember that from the beginning, God put enmity between the serpent and the woman and between the seed of the serpent and the seed of the woman (Genesis 3:15).

If the Lord Jesus had not been born of a woman, if he had not overcome, if he had not ascended to the throne of his Father, there would have been no salvation for any of us – not even for Mary.

The words *son* or *child*, referring to sons of God or to the man child, are understood not to be referring to gender. In Christ there is no male or female, no Jew or Gentile. Everyone born again into the life of Christ is a new creature, though the birth may take place in travail and pain (2 Corinthians 5:17; Galatians 6:15).

Let's look in more detail at those earlier verses in Revelation 12.

> 3b *behold, a great red dragon, having seven heads and ten horns, and seven crowns upon his heads.*

The red dragon is Satan. Seven heads refer to the complete number of heads of all the principalities and powers in his kingdom. Ten horns, which refer to the law, means that he draws his power from the law of sin and death. Note that the crowns are upon the heads of the dragon, upon his principalities. This will change when we come to the dragon's image, which is the beast that comes up from the sea. This new beast, described in Revelation 13:1-5, has its crowns on its horns instead of its heads. In other words, it deifies the law.

> 4a *And his tail drew the third part of the stars of heaven and cast them to the earth;*

In Part I of this book, the case was made for the phrase *the third part* being linked to the amount of oil and wine to offer with a ram as a sacrifice, linked to setting priests into their ministry in the Holy Place, and linked to the Holy Place in general which is symbolically the realm of the church, the realm of the priesthood of all believers (Numbers 15:6-7). Revelation 1:20 says that Jesus has seven stars in his right hand and explains the mystery to mean that the seven stars are the seven angels of the seven congregations. Seven angels mean all the angels pertaining to all seven congregations.

When the dragon, the Devil, casts down the third part of the stars, it's the stars having to do with the Holy Place, which is contaminated with the abomination of desolation. All of the members of the *man child* are immune to this because they are caught up to God and his throne in the heavenly realm of the Holy of Holies.

> 4b *and the dragon stood before the woman who was ready to be delivered, to devour her child as soon as it was born.*

> 5 *And she brought forth a man child, who was to rule all the Gentiles with a rod of iron; and her child was caught up unto God and to his throne.*

> 6 *And the woman fled into the wilderness, where she has a place prepared of God, that they should feed her there a thousand two hundred and sixty days.*

This *man child* has been being born for quite some time now. There is a reason why this appears in Revelation 12, right after Chapter 11, which was discussed in detail in Part I.

In the book of Revelation and as modeled in the temple,

people have the possibility of dwelling in one of three spiritual realms: the outer court (the sea), the inner court or Holy Place (the earth), and the Holy of Holies (the heavens) which contains the direct presence of God. Remember, Solomon's temple had a brazen sea in the outer court (2 Chronicles 4:1-5). And just as only the priests born into the tribe of Levi could enter the Holy Place, so only those who are born again may enter the priesthood of all believers.

The children of Israel were under the Law for fifteen hundred years and are typed with the outer court of the temple. The church age, linked to spiritual adolescence and to the Holy Place, is typed with two thousand years. And some believe the coming day of the Lord, typed with entrance into the Holy of Holies, will last a thousand years.

In the example of these verses in Revelation, the children of Israel (the woman) leave Egypt, which symbolizes bondage to the flesh, the world, and the Devil. They journey into the wilderness or desert, which symbolizes voluntarily coming under the leading, guidance, correction, and discipline of Father God. Until they come to maturity as a people and enter the Promised Land, which has to do with the kingdom of God and symbolizes our inheritance in Christ.

The wilderness is prophetically linked to the Holy Place, which is the part of the temple that the Lord said not to measure (Revelation 11:1-2). This woman, or congregation, must face many problems and dangers in the wilderness, but there is also special provision from God for 1,260 days. Elsewhere, we already spiritually defined 1,260 as forty-two (the required correction factor when the presence of God is missing) multiplied by thirty (maturity or perfection).[3] In order to enter the fullness of the promised inheritance, which has to do with the Spirit without measure, this congregation must be nourished in

3 See *The Correction Factor*, Russell Stendal, Aneko Press.

the desert or wilderness until they come to maturity in Christ. This links with Revelation 11:3 in the introduction. *And I will give my two witnesses and they shall prophesy a thousand two hundred and sixty days, clothed in sackcloth.*

It's also interesting to remember that their 1,260 days of prophecy end like this:

> 18 *And the Gentiles were angry, and thy wrath is come, and the time of the dead, that they should be judged, and that thou should give the reward unto thy slaves the prophets and to the saints and those that fear thy name, to the small and to the great, and should destroy those who destroy the earth.*

The holy city being trodden under foot for forty-two months, the testimony of the two witnesses, and the time that the woman spends in the wilderness are all likely the same spiritual time frame. There have been many types and shadow fulfillments of this throughout history, but I am convinced that the fullness of this prophecy, in Revelation 12:6-9, still lies ahead, because the fullness of the anointing without measure for the body of Christ is still in the future. This is why this Scripture is located in Revelation 12.

What will come is not a little dab of anointing. It is not a single or even a double portion. Zechariah saw golden tubes conducting *unlimited* oil to the lampstand (Zechariah 4:12). This is a symbol of the written word of the Scriptures coming alive in us under the anointing of the Holy Spirit. There are sixty-six books in the Bible, and if we were to make a lampstand according to the instructions in the Book of Exodus, there would be sixty-six features of gold that make up that lampstand (Exodus 25:31-37). And we are to have unlimited oil for it – that is, an unlimited supply of light and power from the Holy Spirit to bring the Scriptures to life within us.

In the Old Testament, the priests had to carefully prepare the oil, meticulously supply the lamps, and trim the wicks so there would be light in the Holy Place. We are coming to a time when this will depend directly upon God, who causes the two olive trees to grow and blossom and give fruit. He causes the golden oil to flow through golden tubes directly into what is now two lampstands (two witnesses) which, at the end of the Book of Revelation and in the highest sense, are the Spirit and the bride (Revelation 22:17). The bride is a citizen of the heavens even though some of the individuals who form part of her may still walk here upon the earth.

This means that the content and revelation of the message going forth no longer depends upon the wisdom of human ministry which relies on extensive theological study in order to provide a Sunday morning message once a week. God will fulfill prophesy for his own name's sake, not because we have been extra wise or extra diligent. He is preparing those who will allow him to do the work. Elijah and John the Baptist are examples of this, and it's summed up in Malachi 4.

After the 1,260 days are over, there is another marker regarding what will happen next:

Revelation 11

> 14 *The second woe is past; and, behold, the third woe comes quickly.*

Remember that these woes are to the *inhabiters of the earth* and each woe is linked to a trumpet, starting with the fifth trumpet (Revelation 8:13). These *inhabiters* are those who think they have a religious legal covenant with God but who do not dwell in the heavens like the victorious overcomers who make up the man child. These overcomers may be men, women, or even children.

> 15 *And the seventh angel sounded the trumpet, and there were great voices in the heaven, saying, The kingdoms of this world are reduced unto our Lord and to his Christ; and he shall reign for ever and ever.*

This is clearly the beginning of the new day in God, and the church age is definitely ended. The seventh trumpet is the last trumpet and is indelibly linked with the first resurrection and the return of Jesus Christ (1 Corinthians 15:52).

If we return to Revelation 12, we find something else that takes place simultaneously with the forty-two months and the 1,260 days.

Revelation 12

> 7 *And there was war in heaven: Michael and his angels fought against the dragon; and the dragon fought and his angels,*
>
> 8 *and did not prevail; neither was their place found any more in heaven.*
>
> 9 *And the great dragon was cast out, the serpent of old, who is called Devil and the Satan, who deceives the whole world; he was cast out into the earth, and his angels were cast out with him.*

Just in case someone is not exactly clear about who this dragon is, Scripture explains that *he is the serpent of old, who is called Devil and the Satan, who deceives the whole world*. He is cast out into the earth, into those who claim to be the people of God (Israel and the church).

Look, this verse doesn't say that the dragon (Satan) deceives just part of the world. No! He deceives the *whole* world, with absolutely no exceptions. He deceives the religions of this world. He deceives the governments of this world. He deceives the multinational companies of this world. He deceives the courts of this world, and so on.

Is this clear? Can you think of any institution of man that has *not* been deceived by the Enemy?

The gospel states that he will deceive and seduce even the very elect if possible (Matthew 24:24; Mark 13:22).

Brethren, is it clear that we can be deceived and that the Enemy will make every effort to deceive us? If we are part of the world, then we will *all* be deceived. The only one Satan cannot deceive is the Lord Jesus Christ. And the only way *we* can be saved from his deception is if the Lord Jesus is our head, and we voluntarily submit to the control, discipline, and chastening of our heavenly Father.

> 9b *he was cast out into the earth, and his angels were cast out with him.*

The Lord Jesus said that he saw Satan fall from heaven (Luke 10:18). He saw it in a vision as the consequence of what would eventually happen as a result of his death and resurrection. The judgment, however, must still be executed. Until that time, Satan continues to manage the things of this world.

We receive a glimpse of this when Jesus cast out demons. The demons complained that he was expelling them *before the time* (Matthew 8:29). They thought the time was not fulfilled for them to be completely uprooted and knew that their master, Satan, had not yet been dispatched.

God, in his wisdom, has allowed the Devil and his fallen angels to retain access to the heavenly realm all throughout the church age. But why?

Job wondered the same thing. In his case, all of the diabolical attack against him, authorized by God, served so that Job could progress from only being able to hear the voice of God to being able to see God with great clarity. The result was that

Job had a credible ministry to his religious friends who neither heard nor saw clearly on spiritual matters (Job 42:5,10).

The Book of Job is also a portrayal of the church age and how it will end.

The Lord has allowed the Devil to continue managing the things of this world for many reasons, and since those reasons are God's, they are good. It is not the case that God is in agreement with the Devil, nor that he created Satan evil in order to demonstrate his power. Certainly not!

When the Devil was created, he was very good like all of the original creation (Genesis 1:31). He had free will and used it to choose evil. He didn't want Adam and Eve to rule over him, so he sought a means to take them out of the way without appearing to be directly responsible. When Satan deceived Eve, he created a difficult situation for Adam, who openly rebelled and chose Eve instead of God. This left him naked and stripped of his authority, which was then usurped by the Devil. The Lord Jesus, however, will have a bride who has overcome all trials and temptations and has been proven to be faithful to him. Where does this bride come from? We shall see.

All of those who have been caught up to the throne of God, and are now citizens of the heavenly realm, form the body of Christ. A new-creation man child is brought forth out of an old-creation woman or congregation, such as the Jews and elements of the church that remain under law instead of grace. She is subject to the government of the natural man and to the curse (Genesis 3:16-19). She is clothed with the sun, which is a central symbol of the prosperity of this world. The moon is under her feet (Revelation 12:1). The inner court, or Holy Place, of the temple is being trampled under her feet for forty-two months, until the correction factor – the direct presence of God – brings forth the mature generation of Christ, which is the forty-second generation (Matthew 1:1-17). She cries out in pain and travails to be delivered of a *man child.* This phrase denotes a free-born, mature son. The woman is obviously corporate and includes all that Eve represents in the natural realm. The overcoming son, the body of Christ, is also corporate and heir to key promises of God. Just as the Jews insisted on trying to fulfill the law in their own strength, so has much of the church. They distill what they believe are the godly principles of the New Testament and attempt to implement them in the flesh. The woman, or the sum of the congregations, doing this now writhe in pain and travail as end-time events close in around them. God promises to deliver her and that she will give birth to an overcoming man child.

> 5b *and her child was caught up unto God and to his throne.*

Notice that this is linked to the war in heaven and to the dragon and his angels being cast out of heaven. Jesus entered his ministry under the law when he turned thirty (symbol of maturity), and he delegates ministry *until we all come forth in the unity of the faith and of the knowledge of the Son of God unto a perfect man, unto the measure of the coming of age of the Christ* (Ephesians 4:13).

Consider the fact that this man child is delivered in the midst of much travail and pain.

Note that this comes on the heels of the announcement in Revelation 11:12 after the two witnesses are resurrected and caught up to heaven. This verse is very likely describing the same event from a different angle.

Isn't this interesting?

On the one hand, Jesus and his overcomers will rule all the Gentiles with a rod of iron. He will bring all the Gentiles forcibly in line with what God says.

On the other hand, Jesus said that his kingdom is not of

this world (John 18:36). He said that his kingdom is within us. To those who desired to enter his kingdom, he said, *Blessed are the poor in spirit, for theirs is the kingdom of the heavens* (Matthew 5:3).

There will be an abrupt transition when the kingdoms of this world are brought down and the kingdom of God is imposed over everyone.

Who will do this?

The many-membered man child of whom Jesus is the head.

> 10a *And I heard a loud voice saying in heaven,*

(Remember that this is from a heavenly perspective.)

> 10b *Now is come salvation and virtue and the kingdom of our God and the power of his Christ; for the accuser of our brethren is cast down, who accused them before our God day and night.*

It appears that these accusations went on day and night until something happened. When the seventh seal was opened, it says there was silence in heaven for about half an hour (Revelation 8:1). It appears that when the overcomers of God are sealed in Revelation 7, this sets the stage for the seventh seal to be opened, and for God to be able to put a people on display that the Devil is no longer able to accuse. When both the bride and the Spirit give forth the same clear witness from heaven, the stage is set for the Devil and his followers to be cast down to earth.

There is silence in heaven when the plan of redemption, which is the fullness of his life in us, is fully unsealed (Colossians 1:27). Our life cannot bring us into complete victory; only Christ's life can (Romans 5:10). When the Lord effected redemption, it didn't happen just in theory or by some kind of magic decree. No, it's necessary to walk, and walk with him, until we have to be carried along by the Spirit of God, until we have to ride, until at the opening of the fourth seal a horse is provided that has no counterpart in the natural creation. This horse is described as a green horse. The Greek word used is the precursor for our word chlorophyll (Revelation 6:8). Christ takes us from being dead in trespasses and sin to being carried by his resurrection life.

Jesus' resurrection life is linked to the death of the old man, the death of the old nature, so we may also take part in the new man in Christ as a citizen of heaven. Jesus now has the keys to death and Hades and can effectively use death to overcome the old man and the old nature (Revelation 1:18).

This new man, born of God, doesn't shoot at the wrong target. He has a perfect heart for God, because his heart has been transformed (1 John 3:9).

How long until this corporate new man receives the kingdom?

When the fifth seal is opened, this is the question posed by the souls of those under the heavenly altar who are covered by the blood of Jesus Christ.

Lord, How long? How long until you intervene, judge, and avenge all the innocent blood the Devil and his followers have shed upon the earth?

They must wait until the number of their fellow servants and brethren that should be killed is fulfilled (Revelation 6:11; 11:7-12).

> 11 *And they have overcome him by the blood of the Lamb and by the word of their testimony; and they loved not their lives unto the death.*

The blood of the Lamb has to do with the death of Jesus for us. It also has to do with his resurrection life, because the life of the flesh is in the blood (Leviticus 17:11,14). *For if, when we were enemies, we were reconciled with God by the death of his Son, much more, now reconciled, we shall be saved by his life* (Romans 5:10).

> 11b *the word of their testimony;*

In the highest sense this also has to do with Jesus, who is the Word of God, and who will flow in us and through us as we yield to the Holy Spirit (John 1:1).

11c *and they loved not their lives unto death.*

The *two witnesses* along with all the souls under the heavenly altar gave up their own lives in order to live the life of Jesus Christ. They underwent physical death, but after that death they did not remain trapped in Sheol (in Greek, *Hades*), which served as a jail for souls administered by the Devil who had the keys to death before Jesus descended into Hades and led captivity captive (Ephesians 4:8-10 – see Appendix A). Instead, they waited under the heavenly altar. The altar is where the blood is applied. It's the equivalent of the gospel. These souls are those who have been *beheaded* (some literally, but more important metaphorically) for the cause of the Lord and the gospel (Revelation 6:9; 20:4). They have come out from under their own headship, so that they might be under the exclusive headship of Jesus Christ.

I am convinced that it is possible for God to bring people like us into compliance with these requirements for victory while we still walk right here upon the earth without coming to a violent physical end. The Scripture calls the apostle John a faithful witness (in Greek, *martyr*) before he died (Revelation 1:1-2). Yet, according to tradition, John was possibly the only original apostle to *not* die a violent death for the cause of Christ. The same word, *witness*, is applied to Jesus Christ in verse 5.

John risked his life many times for the Lord and for the gospel, and this was enough to get him listed as a martyr in God's book. The apostle Paul wrote that *though I give my body to be burned and have not charity* (the love of God*), it profits me nothing* (1 Corinthians 13:3).

12 *Therefore, rejoice, ye heavens, and ye that dwell*

> *in them. Woe to the inhabiters of the earth and of the sea! For the devil is come down unto you, having great wrath, knowing that he has but a short time.*

It is possible to secure our dwelling place in heaven even if our feet are still here upon the earth. The Lord Jesus taught that where our treasure is determines where our heart is (Matthew 6:21).

If we are citizens of heaven and desire heavenly things, we will use our time and resources here below to invest in heavenly things. The things of this world are not eternal. Only the Lord can show us how to convert them into heavenly riches. If we know the Lord, we have the opportunity to make much better investments than those available in any earthly stock market, business venture, or real estate deal. We can invest in the lives of those the Lord shows us to help, and it will be counted as unto the Lord.

When the life of the Lord dominates our being, when we operate by the blood of the Lamb and His Word is our testimony, and when our own life doesn't matter, then we are no longer slaves of sin, the world does not move us, and the devil has no entrance. He cannot overcome anyone who is dead if Jesus Christ is alive in them.

Where this is the case, brethren, we are servants (slaves) of righteousness even though it's still possible for us to make human mistakes. We are moved by inner conviction to do what pleases God and immediately repent if any of our behavior needs to be rectified. When this is the nature of our relationship with the Lord, it's not necessary to calculate and put together our own plans and proposals to further the kingdom of God. They flow as a natural result of the blood of the Lamb and the Word of his testimony.

> 12a *Therefore, rejoice, ye heavens, and ye that dwell*

> *in them. Woe to the inhabiters of the earth and of the sea!*

First, the Lord will fix the situation in the heavens by kicking out the Devil and his angels. Then he promises to deal with those who inhabit the earth and sea. This is the order of events.

He will not judge the world, those who are on the outside, or those who are not in covenant with him until he puts his own house in order. This is why he measures the temple and the altar, and why he leaves the inner court (the Holy Place) out of the measurement. This is where many people exercise gifts and ministry from God who are not in alignment with what God desires and cannot be measured. It does not comply!

When he opens his heavenly temple and the veil between heaven and earth is removed, the revelation of the glorious, resurrected Jesus Christ will destroy any unclean inhabitants of the earth who do not run and hide (Revelation 6:15). We cannot ever be clean in our own life, only in *his* life. We must choose between our life and his life, between self-righteousness and his righteousness.

> 12a *Woe to the inhabiters of the earth and of the sea! for the devil is come down unto you, having great wrath, knowing that he has but a short time.*

The day of the Lord is now come, and the Devil has lost his capacity to be in the heavenly realm. He and his demons aren't able to accuse those who are dead to sin and the old man, those who are part of the new man, part of the new creation (Romans 6:2,11). In such men, and women, the Scripture is fulfilled that declares, *Behold, all things are made new* (2 Corinthians 5:17).

> 13 *And when the dragon saw that he was cast unto the earth, he persecuted the woman who brought forth the man child.*

This woman, like Adam, is of the earth and has numerous problems.

> 14 *And to the woman were given two wings of the great eagle that she might fly from the presence of the serpent into the wilderness, into her place, where she is nourished for a time, and times, and half a time.*

The *wings of the eagle* are mentioned by Isaiah and the *time, times, and half a time* is from Daniel 7:25; 12:7. Notice that the great dragon loses his *wings* and is cast down to the earth. Then, the woman who was cast out of the presence of God, and who has been prophesied to be a key to realizing the plans and purposes of God, received the sentence that her seed would crush the head of the serpent, and that she would bring forth children with pain and travail, yet she would be saved in child bearing. This same woman is delivered of a man child and receives the two wings of the great eagle, by which she attains access into the spiritual realm that she never had before. So she finally escapes the presence of the serpent that hounded her for six thousand years.

Isn't this a very interesting prophecy?

This woman was linked to the fallen creation when she was deceived, because she listened to the Devil when he told her, "You may eat of the forbidden fruit, and you will become like God and not die."

This woman in the midst of much tribulation delivered a son, who was caught up to the throne of the presence of God. Yes, the Lord Jesus is the head, but he will also have brethren in the body of Christ who, according to Scripture, will be joint heirs (Romans 8:17).

The woman escapes from the dragon and is nourished in the wilderness for a time, times, and half a time. On the surface, some interpret this as three and a half years, which jibes with forty-two months and with 1,260 days. However, the Hebrew presents the possibility of a slightly different literal interpretation: a time, times, and the division of time (Daniel 7:25; 12:7).

The first *time* has to do with what was left of the age of the Jews under law (from the perspective of Daniel 12:7).

The Scripture also speaks of the *times* of the Gentiles (Luke 21:24). This speaks of two prophetic days of a thousand years each (2 Peter 3:8).

The *division of time* is what is coming. This will take place at the blowing of the seventh trumpet when the mystery of God shall be finished (Revelation 10:7).

The Lord will have a clean people. A people who, by the blood of the Lamb and the word of their testimony, loved not their lives unto death but overcame and caused the Devil to be cast out of heaven with all his fallen angels (demons).

This brought about war in heaven. The heavenly hosts, under the command of Michael, overcome the Devil and his angels. Michael is the archangel mentioned in Scripture that remains faithful before the throne of God. Revelation, however, speaks of four living creatures or animals (from the Greek, *zoos*) that are in reality cherubim.

At the time of Daniel, war was already taking place in the realm of the heavens, and only Michael stood with Gabriel against the princes of this world (Daniel 10:12-21). Now, the woman continues to travail, and overcomers have been added one by one throughout history until the number is almost complete.

Ever since Jesus descended into Hades and led captivity captive, between the overcomers who have physically died, been literally martyred, and those overcomers who are alive and remain here on earth, the heavenly forces under the command of Michael have greatly increased (1 Thessalonians 4:15). The tide of the battle is turning, and Satan, the accuser of the brethren, is about to be cast down as the number is completed.

14a *And to the woman were given two wings of the great eagle*

This refers to being lifted up and carried unto himself by the Lord, when we are unable to break free of the bondage we are in.

A historical interpretation of this could have to do with the United States of America (originally a wilderness). It has functioned as a refuge for hundreds of years for those who sought freedom to worship God. The symbol of the United States is, of course, the great eagle. We see in Scripture how eagle's wings illustrate this concept. *Ye have seen what I did unto the Egyptians and how I bore you on eagle's wings and brought you unto myself* (Exodus 19:4). The prophet Isaiah paints this picture, *but those that wait for the LORD shall have new strength; they shall mount up with wings as eagles; they shall run and not be weary; and they shall walk, and not faint* (Isaiah 40:31).

Prophetically, this doesn't necessarily mean that we're going to fly around like eagles, although something similar to that literally happened to Philip in the book of Acts. It does mean that we will regain access to a spiritual realm of protection beyond the reach of the dragon. This is the access to the throne of God that Adam and Eve lost. In a certain sense, as individuals we have spiritual access in Christ to the realm of the Holy of Holies. We obtain our access through his covering, so the presence of God does not destroy us. This is different. This is a woman, a corporate people, who will dwell in the presence of God as the final end time fulfillment of this prophecy takes place. The reason the Devil fights so hard is because much of the inheritance that God promises his people is what the Devil currently controls. Satan must lose what he has in order for the Lord to fulfill his promise to us.

14 *And to the woman were given two wings of the great eagle that she might fly from the presence of the*

> *serpent into the wilderness, into her place, where she is nourished for a time, and times, and half a time.*

The wilderness corresponds to the Holy Place. But God plans to open his temple in heaven and allow his ark to be revealed (Revelation 11:19). His ark of salvation is Jesus Christ! God intends to remove the veil that provides the barrier between heaven and earth due to the sin of Adam and Eve. Since that time, the veil has separated the earth from the presence of God (Isaiah 51:6; 2 Peter 3:10; Revelation 6:14).

In the temple described by Ezekiel, called the millennial temple by some, there is no division between the Holy Place and the Holy of Holies. There is no veil to hide those who commit abominations and contaminate that which is downtrodden by the Gentiles. For now, the veil separates those who are not in a real covenant with God and, therefore, do not have circumcised hearts. As long as the veil is in place, this veil is linked to our flesh, the inner court will not measure up. It is impossible to measure this court with the rod of the righteousness of Christ.

When the Lord rolls up the heavens like a scroll, when they vanish like smoke and disappear with a loud noise, when the ark of his covenant is seen in the form of a glorious resurrected Jesus Christ, then Scripture states that when we see him we shall be like him, for flesh and blood cannot inherit the kingdom of God (1 Corinthians 15:50). The presence of God transforms those who possess clean hearts, but the same presence destroys those who are not clean and attempt to pass themselves off as representatives of God.

The fullness of the presence of God didn't enter the temple described by Ezekiel until everything measured up. When this happened, there were no longer three realms. There only remained inside and outside of the presence of God. This temple has no Holy Place. It only has the Holy of Holies and the outer court.

Isn't this interesting?

By the time the Bible ends, the holy city has only one realm. The entire city becomes the equivalent of the Holy of Holies (Revelation 21:22).

According to Ezekiel, for a time, which some think is a thousand years, the priests who led God's people astray and failed to distinguish between the clean and unclean will be allowed to minister outside. They will do the dirty work of killing and offering the sacrifices of the flesh but won't be allowed inside the temple into the presence of God. Only one family of priests, the sons of Zadok (righteousness), will be allowed to go in and out. They are the only priests who remained faithful to God when everyone else became apostate and contaminated.

The temple described by Ezekiel would be impossible to construct physically because the inside dimensions are much larger that the outside. The further you go in, the more it expands. It serves as a spiritual description of the body of Christ on the threshold of the age to come.

After the presence of God is restored, the river of God flows, cleanses, and heals throughout the wilderness and all the way to the Dead Sea (Ezekiel 47). Fruitful trees grow on both banks of the river, and everyone who swims in the river shall live.[4] Even the leaves of the trees are used for medicine.

In Eden, the life of God, represented by the tree of life, was external. Now, God will place his presence in fullness within his martyrs, witnesses, and overcomers. Therefore, every fruitful tree will grow along both banks of the river of God as it flows through the *wilderness*. Jesus said that rivers of the water of life will flow from the depths of our innermost being. This is the river of God that flows by the Holy Spirit. The fullness of the Spirit has yet to be poured out, because it's reserved for the time of the end.

---

4 See *The River of God*, Russell Stendal, Aneko Press.

The river will flow in fullness through the same wilderness where the woman is nourished for a time, and times, and half a time. This will happen at the end of the 1,260 days, or the forty-two months at the time of the end.

In addition to the possibility of a direct literal meaning, forty-two months also refers spiritually to a correction factor.[5] Since months can also be symbolic of generations, there is yet another facet. There are forty-two generations from David to Christ. Jesus is generation forty-one. Christ, including the body of Christ, is generation forty-two (Matthew 1:1-17). The only way for the temple to measure up is if it consists of the mature generation of Christ. This is the generation that will not pass away until all that Jesus said in Matthew 24 is fulfilled.

The plan of God is consistent throughout Scripture. Beginning with Cain, there is a consistent pattern. He worked hard farming and offered the work of his hands to God. God didn't receive Cain or his present. This made Cain so angry that he went out and killed his brother, Abel, who God received because he sacrificed a lamb. The word for Cain's present was mistranslated throughout the Bible as *grain offering*. In the Jubilee Bible, it is translated as *present* and shows a clear pattern that the work of our hands is not acceptable unto God unless it is accompanied by a blood sacrifice. This shows us that only the work done in and through us by Jesus Christ, who was the supreme blood sacrifice, will ever be acceptable to God.

Unless we are in a blood covenant where the life of the Lord can overcome our own life, and by the Spirit, we put to death the deeds of the flesh, the work of our hands will never be acceptable to God. The only work acceptable to the Lord is the work that he performs in us and through us.

When he does this work and by his nature in us, we will measure up and not be excluded, because the final judgment of

---

5 See *The Correction Factor*, Russell Stendal, Aneko Press.

God is according to our works (Revelation 20:11-15). Of course our own good works cannot save us or anyone else. But if we are included as joint heirs to reign and rule with Christ, there will be ample evidence of his work in and through us.

> 15 *And the serpent cast out of his mouth water as a river after the woman, that he might cause her to be carried away by the river.*

The river that flows from the mouth of the serpent has many ties. For instance, at the sound of the third trumpet, the third part of the rivers and fountains is poisoned by a fallen star named Wormwood, or Hemlock (Revelation 8:10-11). Additionally, water symbolizes the Word of God. Now the Devil proclaims a false word that seems very real. Many spew forth a word in the name of God that is really from the enemy. However, if we're in the wilderness of the dealings of God, if he has us in a situation that isn't all that comfortable, or if we're being sustained by the Lord in a very dry realm, then look at what can happen:

> 16 *And the earth helped the woman, and the earth opened up her mouth and swallowed up the river which the dragon had cast out of his mouth.*

Had the woman relaxed in the delicious parts of this world where there is lavish rainfall (blessing) and all the rivers flow high up on their banks, then the Devil could have caused a flood that would have swept her away. Similarly, those who are overboard into a gospel of prosperity of the things of this world may quickly be swept away by the false river of the Devil. On the other hand, those who allow the Lord to maintain them in a dry desert through his direct dealings, like Elijah and John the Baptist, will find that the very earth will help them by swallowing up the river that flows from the mouth of the serpent.

It is the *wings of the great eagle* provided by God that allow her to fly into her place of safety in the wilderness in the first place.

> 17 *And the dragon was wroth with the woman and went to make war with the remnant of her seed, who keep the commandments of God and have the testimony of Jesus Christ.*

In the gospel of John, Jesus stated that he has other sheep in other places. And at the time of the end, there will be only one shepherd and one sheep fold (John 10:16).

The Devil is unable to do anything to the woman who caused him so much damage by bringing forth the man child, because she uses the wings provided by God and refuses to go into the prosperous places of this world. She remains in an apparently dry and desolate (economically and/or spiritually) place where God continues to nourish her.

During this time, the two witnesses have power to shut up the rain (blessing) in the days of their prophecy. They bring a screeching halt to the prosperity of this world, including the religious realm. This is a major reason why the world and the religious realm hates them and kills them in the end.

But God continues his perfect plan for victory. Even though a beast, which represents the paganism of the nations, comes up out of the sea. And another beast comes up out of the land, which is a false prophet with two horns or sources of power. These two sum up the history of all those who congregate the people in religious fortresses of one type or another all over the planet. God plans to bring this all to a wonderful and incredible finish.

Let us pray

Heavenly Father,

We look forward to the days ahead. We look forward to each step, to each trumpet, to each event, to each sign that shows us that we are one step closer to your direct government here upon the earth.

Thank you for revealing yourself to those who are pure in heart. Our desire is to hear Jesus say, "Well done, good and faithful servant," when our time of service here upon the earth is done. We place our lives upon your altar that you may intervene and correct anything in us that does not measure up to your standards.

May we find our dwelling place in Sion, in your presence, in the Holy of Holies, and not in the corrupt Holy Place that has suffered so many abominations for such a long time.

We ask this in the name of our Lord Jesus Christ. Amen.

Chapter 17

The Beast and the False Prophet

Revelation 14

1 *And I saw and, behold, the Lamb stood upon Mount Sion and with him a hundred and forty-four thousand, having the name of his Father written in their foreheads.*

This symbolic number is now complete and represents the unlimited perfect number of all the redeemed in the Old Testament plus all the redeemed of the New Testament: twelve times twelve times one thousand.

The number may be symbolic, but the Lamb is on Mount Sion. This means that Jesus is once again here upon the earth in person, and Sion is his true habitation. More specifically, his true habitation is his clean, overcoming people who walk upon this earth yet are citizens of heaven.

Why does this say *Sion* and not *Zion*? While it's true that the majority of Bibles today use the spelling *Zion* in this verse, the Jubilee Bible, and a handful of others, has elected to use *Sion*. As the editor of the Jubilee Bible, allow me to explain my reasoning. In the Old Testament, there are one hundred and fifty-three references to Zion, the stronghold David captured in Jerusalem, and two references to Sion, which is Mount Hermon (Deuteronomy 4:48; Psalm 65:1). The New Testament contains seven references to this word, all of which are spelled with the Greek letter sigma instead of zeta. Therefore, they are properly translated in the KJV as Sion, even when they are a direct quote of an Old Testament passage that clearly started out as Zion. Sion, or Mount Hermon, is a type and shadow of the Jerusalem above that Paul says is free and the mother of us all (Galatians 4:26). This is a portrayal of God's heavenly people who live upon this earth. This is what Isaiah referred to when he described God as living *upon the mount of the testimony and in the sides of the north* (Isaiah 14:13). Zion, the stronghold, eventually became so religious and corrupt that on two occasions, the temple was completely destroyed. Sion, the highest mountain in the holy land, remains a beautiful example of the fullness of the lofty spiritual realm where God desires to live in and with his people.

So, where are we now?

The Lord Jesus will accomplish whatever the Father desires and conclude the perfect fulfillment of all the prophecies.

In times past, the Lord gave the children of Israel the opportunity to enter into their inheritance in the Promised Land. But they failed, in that they didn't believe the good report of the two faithful spies. Their unbelief meant forty more years in the wilderness. Nevertheless, at the age of eighty-five, after a delay of forty-five years, Caleb came into the mountain of his inheritance. God eventually made good on all his promises, as recorded in the Book of Joshua.

Because God granted us free will, there have been many setbacks to his plan for us along the way. These setbacks took the form of human failure, human arrogance, and fierce opposition from the Devil. Many have been deceived by Satan's wiles and have sought the things of this world instead of the things of God. Still, the Lord will fulfill his purpose.

Each passing day brings us closer to the fulfillment of the purpose of God. Each passing day brings us closer to the Lord possessing the testimony he desires. Each passing day we are closer to the Elijah that is to come, which, I am convinced, is not a single individual.

Each day we are closer to becoming a man child of many members with the Lord Jesus at the head, who will govern the Gentiles, anyone without a circumcised heart, with a rod of iron.

It's possible that there may be a little more delay if God desires to grant more time, because the plan of God is that people are saved and not lost. This requires a clear message that cuts through all of the confusion, coupled with conviction of the Holy Spirit. We do know, however, that some people will be lost. Some will be found in the same kind of rebellion as the Devil.

In the end, the man child born of the woman, who was deceived (fallen humanity), will completely crush every head of the serpent. Before that final victory, one of the heads of the beast, representing human government authorized by the dragon, received a mortal wound. But the beast recovered. Scripture says that *all the earth marveled, and followed the beast,* including the entire religious world that is typed with the *earth* in Bible prophecy.

We, more or less, know how this came about in a historical sense with the fall of the Roman Emperors and their recovery as the papacy, but now there isn't very much time left. The dragon is about to be cast out of heaven. Then there will be a huge problem here upon the *earth.*

The *earth* has become a very religious realm. The people, churches, temples, congregations, synagogues, mosques, and institutions that have been contaminated by man, fight with one another and refuse to submit to the correction of God.

Yet, that correction is of critical importance. It isn't possible to avoid the Devil's deception unless we place ourselves under the direct authority of Jesus Christ. He is the only one able to save us. Jesus is the only way. Not only can he save us, but he allows us to participate in the great victory that is about to take place by the blood of the Lamb and the word of our testimony, if we do not love our lives unto death.

Revelation 13

> 1 *And I stood upon the sand of the sea and saw a beast rise up out of the sea, having seven heads and ten horns, and upon its horns ten crowns, and upon its heads the name of blasphemy.*

The vision of Revelation chapter 13 is from the perspective of the dividing line (the beach) between the land and the sea. From a human point of view, the situation appears very grim.

Abraham was promised descendants as numerous as the stars of the heavens or the sand upon the seashore (Genesis 22:17). Abraham's grandson, Jacob (before God changed his name to Israel), was only promised that God would make his seed like the sand of the sea (Genesis 32:12). Here we see these themes reflected in Revelation.

The sand of the seashore demarcates the separation of the land, or earth, from the sea. Those who are under the Old Covenant of law, without the indwelling Spirit of God, fit this description. Many in the church have made the New Testament into law instead of grace. They distill Bible principles and apply them according to their human mind instead of depending on the Holy Spirit to lead and guide them into all truth.

The sea refers to the sea of lost Gentile humanity. Without God, the natural man is really a beast. The seven heads represent all the heads of humanistic, secular, pagan, or religious government. The ten horns mean that the beast derives its power from law. This has been the case of virtually all the governments of the world since the Medes and Persians elevated the law above the power of the king, so the king couldn't change established law (Daniel 6:8,15; Esther 8:8).

The crowns are not on the heads of this beast, as they were with the dragon. These crowns are on the beast's horns. This beast crowns the law rather than individual heads. The heads have *the name of blasphemy*, meaning they are competing with God. Modern-day leaders of western democracies are not above the law. Though some of them may wish to be and act as if they are. Over the centuries, national, religious, and international law has deviated more and more from God's law as the corruption of the beast – the natural, carnal man – has increased over time (Daniel 7:25).

> 2 *And the beast which I saw was like unto a leopard, and its feet were as the feet of a bear, and its mouth as the mouth of a lion; and the dragon gave it his power and his throne and great authority.*

Daniel saw four beasts that were prophetic interpretations of four coming world empires. This beast John saw appears to be a composite of the four beasts that Daniel saw, which also had a total of seven heads. Three of them had one head each, but the fourth had four heads. Daniel's beasts portrayed the Babylonians, the Medes and Persians, the Greeks, and the Romans. Daniel wrote down this dream and referred to this as *the sum of the matters* (Daniel 7).[6]

This final beast portrays aspects of the four previous empires that have filtered into all the governments of the world. This beast represents all the heads and all the horns of all the leaders and all the laws of the entire world system at the time of the

---

6 See *The Book of Daniel*, by Russell Stendal, Aneko Press.

end. In this way, it's similar to the statue King Nebuchadnezzar saw in his famous dream that God revealed and interpreted to Daniel (Daniel 2).

The statue portrayed the head of gold (Babylon), the arms and shoulders of silver (Media and Persia), the belly of bronze (Greece), the legs of iron (Rome), and feet and toes of iron mixed with clay. The ten toes represent the democracies and other governments of today that make laws (iron) that the people (clay) cannot keep, because the natural man needs a change of heart. Then, in the dream, a stone cut without hands smote the statue upon its feet of iron and clay, and all the pieces of the statue became like chaff on a threshing floor.

The wind carried all the chaff away. The stone, representing the kingdom of God, became a great mountain that filled all of the earth (Daniel 2). Note, this image ends with feet and toes of iron mixed with the clay that is partly strong and partly fragile (Daniel 2:42-43). It doesn't meld into a homogenous, all-encompassing, one-world government at the time of the end.

The Devil, even after giving this seven-headed monster his power, throne, and great authority, still has not been able to consolidate his power and kingdom under one head. After six thousand years as the prince of this world, the Devil hasn't been able to do any better than this seven-headed monster. Seven heads mean *all* the heads. Jesus said, *If a kingdom is divided against itself, that kingdom cannot remain. And if a house is divided against itself, that house cannot remain. And if Satan rises up against himself and is divided, he cannot remain, but has an end* (Mark 3:24-26). The Devil's kingdom doesn't run on love and trust. All of his followers are always at each other's throats.

> 3 *And I saw one of its heads as it were wounded to death; and its deadly wound was healed; and all the earth marveled, and followed the beast.*

We know about the head that was wounded to death and recovered from its deadly wound. The earth (the religious realm) continues to marvel and follow the natural man with all his seemingly great philosophical ideals.

> 4 *And they worshipped the dragon which had given authority unto the beast: and they worshipped the beast; saying, Who is like unto the beast? who is able to make war with it?*

Humanistic government, with its heads ruling over countries and institutions all over the world, continues to prevail. The worship of man prevails. Anyone who refuses to worship man is hated and persecuted without mercy. Yet, worship of man is worship of the beast.

> 5 *And there was given unto it a mouth speaking great things and blasphemies; and power was given unto it to continue forty and two months.*

The beast's mouth speaks through all of its seven heads. It has power for forty-two months. Which is the same time frame that the *holy city* will be trodden under foot by the Gentiles (Revelation 11:2). Spiritually, the forty-two months continue until the correction factor, the direct presence of God through the mature generation of Christ, is applied to cleanse this realm.

In prophecy, months can have to do with women, who have the same monthly cycle as a lunar month, and therefore with generations. This beast will operate through all the generations of the natural, carnal man. The only thing that will stop it is the effects of the seventh trumpet. This is when the forty-second generation, the generation of Christ, comes to maturity and is transformed by resurrection. For when we see Jesus, we shall be like him.

This is when the mystery of God will be revealed, and there will be war in heaven in which the Devil will not prevail. He will be cast down to the earth and jailed in what used to be his own prison for *a thousand years* followed by a general resurrection unto final judgment.

> 6 *And it opened its mouth in blasphemy against God, to blaspheme his name and his tabernacle and those that dwell in heaven.*

The blasphemy from the mouth of all the heads of the humanistic monster that controls all the kingdoms and institutions of the world, against God and those that dwell in heaven, is deafening. The monster is particularly harsh in its blasphemy against those who live here on earth yet are true citizens of heaven.

> 7 *And it was given unto it to make war with the saints and to overcome them; and power was given to it over all kindreds and tongues and nations.*

Read the above verse again. The monster not only makes war with the saints but overcomes them, and great power has been given to it. What, then, will happen to the faithful? Consider the words of Daniel 12:7. *And I heard the man clothed in linens, who was upon the waters of the river, who raised his right hand and his left hand unto heaven, and swore by the living one in the ages that it shall be for a time, times, and a half; and when the scattering of the holy people shall be finished, all these things shall be fulfilled.*

Can *the scattering of the holy people* be a true prophecy? Indeed, it can, brethren. It's when the holy people of God have finished being scattered all over the globe in countless sects and denominations, and when they have come to a complete end of their human resources, that God will step in and intervene. The natural man, even with powerful gifts and ministries from God, will never be able to overcome the beast (Job 41:26-29).

Revelation 13

> 8 *And all that dwell upon the earth shall worship it, whose names are not written in the book of the life of the Lamb that was slain from the foundation of the world.*
>
> 9 *If anyone has an ear to hear, let him hear.*

Those who dwell in the sea worship the dragon. Paganism is essentially Devil worship. But all those who dwell upon the earth, in the religious realm, worship the humanistic beast set up by the Devil. Those who dwell in the religious realm don't have their names written in the book of the life of the Lamb, because the life of the Lamb gives citizenship and access to the heavenly realm.

The Lamb was slain from the foundation of the world (Revelation 13:8). But when *was* the foundation of the world?

The world of fallen humanity is the kingdom of the Devil. It was founded when the serpent deceived Eve and Adam rebelled against God. From the time of the fall, God decided to redeem mankind. Even though he knew that redemption would require the death of his son, Jesus Christ, to pay for the sins of the world (John 3:16). *For if, when we were enemies, we were reconciled with God by the death of his Son, much more, now reconciled, we shall be saved by his life* (Romans 5:10).

The Lamb has a book that records all of those who have his life. *He that has the Son has life; and he that does not have the Son of God does not have life* (1 John 5:12).

Despite Jesus' sacrifice, religious people who are not citizens of the heavens will all worship the beast. Even atheists worship the beast of humanism. This has clearly been going on for quite some time. All those who dwell on the earth will worship it. These are the same people who will run and hide when the Lamb is revealed from heaven (Revelation 6:15-17). Citizens of heaven have their names written in the book of the life of the Lamb that was slain from the foundation of the world. From the foundation of the world, from the beginning of Adam's rebellion, from the beginning of Satan's usurpation of the authority that God gave to Adam, Jesus had already decided that the only way to redeem mankind and creation would be to give his life for us so that his life could come forth in us.

What about those who aren't citizens of heaven?

> 10 *He that leads into captivity shall go into captivity; he that kills with the sword must be killed with the sword. Here is the patience and faith of the saints.*

Everyone is definitely going to reap what they sow. Patience is a fruit of the Spirit. Faith is depending on the Lord instead of trusting in man or ourselves. Pagan Rome is reported to have martyred millions of Christians. Many saw one head of the beast recover from a deadly wound when, at the fall of the Roman Empire, according to *Foxe's Book of Martyrs*, Christian Rome rose up and killed ten times more martyrs in the Spanish Inquisition alone. It is also interesting to note that the Spanish Inquisition lasted exactly 1,260 years. The beast, with all seven heads still intact, continues to devour. The heads of all the different governments, religions, and institutions of the world are more and more divided. Jesus' prophecy that *if Satan rises up against himself and is divided, he cannot remain, but has an end* is very close to fulfillment.

The False Prophet

> 11 *Then I beheld another beast coming up out of the land; and he had two horns like the Lamb, but he spoke as the dragon.*

The phrase *two horns* occurs five times in Scripture. This is the last mention. The previous four references all occur in the book of Daniel and refer to the ram that represents the kingdom of the Medes and Persians (Daniel 8).

There is significant and interesting typology, particularly in the Book of Esther, regarding events at Shushan, the palace at the head of the empire of the Medes and the Persians.[7] Shushan, meaning *lilies* and linked in typology to Christ and the church, is where two realms come back together. They are the realm of Media (center of the earth) and the realm of Persia (the eternal). This is also a central theme in Revelation as the veil between the heavens and the earth is removed, and Jesus Christ is revealed in the fullness of his glory (Revelation 6:14; 11:19).

According to Daniel, he saw a ram with one horn, or one source of power, that was higher than the other (speaking of the Medes eventually having more power than the Persians). The higher one, with the greater capacity, *came up last* (Daniel 8:3). The Lamb, Jesus Christ, has two horns. He has power through his Spirit in his people here upon the earth and power through his heavenly hosts.

The horn that comes up last is the power of God's heavenly people here on earth. As God's people mature, it becomes more and more apparent that *whatsoever we bind on earth shall be bound in the heaven and whatsoever we loose on the earth shall be loosed in the heaven* (Matthew 18:18).

This second beast, that some call the antichrist, has two horns like the Lamb. He has powerful capabilities on earth and also in the spiritual realm. He looks like the Lamb but talks like the Dragon (Satan). One of the ways in which Satan tries to trick the faithful is by sending his ministers in and among religious people posing as angels of light. Their power, at first glance, may seem similar to the power of God. In Greek, the prefix *anti-* (as in antichrist) does not mean the opposite. It means false or counterfeit. Thus, *antichrist* doesn't mean the

7 See *Queen Esther and the Ring of Power*, Russell Stendal, Aneko Press.

opposite of Christ but rather a counterfeit Christ, which is much harder for the natural man to detect. Antichrist can operate as a spirit through people. It was already in the world at the time of the early church (1 John 4:3).

False, or counterfeit, prophets may operate in prophecy, miracles, and many other things that people tend to associate with the ministry of God. Such prophets distort and abuse gifts and ministries that originate from God. As you are probably aware, this has been happening in many places. Those who dwell upon the earth are deceived when they hear what seem to be great preachers, with signs and wonders, who tell them how to use God to obtain the things of this world. The dwellers of the earth are deceived by the supernatural *fire from heaven* of the false prophets and never contemplate Jesus' warning that we shall know them by their fruits (Matthew 7:20).

> 12 *And he exercised all the power of the first beast in its presence and caused the earth and those that dwell therein to worship the first beast, whose deadly wound was healed.*
>
> 13 *And he does great signs, so that he even makes fire come down from heaven to the earth in the sight of men*

Starting with the golden calf, every religious shrine, avocation, movement, or sect craves supernatural approbation.

When asked by a furious Moses to explain the golden calf, Aaron replied, "I cast our gold into the fire and this calf came out!" In essence, he implied that it was a miracle. What else could they do but worship it? (Exodus 32:24). Virtually every deviant icon, image, shrine, church, mosque, synagogue, etc. has some version of a *fire from heaven* moment claiming supernatural beginnings or approval.

The strange fire of false anointing continues to sweep through most of the religious world today.

> 14 *and deceives those that dwell on the earth by those signs which were given unto him to do in the presence of the beast, commanding those that dwell on the earth to make an image of the beast, which has the wound by the sword, and did live.*

It's not the dwellers of the sea who are deceived by this beast but the dwellers of the earth. This is not, therefore, a problem for Hindus or atheists. It's those who consider themselves to be among the people of God who are deceived.

Historically, if the head of the beast which had the deadly wound by the sword was the Roman line of Caesars, then the image of the beast includes the line of popes who claim to be the vicar of Christ and thereby displace the Holy Spirit and set themselves up to be worshipped as God. *Vicar of Christ* means *in the place of Christ*, but only the Holy Spirit can take the place of Christ upon the earth.

Those who, like King Saul, crave the supernatural and displace the Holy Spirit rarely remain alone. King Saul received a supernatural evil spirit from the LORD when the Spirit of the LORD departed from him (1 Samuel 16:14-15).

> 15 *And it was given unto him to endue the image of the beast with spirit, so that the image of the beast should speak, and he shall cause those that do not worship the image of the beast to be killed.*

Just as the dragon and the first beast manifest themselves through a great variety of humanistic sources, so does this second beast.

This false prophet attempts to recreate God in the image of fallen man. This happens not only in Islam but also at the core of many sectors of Christianity, starting with papal Rome and the Orthodox Church. Today, we are shocked by groups like

ISIS with their wholesale killing of those whom they consider to be infidels. But not too many years ago, the Spanish and Portuguese Inquisitions brutally tortured and slaughtered millions in the name of God.

Even John Calvin, angered by doctrinal differences with the theologian, physician, and humanist Miguel Servet, declared in writing, "I hope that sentence of death will at least be passed on him." Although Calvin went on to express the wish that the severity of the punishment be mitigated, Servet was subsequently burned at the stake.

This beast has the backing of the secular humanistic realm. It brings a supernatural flair to religion, with the object of promoting the worship of man and the pursuit by religion of temporal power.

> 16 *And he caused all, both small and great, rich and poor, free and slaves, to receive a mark in their right hand, or in their foreheads;*
>
> 17 *and that no one might buy or sell, unless he has the mark or the name of the beast or the number of its name.*
>
> 18 *Here is wisdom. Let him that has understanding count the number of the beast: for the number of man; and its number is six hundred sixty-six.*

What is the name of the beast?

It's the same as the nature of the beast, which in turn is the nature of fallen Adam and not the nature of Christ.

Many are familiar with the link between the number 666 and the Devil. Fewer are aware that its first appearance in Scripture is not in Revelation, but in 2 Chronicles 9:13. *Now the weight of gold that came to Solomon in one year was six hundred and sixty-six talents of gold.*

This number originally represents all the gold (tribute) from all over the world that came to Solomon during the Golden Age of Israel.

If we dissect this number, we find that it's the sum of (6x100) + (6x10) + (6x1). That is, six times one hundred plus six times ten plus six times one.

The number one (symbolic of light) multiplied by one hundred, has to do with the plan of God. Noah spent one hundred years building the ark. And Isaac was miraculously born when Abraham was one hundred years old, according to the plan of God. The number six hundred, however, means man's plans.

The number ten has to do with the law, such as the Ten Commandments. Whereas, sixty can mean man's law or man's commandments.

The number one is linked to light in Scripture. On the first day, *God said, "Let there be light"* (Genesis 1:3). Therefore, six can represent man's light. Thus 666 would mean man's plans according to man's laws in man's light.

If all of this is submitted to God, as was done when the 666 talents of gold were sent to King Solomon every year, then God will correct us as necessary and bless us. However, if man attempts to take all of this for himself, then we have the mark of the beast. *I said in my heart concerning the estate of the sons of men that God might manifest them and that they might see that they themselves are beasts to one another* (Ecclesiastes 3:18).

This *mark of the beast* is to be placed *in* (not on) the right hand or *in* (not on) the forehead. It is primarily a way of acting and thinking according to the ways of the natural man, who is really a beast. Remember, this second beast that requires the mark has two horns. One of those horns symbolizes the spiritual power of the Devil and his demons, or fallen angels.

When the servants, or slaves, of God are sealed *in* their foreheads (not *on* their foreheads), it's because they receive the mind of Christ by the Holy Spirit. The seal of God is not 777 or some other representation of the name of God branded or tattooed on the foreheads of those who belong to him (Revelation 7:3).

Anyone who has the seal of God in their forehead and who is a true citizen of heaven doesn't have to worry about the mark of the beast. Those who are busy buying and selling in the temple and making a religious marketplace according to the ways of the world, already have the mark of the beast. And only those who have the same mark can do business with them. If those who carry the mark of God attempt to do business with those who carry the mark of Satan, they will find themselves being taken to the cleaners unless they also think and act like a beast.

Revelation 14

> 1 *And I saw and, behold, the Lamb stood upon Mount Sion and with him a hundred and forty-four thousand, having the name of his Father written in their foreheads.*
>
> 2 *And I heard a voice from heaven as the voice of many waters and as the voice of a great thunder; and I heard the voice of harpers harping with their harps;*
>
> 3 *and they sang as it were a new song before the throne and before the four animals and the elders; and no one could learn that song but the hundred and forty-four thousand, who were redeemed from the earth.*

David mentioned this song in this psalm dedicated to the overcomer. *And he has put a new song in my mouth, even praise unto our God; many shall see it and fear and shall wait on the LORD* (Psalm 40:3).

Mount Sion, on the sides of the north, is where the Lord dwells in and among all of his redeemed. They have the *name* (nature) *of his Father written in their foreheads.* As we mentioned earlier, one hundred and forty-four thousand is a number that is symbolic of all of the redeemed.

> 4 *These are those who are not defiled with women, for they are virgins. These are those who follow the Lamb wherever he goes. These are redeemed from among men, being the firstfruits unto God and to the Lamb.*
>
> 5 *And in their mouth was found no guile, for they are without blemish before the throne of God.*

In prophetic language, women represent entire groups or congregations of people. Those who are defiled with "women" are those who are absorbed into a given group, movement, congregation, or denomination in such a way that their direct relationship with God has been betrayed and compromised (2 Corinthians 11:2-4). This can happen any time our commitment to one another supersedes our commitment to God.

There are also those who think that because they are in charge of the congregation(s) (the women) their ministry is a "husband ministry." Imagine the problem some will have on the judgment day if Jesus accuses them of making indecent advances to his bride! Truly, the fear of the LORD is the beginning of wisdom.

True pastors (*shepherds* in Greek) have authority from God to watch for the wellbeing of the souls of the flock belonging to the Lord (Hebrews 13:17). Jesus is the great shepherd. Any pastoral ministry that he delegates is under him and not a replacement of him. True ministry seeks to join the people to the Lord and watch for their souls so that nothing interrupts their walk with God. True ministry does not involve placing oneself between the people and God.

Those who are not defiled with women and are spiritual virgins are those who follow the Lamb wherever he goes. Paul wrote, *For I am jealous over you with the jealousy of God, for I have espoused you to one husband, that I may present you as a chaste virgin to the Christ* (2 Corinthians 11:2).

> 6 *And I saw another angel fly in the midst of heaven, having the eternal gospel that he might evangelize those that dwell on the earth and every nation and kindred and tongue and people,*
>
> 7 *saying with a loud voice, Fear God and give glory to him, for the hour of his judgment is come; and worship him that has made the heaven and the earth and the sea and the fountains of waters.*

When Jesus came the first time, he spoke from the earth and shook the earth. Now, he is going to shake the heavens *and* the earth (Haggai 2:6; Hebrews 12:26). Now that he has a clean, heavenly people who have not been defiled by "women," the eternal gospel will go forth from the midst of heaven to evangelize those who dwell on the earth, which includes every nation, kindred, tongue, and people. Wherever Israel and the church have confused, mixed up, or perverted God's message, it will be set straight.

> 8 *And another angel followed, saying, Babylon is fallen, is fallen, that great city, because she has given all the Gentiles to drink of the wine of the wrath of her fornication.*

Mystery Babylon is the mother of the harlots and of the abominations of the earth. At the time John saw this vision, her headquarters was located in Rome. Simon Peter, writing from Rome, closes his first epistle by saying, *Those here at Babylon...salute you* (1 Peter 5:13). Babylon is the mother of many daughter cities that are now spread all across the planet.

She claims to represent God, yet she has given all the Gentiles to drink of the wine of the corrupt and carnal old life of Adam instead of the wine of the new life of Christ. This will finally come down upon her head. All of the blood of all of the martyrs has been found in her. Instead of setting a good example, instead of sharing the true gospel, instead of providing the life of the Lord, Babylon and her daughter cities have pursued the opposite. They cater to the old man and consent to manipulation by religious demons while claiming this behavior is of God. They proclaim their own righteousness in the midst of their fornication with the kings of the earth, which are those who manage the religious, political, and economic kingdoms of the earth.

> 9 *And the third angel followed them, saying with a loud voice, If anyone worships the beast and its image and receives the mark in his forehead or in his hand,*

Notice again that the mark is received *in* the forehead or *in* the hand, not *on* the forehead or *on* the hand. This reinforces the case that the *mark* is primarily a way of thinking and a way of acting having to do with the natural unconverted man (beast).

> 10 *the same shall drink of the wine of the wrath of God, which is poured out without mixture into the cup of his indignation; and he shall be tormented with fire and brimstone in the presence of the holy angels and in the presence of the Lamb;*

This sets the stage for the wrath of God that will be poured out. It's important to bear in mind, however, that God never destroys the righteous along with the wicked (Genesis 18:25).

God's indignation has been a central theme for many prophets, including Isaiah, and *the wine of the wrath of God* means that God is about to give the wicked a double dose of their own medicine. The *holy angels* referred to are the angels or messengers sent from God that are for the exclusive service of the Lord. In Scripture, brimstone is always linked to the righteous judgments of God and is never associated with anything that proceeds from the Devil.

> 11 *and the smoke of their torment ascends up for ever and ever; and those that worship the beast and its image and whosoever receives the mark of its name, have no rest day or night.*

These examples will be remembered for ever and ever. Those who worship the natural man, and those who worship the god that they have made in the image of man, and those who think and act according to the nature of the natural man will have no rest, day or night. The first example of this was Cain. God sentenced him to wander as a fugitive and vagabond, to never be at rest, after he murdered his brother, Abel (Genesis 4:12).

> 12 *Here is the patience of the saints; here are those that keep the commandments of God and the faith of Jesus.*

Patience is a fruit of the Holy Spirit. The saints have been waiting six thousand years for God to turn this around. The day of man has endured for six prophetic days (six thousand years). Those that keep the commandments of God are linked to the faith *of* Jesus, which is beyond faith *in* Jesus. The faith of Jesus must come forth in us if we are to overcome.

> 13 *And I heard a voice from heaven saying unto me, Write Blessed are the dead who die in the Lord from now on; Yea, saith the Spirit, that they may rest from their labours, and their works do follow them.*

This is the second beatitude in the Book of Revelation. It coincides with Jesus' second beatitude, *Blessed are those who mourn for they shall be comforted* (Matthew 5:4). The word *mourn* means mourning a death (i.e., the death of the old man, of the old nature). The comforter is the Holy Spirit.

We are to cease and desist from our own works and rest, so the Holy Spirit may work in and through us. Noah's name meant rest. He was an example of this. Then the works that God does in and through us will follow us.

> 14 *And I looked, and, behold, a white cloud, and upon the cloud one sat like unto the Son of man, having on his head a golden crown and in his hand a sharp sickle.*

God led the children of Israel from a pillar of cloud. Jesus will return *in a cloud with power and great glory* (Luke 21:27; Revelation 1:7). Scripture also declares that *we are compassed about with so great a cloud of witnesses* (Hebrews 12:1).

Jesus called himself the Son of man. He is seated at the right hand of the Father with all power and authority, with a great cloud of witnesses who have gone on before. He is about to conduct the harvest, which has to do with judgment, and witnesses are required in order for judgment to be passed.

> 15 *Another angel came out of the temple, crying with a loud voice to him that was seated on the cloud, Thrust in thy sickle and reap; for the harvest of the earth is dry.*

The cloud is symbolic of the nature of God. When the harvest of the earth is dry, this means that it is mature and the time has come to reap (Galatians 6:7-9).

> 16 *And he that was seated on the cloud thrust in his sickle upon the earth; and the earth was reaped.*

The earth is the realm of the people of God, Israel, and the church. Do not be confused, however, when God labels those with uncircumcised hearts in Israel and in the church as Gentiles.

> 17 *And another angel came out of the temple which is in the heaven, he also having a sharp sickle.*

The harvest proceeds. First, the tares are reaped into bundles and then burned (Matthew 13:30).

Here is Jesus' interpretation of the parable of the wheat and the tares:

> *He answered and said unto them, He that sows the good seed is the Son of man; the field is the world; the good seed are the sons of the kingdom, but the tares are the sons of the wicked; and the enemy that sowed them is the devil; the harvest is the end of the age, and the reapers are the angels. As therefore the tares are gathered and burned in the fire, so shall it be in the end of this age. The Son of man shall send forth his angels, and they shall gather out of his kingdom all things that offend and those who do iniquity and shall cast them into the furnace of fire; there shall be wailing and gnashing of teeth. Then shall the righteous shine forth as the sun in the kingdom of their Father. He who has ears to hear, let him hear* (Matthew 13:37-43).

Have you ears to hear? Have you eyes to read? Then let's return to the revelation that was shown to John.

> 18 *And another angel came out from the altar, who had power over the fire, and cried with a loud voice to him that had the sharp sickle saying, Thrust in thy sharp sickle and gather the clusters of the earth; for her grapes are fully ripe.*

> 19 *And the angel thrust in his sickle into the earth and gathered the vine of the earth and cast it into the great winepress of the wrath of God.*

There are two kinds of grapes in Scripture that produce two very different kinds of wine. Wine is a symbol of life, but there is a huge difference between the life of Adam and the life of Christ. Note that these grapes come in *clusters*. Only those who understand and submit to the altar (the gospel), which is linked to the fire of God, will produce the right fruit. The *clusters* of the earth represent those who congregate in places where they obtain their doctrine, directives, and guidance from one another and from false prophets instead of from God. The only wine these *clusters* can produce is the wine of the life of Adam.

> 20 *And the winepress was trodden outside the city, and blood came out of the winepress, even unto the bits of the horses, for a thousand six hundred furlongs.*

Psalm 32:9 offers an explanation about the bits of the horses. *Be ye not as the horse or as the mule, which have no understanding: whose mouth must be held in subjection with bit and bridle, or they will not come near unto thee.* The horse without understanding, that must be held in subjection with a bit, is a symbol of those who must be controlled under law. Those who are led by the Spirit are the sons of God and are not under the law (Romans 8:14; Galatians 5:18).

When the judgment of God falls, it will affect all those who, like the horse in Psalm 32, have no understanding and must be controlled by the iron bit of the law for a distance of one thousand six hundred furlongs. A furlong is about one eighth of a mile or forty rods. Spiritually, if six hundred represents man's plans, then one thousand six hundred means that the fullness of man's plans for human control and dominion will be completely judged as they come to fruition and maturity.

In the natural world, one thousand six hundred furlongs equal about two hundred miles. If the city were Jerusalem, a two-hundred-mile radius would mean that this judgment would affect everyone in the land of Israel, which symbolically is another picture of the earth or the realm of the people of God. This is the area that would fall under the law, and the letter of the law kills. Under the law, some things could be purified with water and others with fire, but *without the shedding of blood there is no remission* (Hebrews 9:22). Without remission, *the soul that sins, it shall die* (Ezekiel 18:4).

Many disguise their addiction and bondage to law under the pretense of distilling apparently righteous principles and values from the Scriptures. They proceed to apply these principles and values in the flesh, according to the desires of their own soul, or according to the dictates of their spiritual director(s) instead of being led by the Spirit of God in good conscience. Yet, it's only the Spirit that brings forth life.

Revelation 15

> 1 *And I saw another sign in the heaven, great and marvelous, seven angels having the seven last plagues; for in them is completed the wrath of God.*

The seven angels with the seven last plagues are another sign. They come from the presence of God.

If we add the three woes linked to the last three trumpets to the seven last plagues, that totals ten plagues in the book of Revelation, just as God unleashed ten plagues against Egypt. The first three Egyptian plagues had the potential to affect everyone, but the final seven plagues didn't affect the people of God who lived in Goshen (Exodus 9:4).

> 2 *And I saw, as it were, a sea of glass mingled with fire and those that had gotten the victory over the beast and over its image and over its mark and over the number of its name stand on the sea of glass, having the harps of God.*

God's overcomers are unaffected by the problems related to the sea of humanity. They are at peace and don't have to worry about the beast, the image of the beast, its mark, or the number of its name, because they are victorious in Christ and sealed. Note that the mark of the beast and the number of its name are listed separately. Therefore, the mark isn't exactly the same as the number 666.

> 3 *And they sing the song of Moses, the slave of God, and the song of the Lamb, saying, Great and marvellous are thy works, Lord God Almighty; just and true are thy ways, thou King of saints.*

This *song of Moses* is the song of victory Moses composed at the end of his long life of ministry (Deuteronomy 31:19-22).

> 4 *Who shall not fear thee, O Lord, and magnify thy name? for thou only art holy; therefore, all the Gentiles shall come and worship before thee; for thy judgments are made manifest.*

This song celebrates the victory when every knee shall bow and every tongue shall confess that Jesus is Lord (Romans 14:11; Philippians 2:10). This is what God said through the prophet Isaiah:

> *Assemble yourselves and come; draw near together, all ye that are escaped of the Gentiles. They have no knowledge that set up the wood of their graven image and pray unto the god that does not save. Tell ye, and bring them near; yea, let them take counsel*

> *together; who caused this to be heard from the beginning and has declared it from that time, except me, the LORD? and there is no God beside me; a just God and a Saviour; there is no one besides me. Look unto me, and be ye saved, all the ends of the earth; for I am God, and there is no one else. I have sworn by myself; the word is gone out of my mouth in righteousness and shall not return, That unto me every knee shall bow; every tongue shall swear. And unto me he shall say, Surely in the LORD is the righteousness and the strength; until he shall come; and all that are incensed against him shall be ashamed. In the LORD shall all the generation of Israel be justified and shall glory* (Isaiah 45:20-25).

Israel, which means *God prevails* or *he who prevails with God*, is linked to the name of God. It represents all the people of God, Jews and Gentiles, who are truly converted and have clean, circumcised hearts.

There is another parallel passage in Joel:

> *Assemble yourselves and come, all ye Gentiles, and gather yourselves together round about; there cause thy mighty ones to come down, O LORD. Let the Gentiles be wakened and come up to the valley of Jehoshaphat for there I will sit to judge all the Gentiles round about. Put in the sickle for the harvest is ripe; come, go down for the press is full, the vats overflow; for their wickedness is great. Multitudes, multitudes in the valley of decision for the day of the LORD is near in the valley of decision. The sun and the moon shall be darkened, and the stars shall withdraw their shining. The LORD also shall roar out of Zion and utter*

> *his voice from Jerusalem; and the heavens and the earth shall shake; but the LORD will be the hope of his people and the strength of the sons of Israel. So shall ye know that I am the LORD your God, that I inhabit Zion, the mountain of my holiness: then shall Jerusalem be holy, and no strangers shall pass through her any more* (Joel 3:11-17).

Jerusalem continues to be profaned by many *strangers.* But a radical change will soon take place, when *Mount Zion* and *Jerusalem* become a place of salvation and safety instead of their current mixture of the holy with the profane.

What else does Revelation tell us about this time that is to come?

Revelation 15

> 5 *And after these things I looked, and, behold, the temple of the tabernacle of the testimony in the heaven was opened;*

The tabernacle of the testimony in heaven has been closed or veiled off from the inhabitants of the earth, because it contains the direct presence and glory of the Lord that will destroy anyone who is contaminated or unclean. When it's opened, it sets the stage for immediate judgment, described as the wrath of God, as seven cups or vials are poured out.

This correlates with Revelation 6:14 and 11:19 and is the fulfillment of Yom Kippur, the Day of Reconciliation (or atonement), when anyone who does not afflict their soul (repent) shall be cut off from among their people. Anyone who does not desist from their own works shall be destroyed. As Leviticus 23:27-28 describes it, *and ye shall afflict your souls and offer an offering made on fire unto the LORD. And ye shall do no work in this same day; for it is a day of reconciliations, to reconcile you before the LORD your God.*

Reconciliation means us being lined back up straight with God. It doesn't mean that God will meet us half-way, somewhere between our *mortal* and our *venial* sins. It means that he has standards that we have to meet, as the next verses make clear. *For every person that shall not afflict themselves in that same day, shall be cut off from among his people. And any person that does any work in that same day, the same person will I destroy from among his people. Ye shall do no manner of work; it shall be a perpetual statute throughout your ages in all your dwellings* (Leviticus 23:29-31).

The fullness of this day is the day of the Lord. Note that it is a perpetual statute and, as such, it applies throughout all the ages of the people of God, including the ages of the law, of grace, and of the kingdom. Also note that it applies to *all* dwellings, whether they are of heaven, of the earth, or of the sea.

No one who is unrepentant and uncircumcised of heart will be able to continue to do their own work in the name of the LORD.

Here is what Joel wrote concerning that day: *The sun shall be turned into darkness and the moon into blood before the great and terrible day of the LORD comes. And it shall come to pass that whoever shall call upon the name of the LORD shall escape; for in Mount Zion and in Jerusalem shall be salvation, as the LORD has said, and in those who are left, to whom the LORD shall have called* (Joel 2:31-32).

Again and again the prophets warn us, sometimes in plain words and sometimes in metaphor. Here are more striking images from the revelation seen by John:

6 *and the seven angels came out of the temple, having*

> *the seven plagues, clothed in pure and white linen, and having their breasts girded with golden girdles.*

We are the temple, and the seven angels that come out are described as having breasts. In Greek, this means the breasts of women. As the people of God are this temple, so the seven female angels represent all the congregations that dwell in the heavenly realm of the Holy of Holies. The word *angel* denotes that they have been commissioned and sent by God. They are now clothed with pure, white linen representing the righteous acts of the saints, and golden girdles representing the nature of God.

This is a corporate, clean people of God who now flow in the heavenly fullness of the Spirit of God. This is vastly different from the earthly outpouring on the Day of Pentecost (typed with the Holy Place) that was described by the apostle Paul as the *earnest* or down payment of our inheritance in the Spirit (2 Corinthians 5:5; Ephesians 1:13-14).

> 7 *And one of the four animals gave unto the seven angels seven golden vials full of the wrath of God, who lives for ever and ever.*

The golden vials are the prayers of the saints (Revelation 5:8), which have been long held in remembrance before the throne of God. On the fulfillment of the Day of Reconciliation, those prayers will all be answered in full. The clean, corporate congregations of God that dwell in the heavenly realm will be given the authority to judge the false church and the corrupt world.

The Passover had its fulfillment when the death and resurrection of our Lord Jesus Christ made possible our salvation and redemption. Pentecost was fulfilled at the outpouring of the Holy Spirit upon the early church of the Day of Pentecost, starting with one hundred twenty believers in an upper room. The fullness of the Feast of Trumpets is now upon us. The next prophetic event to be fulfilled among the people of God prior to the Feast of Tabernacles, the feast at the end of the harvest, is Yom Kippur or the Day of Reconciliation (Leviticus 23).

> 8 *And the temple was filled with smoke from the majesty of God and from his power; and no one was able to enter into the temple until the seven plagues of the seven angels were fulfilled.*

We can see the type and shadow fulfillment of this during the dedication of Solomon's temple. Note that it also began with a song. *And when the priests came out of the sanctuary (for all the priests that were present were sanctified and did not then wait by course, and the Levite singers, all of those of Asaph, those of Heman, and those of Jeduthun, together with their sons and their brethren being clothed in white linen, having cymbals and psalteries and harps, stood at the east end of the altar, and with them one hundred and twenty priests sounding with trumpets).* (2 Chronicles 5:11-12).

The trumpets link this to the Year of Jubilee, which began on the Day of Reconciliation (Leviticus 25:9).

Here's an interesting thought:

Consider that 120 trumpets may be symbolic of the 120 fifty-year Jubilee periods since Adam and Eve got the entire human race into trouble in the garden. A year of Jubilee was to take place every fiftieth year (Leviticus 25:10). If 1967 was the 119th Jubilee, or the 69th Jubilee since the writing of the Book of Leviticus circa 1883 BC, then the 120 trumpets will be fulfilled in 2017, beginning on Yom Kippur in the fall of 2016. This would be the 70th Jubilee since the writing of the Book of Leviticus. We will soon see if this is indeed the right timetable.

I feel, for many reasons, that 1967 was a Jubilee year when many prophecies converged along with the six-day war and the beginning of important ministry and revival.[8] However God chooses to work all of this out, I expect next year (2017) to be a very special prophetic year that in hindsight will undoubtedly prove to be even better than 1967 for anyone who has a clean heart.

And what a wonderful picture of celebration is painted in 2 Chronicles 5:13-14. *And they sounded the trumpets and sang with one voice, all together as one man praising and thanking the LORD, when they lifted up their voice with trumpets and cymbals and instruments of music, when they praised the LORD, saying, For he is good, for his mercy endures for ever; and the house was filled with a cloud, even the house of the LORD, so that the priests could not stand to minister by reason of the cloud, for the glory of the LORD had filled the house of God.*

Once the number of the martyrs (witnesses) is complete, and once God's true people are cleansed, then the temple of God of living stones will measure up, and the fullness of the glory of God will return to his house (his people). This is when the vials of all the prayers that have gone up over the past millennia will be answered, as God commands his angels to pour out the vials of his wrath and judgment upon those who have killed and mistreated his children. The enemy's deception will completely collapse, and anyone who calls upon the name of the LORD shall be saved.

Let us pray

Heavenly Father,

We ask that we might understand this revelation. We ask that all those who are not happy with the way things are being run here upon the earth, all those who cry out and sigh regarding what they see

8 See *The Book of Daniel*, by Russell Stendal, Aneko Press.

all around them, will receive your mark, your seal. We ask that they may have your heart and your mind, Lord; that they may be dressed with fine linen and be covered by the righteous work that you are doing in and through them. Amen.

Chapter 18

The Vials

Revelation 16

> 1 *And I heard a great voice out of the temple saying to the seven angels, Go and pour out the vials of the wrath of God upon the earth.*

This is the voice of God giving direct orders to the seven angels that represent his people.

> 2 *And the first went and poured out his vial upon the earth; and an evil and grievous sore fell upon the men who had the mark of the beast and upon those who worshipped its image.*

This judgment only falls upon those who have the mark of the beast, which is primarily a way of thinking and acting according to the nature of the flesh.

Those who have the mark of the beast and worship its image are linked to *buying and selling* (Revelation 13:17). Jesus overturned the tables of the moneychangers and drove the buyers and sellers from the temple on two occasions. This judgment will make it very difficult for corrupt business to continue as usual in the name of the Lord.

Grievous sore could have been translated *grievous plague.* God told Pharaoh through Moses, *this time I will send all my plagues upon thine heart and upon thy slaves and upon thy people that thou may know that there is none like me in all the earth. For now I will stretch out my hand that I may smite thee and thy people with pestilence, and thou shalt be cut off from the earth* (Exodus 9:14-15).

Pharaoh prided himself in the hardness of his heart towards the people of God. The worst plagues that fell were when God hardened Pharaoh's stubborn heart again and again until he and his entire army were finally destroyed in the Red Sea.

Those who pride themselves in being tough, ornery tightwads who abuse and enslave others – and many religious leaders are like this – should take note.

> 3 *And the second angel poured out his vial into the sea; and it became blood as of a dead man, and every living soul died in the sea.*

When the second trumpet sounded, the third part of the sea became blood. What began as judgment from the house of the Lord within the realm of the Holy Place, extends to cover every living soul in the sea of the outer court. The soul that sins shall die. This law is immediately enforced. It's impossible for anyone to keep their soul alive in the realm of the sea when the sea has turned to blood. It's also extremely difficult for their soul to stay alive on the earth, because the temple of God is open. The blinding light and glory of the presence of God, linked to the revelation and return of Jesus Christ, streams forth unchecked from the Holy of Holies and will destroy the man of sin (2 Thessalonians 2:8).

The dwellers of the earth have already had to run and hide in caves and under the rocks (Revelation 6:15). The mountain of religiosity has already cast itself into the sea after the presence of God caused it to smoke and burn (Revelation 8:8). The only hope for lost humanity is to cry out and call on the name of the Lord (Joel 2:30-32).

> 4 *And the third angel poured out his vial into the rivers and fountains of waters; and they became blood.*
>
> 5 *And I heard the angel of the waters say, Thou art righteous, O Lord, who art and wast the Holy one because thou hast judged these things;*
>
> 6 *for they have shed the blood of saints and prophets, and thou hast given them blood to drink; for they deserve it.*
>
> 7 *And I heard another out of the altar say, Even so, Lord God Almighty, true and righteous are thy judgments.*

The altar is linked to the gospel because it's on the altar that the old man, the old nature, must be repented of, surrendered to God, and done away with. So that we may come forth in the name (nature) of the new man in Christ. Jesus said, *Think not that I am come to undo the law or the prophets; I am not come to undo, but to fulfill. For verily I say unto you, Until heaven and earth pass away, not one jot or one tittle shall pass from the law until all is fulfilled* (Matthew 5:17-18). Jesus died for us and fulfilled the law with his blood as the Lamb of God. Those who reject him may have to pay with their own blood.

Under the law, no one may be put to death unless they have been convicted by the testimony of two or three witnesses (Numbers 35:30; Deuteronomy 19:15). However, here we have the witness of the angel of the waters and the witness of *another out of the altar* of *those that had been slain because of the word of God and for the testimony which they held* (Revelation 6:9).

The third trumpet affected one third of the rivers and fountains. All the rivers and fountains of humanism become blood. No one can drink from any of these waters and keep their soul alive. Those who have been drinking from the water of twisted humanistic philosophy or contaminated religion will have their supply revealed for what it really is: not life but death.

> 8 *And the fourth angel poured out his vial against the sun; and it was given unto it to scorch men with fire.*
>
> 9 *And men were scorched with great heat, and blasphemed the name of God, who has authority over these plagues; and they did not repent to give him glory.*

The heat of the sun, representing the entire world system, becomes completely unbearable. That which once gave life now gives death. The real salt and light are no longer there. There is no one left in the world system who is spiritually alive. It's not possible for anyone to keep their soul alive in the *sea* or on the *earth*. The lamps of the foolish virgins have been faltering and flickering for a long time. Now they are almost all extinguished, because they have run out of oil (Matthew 25:7-12). Every possibility for them to stay lit, apart from a direct relationship with God, has been eliminated. Those whose lamps have gone out are like beasts (Psalm 49:12,20). Yet, God hopes that they will repent and give him the glory.

> 10 *And the fifth angel poured out his vial upon the throne of the beast; and its kingdom was filled with darkness; and they gnawed their tongues for pain,*
>
> 11 *and blasphemed the God of the heaven because of their pains and their sores and did not repent of their deeds.*

Now the world is in pitch-black spiritual darkness. The natural man (the beast) has no light. The lamps of those who operated gifts and ministries from God and did not come under the direct discipline of the heavenly Father are completely extinguished. It's interesting to note that the Shekinah glory of God can appear to the natural man to be pitch-black darkness, because his spiritual senses are not alive (Exodus 20:21). Do you remember when God sent Gideon into the midst of the enemy camp in the dead of night with their lamps hidden inside pitchers of clay? (Judges 7:16-22). He's about to do something similar.

Even after it's no longer possible to sustain living souls in the sea and after there's nothing on the earth but blood (death) to drink on dry land, those associated with the throne of the beast and its kingdom (the world) are still physically alive, with grievous pains and sores in their hearts. Because their hearts is where the full impact of the plagues is felt as they continue to refuse to repent of their deeds (Exodus 9:14).

However, this will be a wonderful time for those who are right with God. Listen to this from Isaiah. *Arise, shine; for thy light is come, and the glory of the LORD is risen upon thee. For, behold, the darkness shall cover the earth, and gross darkness the peoples: but the LORD shall arise upon thee, and his glory shall be seen upon thee. And the Gentiles shall walk to thy light, and the kings to the brightness of thy birth* (Isaiah 60:1-3).

A new light is dawning, and with it, an entire nation, also described as the birth of a man child. And this time, the woman is not under the curse. *Before she travailed, she brought forth; before her pain came, she was delivered of a man child* (Isaiah 66:7).

Malachi 4:1-3 offers this view: *For, behold, the day comes that shall burn as an oven; and all the proud, and all that do wickedly shall be stubble; and the day that comes shall burn them up, said the LORD of the hosts, that it shall leave neither root nor branch. But unto you that fear my name shall the Sun of righteousness be born, and in his wings he shall bring saving health; and ye shall go forth and jump like calves of the herd. And ye shall tread down the wicked; for they shall be ashes under the soles of your feet in the day that I make, said the LORD of the hosts.*

A new day is dawning. A new sun is rising, the Sun of righteousness, and a nation shall be born in a day (Isaiah 60:19-20; 66:8). *The way of the kings from the rising of the sun will now be prepared* (Revelation 16:12). The fullness of the brilliant, dazzling, radiant light of Christ in a many-membered body with the Lord Jesus at the head will soon directly confront, battle, and overcome all the powers of darkness.

Let's return to the scene described in Revelation 16.

> 12 *And the sixth angel poured out his vial into the great river Euphrates; and its water was dried up, that the way of the kings from the rising of the sun might be prepared.*

The river Euphrates, its name means *double fruitfulness*, is the northern boundary that God assigned to the land of Israel. It was considered to be a natural barrier of protection. At the sixth trumpet, four angels that had been bound in the Euphrates were released. These angels were prepared unto the hour and day and month and year, to slay the third part of men (Revelation 9:15).

Preparations are being made to judge everyone.

> 13 *And I saw three unclean spirits like frogs come out of the mouth of the dragon and out of the mouth of the beast and out of the mouth of the false prophet.*
>
> 14 *For they are spirits of demons, working miracles, which go forth into the kings of the earth and of the whole world to gather them to the battle of that great day of God Almighty.*
>
> 15 *Behold, I come as a thief. Blessed is he that*

> *watches and keeps his garments lest he walk naked, and they see his shame.*

The spirits of demons, which work miracles as they operate out of the mouth of the dragon, the beast, and the false prophet, are about to be revealed for what they are. Like wicked Haman, they will attempt to wipe out all of the people of God, and not realize that they are really gathering the kings of the earth and of the whole world to the battle of the great day of God Almighty. In 2 Thessalonians 2:8, we learn what will happen when Jesus Christ returns with all his saints. *And then shall that Wicked one be revealed, whom the Lord shall consume with the Spirit of his mouth and remove with the clarity of his coming.*

The deception of the wicked one will be revealed wherever he is operating, hiding, controlling, or manipulating. He will use all of his proxies and *gather the kings of the earth and of the whole world to the battle of that great day of God Almighty.* They shall all be defeated, and the people of God that they've enslaved shall be set free.

> 16 *And he gathered them together into the place which in Hebrew is called Armageddon.*

This is Har Megiddo or *height of the place of God.* It's primarily a spiritual place that will affect almost everyone on the planet. There will, of course, also be significant natural events in the mid east.

> 17 *And the seventh angel poured out his vial into the air; and there came a great voice out of the temple of the heaven from the throne, saying, It is done.*

After the seventh trumpet, the great dragon, the serpent of old who is called the Devil and Satan, and his angels were cast out of heaven into the earth. After the seventh vial, he will soon be chained and bound for a thousand years in the bottomless pit (Revelation 20:2).

> 18 *Then there were voices and thunders and lightnings; and there was a great earthquake, such as has never been since men were upon the earth, so mighty an earthquake, and so great.*

Thunder is linked to the voice of God. Lightning is linked to the presence of God and to the second coming of Jesus Christ. The first use of the word *earthquake* in Scripture is seen when Elijah fled to the mountain of God and found out that the LORD was not in the wind, the earthquake, or the fire but in the still, small voice (1 Kings 19:11-12). Times of great spiritual significance can be described in Scripture as earthquakes. There was a great earthquake when Jesus died on the cross and another at his resurrection (Matthew 27:51; 28:2).

Now, the greatest earthquake since men were first upon the earth will take place. What could be of greater spiritual seismic significance than the death and resurrection of Jesus Christ? Joel 2:9 may offer a clue. *They shall go through the city; they shall run upon the wall; they shall climb up upon the houses; they shall enter in at the windows like a thief.* Jesus said in Revelation 16:15 that he will return as a thief. Here, Joel sees him entering cities at the head of his army. It is the triumphant return of Jesus Christ that will go down in history as the division of time. Joel's awe-inspiring description continues in the next two verses. *The earth shall quake before him; the heavens shall tremble: the sun and the moon shall go dark; and the stars shall withdraw their shining: and the LORD shall utter his voice before his army: for many are his camps and strong, that execute his word; for the day of the LORD is great, and very terrible; and who can abide it?* (Joel 2:10-11).

Here is another view of the same event found in Isaiah 24, where verses 17 and 18 offer a clear warning. *Fear and the pit and the snare are upon thee, O inhabitant of the earth. And it shall come to pass that he who shall flee from the noise of the fear shall fall into the pit; and he that shall come up out of the midst of the pit shall be taken in the snare: because from on high, windows have been opened, and the foundations of the earth shall shake.*

The phrase *from on high, windows have been opened* means that the veil has been removed and the glory and brightness of the revelation of Jesus Christ from the heavens floods the earth. The results are described in verses 19 and 20. *The earth shall be utterly broken down; the earth is clean dissolved; the earth is moved exceedingly. The earth shall reel to and fro like a drunkard and shall be removed like a cottage; and its transgression shall be heavy upon it; and it shall fall and never rise again.*

The earth – the habitation of the humanistic dominance of Israel and the church – shall fall and never rise again. *And it shall come to pass in that day that the LORD shall visit the punishment upon the host of the high ones that are on high and upon the kings of the earth on the earth* (Isaiah 24:21). In other words, the demons behind the apostasy and deception among the people of God shall be punished along with the *kings* they helped raise up and empower over the people of God. *And they shall be gathered together as prisoners are gathered in the pit and shall be shut up in prison, and after many days they shall be visited* (Isaiah 24:22). Yes, they shall be locked up and imprisoned in the bottomless pit in Hades. After *one thousand years*, at the general resurrection they shall be visited for final judgment (Revelation 20:5-15).

> *Then the moon shall be confounded, and the sun ashamed, when the LORD of the hosts shall reign in Mount Zion and in Jerusalem, and in the presence of his ancients he shall be glorious* (Isaiah 24:23).

It's clear that the primary meaning of the key terminology

is prophetic. The *moon* is confounded and the *sun* ashamed. Therefore, the vividly described *earthquake* means that all the kingdoms of man are shaken and cannot recover, so that we may receive a kingdom that cannot be moved (Hebrews 12:25-29). Since the spiritual and natural realms are related and are being joined together once again, there will undoubtedly be many natural events that correlate with and help mark and identify the spiritual events. Scripture states that *the spiritual is not first, but the natural; and afterward, that which is spiritual* (1 Corinthians 15:46).

Revelation 16

> 19 *And the great city was divided into three parts, and the cities of the Gentiles fell; and Babylon the great came in remembrance before God, to give unto her the cup of the wine of the fierceness of his wrath.*

The great city that should also be the holy city is trodden underfoot by the Gentiles for forty-two months. Forty-two is the correction factor, which means that the main thing lacking is the direct presence of Jesus Christ. This great city is where the two witnesses are killed. It's spiritually called Sodom and Egypt. It's also where our Lord was crucified. This great city, that has been consumed by religion, is divided into three parts. Three parts or three one-third segments means that the clean priests of the Lord are being separated. Among the priesthood of all believers, the sons of Zadok (righteousness) are being separated from those who caused God's people to sin (Ezekiel 44:15; 48:11-12).

Jesus is our redeemer; he redeemed us with his blood. Redemption in typology is linked to wine (a symbol of life). There is something, however, that many have not taken into account as they sip the wine of their little communion cup. The word *redeemer* is the exactly same Hebrew word as *avenger of blood*. For some, the cup is salvation and blessing. For others, it's damnation and wrath (1 Corinthians 11:27,29). Those who have been going through the outward ritual without a close inner relationship (real communion) with Jesus and his Father will face the fierceness of his wrath. The only way to know the Father is to come under his discipline and chastening while there is still time.

> 20 *And every island fled away, and the mountains were not found.*

In prophetic language, islands are private kingdoms and mountains are strongholds.

> 21 *And there fell upon men a great hail out of heaven, every stone about the weight of a talent; and men blasphemed God because of the plague of the hail; for the plague thereof was exceeding great.*

To blaspheme is to take God's name in vain. *The LORD will not hold guiltless anyone who takes his name in vain* (Exodus 20:7).

Matthew 7:21-23 warns us of what will happen to many. *Not every one that saith unto me Lord, Lord, shall enter into the kingdom of the heavens, but he that doeth the will of my Father who is in the heavens. Many will say to me in that day, Lord, Lord, have we not prophesied in thy name? and in thy name have cast out devils? and in thy name done many wonderful works? And then I will profess unto them, I never knew you; depart from me, ye that work iniquity.*

This is what happens to those among the people of God who claim to be sons of God but are really impostors, even if they have gifts, talents, or ministries that appear to be from God. This relates to the *kings of the earth* we discussed earlier.

Isaiah 28:15 describes the perspective of those worldly kings. *Because ye have said, We have made a covenant with death, and with Sheol we are at agreement; when the overflowing scourge shall pass through, it shall not come unto us: for we have made lies our refuge, and under falsehood we have hid ourselves.*

False doctrine claiming to approve of carnal security has permeated large sectors of Israel and the church in our present time.

Isaiah tells us what lies in wait for those kings. *Therefore thus saith the Lord GOD, Behold, I lay in Zion for a foundation a stone, a tried stone, a precious corner stone, a sure foundation: he that believes shall not make haste. Judgment also will I lay to the line and righteousness to the plummet: and the hail shall sweep away the refuge of lies, and the waters shall overflow the hiding place. And your covenant with death shall be disannulled, and your agreement with Sheol shall not stand; when the overflowing scourge shall pass through, then ye shall be trodden down by it* (Isaiah 28:16-18).

This is similar to the scene described in Revelation 16.

> 21 *And there fell upon men a great hail out of heaven, every stone about the weight of a talent; and men blasphemed God because of the plague of the hail; for the plague thereof was exceeding great.*

Rain is likened to the blessing of the Word of God. When the early and later rains fell at the proper time, there would be an excellent harvest. Hail is different. *Hail* is a hard word and a hard rain. It's hail that *shall sweep away the refuge of lies, and the waters shall overflow the hiding place.*

Every stone of hail that comes down in this judgment is about the same weight as a talent. Different types of talents had varying weights. For example, the Greek talent weighed fifty-seven pounds compared to the Roman talent at seventy-one pounds. The common talent used in New Testament times weighed an impressive one hundred thirty pounds – not the sort of thing you'd want falling from the sky!

God has given out many talents, in the modern sense of the word. Yet Jesus took issue with the slave who buried his talent and didn't use it for the Master's gain (Matthew 25:24-30). The primary issue is not how talented a person is but how they use those God-given talents. Some will have prophesied, cast out devils, and even performed wonderful works in Jesus's name, only to hear him say, *I never knew you; depart from me, ye that work iniquity.* Why? Because they didn't realize that sooner or later, there will be an exam to see if their gifts, talents, and ministries produced tangible fruit for the kingdom of God (Ezekiel 46:17). Those who are not true sons will lose their gifts and talents if they haven't produced good fruit of the Spirit, which in the highest sense is godly character in our own lives and in the lives of those to whom we minister.

Some have used their God-given talents for personal gain or the gain of some impersonal movement, organization, or institution. They've taken the name of the Lord in vain by applying his name to their own plans, programs, and institutions. Their work may appear wonderful from the outside. But this counts for nothing if, at the end, Jesus decides that he doesn't know them and that they have really been working iniquity (hidden sin).

It's sobering to think that the Devil still has his talents, he still has his gifts, and they still function. The fact that he openly rebelled didn't cause the Lord to immediately take away his power. For six thousand years, God allowed the Devil to exercise authority over this fallen world and continue to deceive everyone who doesn't completely surrender to God. But this situation is about to come to a very abrupt end for both the Devil and men.

Now is the time when the fruit of each person and of all the kingdoms of this world is ripe unto harvest. Now is the time when the stone that was cut without hands is about to destroy the image that Nebuchadnezzar and Daniel saw, which represents all the kingdoms of the world (Daniel 2). Now is the time of the judgment.

Let us pray

Heavenly Father,

May we find that secret place in you described in Psalm 91, where we may abide under your shadow and be covered under your protection, no matter what happens around us. Allow us to invest our talents, under the guidance of your Holy Spirit, so that we might obtain true riches for your kingdom. We ask this in the name of our Lord Jesus Christ. Amen.

Chapter 19

The Condemnation of the Great Whore

Revelation 17

1 *And there came one of the seven angels who had the seven vials and talked with me, saying unto me, Come here; I will show unto thee the condemnation of the great whore that sits upon many waters,*

The seven angels who had the seven vials represent the true people of God who are inhabitants, or citizens, of the heavens. That it refers to the vials in past tense (had) means that the vials have already been poured out, and that the whore has already been condemned. Now we'll look at the details, as the sentence of God's judgments unfold.

The waters that the whore sits upon are peoples, nations, multitudes, and tongues. The whore and her many daughters have to do with unclean religious congregations (typed as women in prophecy), in all of their many guises. She seduces secular and religious leaders (*the kings of the earth*) to do the will of man, and ultimately the will of the Devil, instead of the will of God. She has intoxicated and subdued all the inhabitants of the earth with her deadly poison as she attempts to neutralize and exterminate the true prophets and people of God.

> 2 *with whom the kings of the earth have committed fornication and the inhabitants of the earth have been made drunk with the wine of her fornication.*

The implication is that all the kings of the earth have committed fornication with her and all the inhabitants of the earth have been made drunk with the wine of her fornication. This is in keeping with the statements made so far in the book of Revelation regarding all the inhabitants, or dwellers, of the earth being linked to the abomination of desolation in the Holy Place. Only those who dwell in the heavenly realm are pure, clean, and safe, even if they're martyred.

> 3 *So he carried me away in the spirit into the wilderness: and I saw a woman seated upon a scarlet-colored beast, full of names of blasphemy, having seven heads and ten horns.*

The wilderness also links this part of the vision to the Holy Place, the age of the church. Spiritually, this is similar to when the children of Israel wandered in the wilderness for forty-two years prior to entering the Promised Land. A woman stands for a people, congregation, or church. A beast means that this conglomerate, which the woman rides, is linked to the realm of the natural, carnal man. The scarlet color is the same as the color of the pomegranate, which symbolizes the fruit of righteousness, but is also similar to the red dragon (Satan) who specializes in self-righteousness. The *names of blasphemy* mean that the name of the LORD is being taken in vain. These people claim to represent God but aren't his true representatives. Seven heads mean many heads, many secular and religious leaders, many nations, and many denominations. Ten horns mean that this beast draws its power from the law of sin and death.

> 4 *And the woman was arrayed in purple and scarlet colour and decked with gold and precious stones and pearls, having a golden cup in her hand full of abominations and of the filthiness of her fornication;*

Purple and scarlet can denote royalty and freedom. On the other hand, they can also represent pride, arrogance, and tyranny. Gold can represent the nature of God or, on the down side, avarice. The gold, precious stones, and pearls with which the woman is decked have been usurped from the history and testimony of the true prophets and saints of God whom she has murdered and then set up as objects of worship.

> 5 *and upon her forehead was a name written, MYSTERY, BABYLON THE GREAT, THE MOTHER OF THE HARLOTS AND OF THE ABOMINATIONS OF THE EARTH.*

This is a representation of the abomination of desolation, or image of jealousy, either in or in front of the Holy Place that caused God to withdraw his presence from the entire realm by the time of the end and to bring down judgment (Ezekiel 8:5-18; Daniel 11:31; 12:11; Matthew 24:15; Mark 13:14). That she is the Mother of the Harlots means that she has many daughters (cities, congregations, and denominations) that are harlots like their mother and fornicate with the kings of the earth. Sometimes her rebellious daughters hate their mother and vice versa.

> 6 *And I saw the woman drunken with the blood of the saints and with the blood of the martyrs of Jesus; and when I saw her, I marvelled with great surprise.*

The word translated here as *martyrs* could also have been translated *witnesses*. This woman has participated in killing the witnesses of Jesus for such a long time that she not only became drunk with the blood of the saints and the blood of the witnesses (martyrs), she made the inhabitants of the earth drunk with it.

> 7 *And the angel said unto me, Why didst thou marvel? I will tell thee the mystery of the woman and of the beast that carries her, which has the seven heads and ten horns.*

The mystery of this woman is also called the mystery of iniquity (2 Thessalonians 2:7-12).

> 8 *The beast that thou sawest was, and is not, and shall ascend out of the bottomless pit, and shall go into perdition; and those that dwell on the earth shall wonder (whose names are not written in the book of life from the foundation of the world) when they behold the beast that was, and is not, and yet is.*

After the seventh, or last, vial of the wrath of God is poured out, *there came a great voice out of the temple of the heaven from the throne, saying, It is done* (Revelation 16:17). This means that the red beast, or dragon, has been judged and *is not.* He is sentenced and locked up by death in the bottomless pit (Revelation 20:1-2). After *one thousand years,* he shall be loosed a little while and ascend out of Hades, the bottomless pit, and shall go into eternal perdition in the lake of fire (Revelation 20:3; 20:7-10).

> 9 *And here is the meaning which has wisdom. The seven heads are seven mountains, on which the woman sits.*

Mountains represent kingdoms or strongholds. Seven mountains are all the kingdoms of the earth.

> 10 *And they are seven kings: five are fallen, and one is and the other is not yet come; and when he comes, he must continue a short space.*

King and *kingdom* are essentially the same word in Greek, and you recall that Daniel saw a vision of four beasts with a total of seven heads. In John's vision, as in Daniel's, the first king is Babylon, and the second and the third are the Medes and the Persians. Each king has a spiritual counterpart (Daniel 8:20-21; 10:13). The fourth king is Alexander the Great from Greece. The fifth is most likely Seleucus I Nicator, one of Alexander the Great's generals who consolidated control of Babylonia, Anatolia, Persia, the Levant, Mesopotamia (including what we call the Holy Land), and much of what is now Kuwait, Afghanistan, Pakistan, and Turkmenistan, forming the Seleucid Empire.

The sixth king, referred to by the words *and one is* in verse 10, is clearly the Romans who ruled at the time of the apostle John. This is the head that received the deadly wound and recovered as the papacy. The seventh world empire, or kingdom, that *must continue a short space* is the United States of America in alliance with western democracies. It became the sole world superpower after the temporal power of the Vatican faded and diminished due to WWI and WWII, and the Soviet Union collapsed, marked by the fall of the Berlin wall. The Roman empire split into east and west, as symbolized by the two *legs of iron* in the image representing all the world empires seen by King Nebuchadnezzar and interpreted by Daniel (Daniel 2:33). The residue of the eastern empire (centered around Constantinople and the Orthodox) and the residue of the Roman Empire (centered around the western European powers) have given way to the supremacy of the United States and its allied democracies, symbolized by the feet and toes of iron mixed with clay. Iron is a symbol of the law and clay of man. Democracies make laws that the people do not and cannot keep because they are still clay and have not had a change of heart (Daniel 2:41-43).

11 *And the beast that was, and is not, is also the*

eighth king, and is of the seven, and goes into perdition.

This appears to be speaking of when the Devil becomes incarnate in a man (Gog), and the peoples of his kingdom (Magog) continue to be portrayed as a seven-headed beast, which incorporates aspects of all seven world kingdoms. Then, as he mobilizes all his forces against the people of God, he is killed and chained in the bottomless pit for *a thousand years* until he is loosed for a little while. After which, he goes to perdition (Revelation 20:3,10). This is again linked to Gog and Magog and the Devil's deception of the Gentiles on the four corners of the earth, when he is released for a short while after having been imprisoned for a thousand years (Revelation 20:7-10). Gog, which means *a high, lofty mountain*, may be another name for Satan, and Magog means *multitude of Gog*. This incident happens after the Devil is released from the bottomless pit and has to do with the final judgment of all the Gentiles. But it also appears to be linked to what the Devil was doing before he got busted (Ezekiel 38; 39:1-7). Attacking God's chosen people is never a wise idea.

We must remember that all the world's kingdoms are in the hands of the Devil. This is made clear by the fact that when Satan tempted Jesus in the wilderness, he offered him all the kingdoms of the world if Jesus would bow and worship him (Matthew 4:8-10). But Satan's realm has always been divided. Therefore, it isn't necessary for a homogenous one-world government to come together at the time of the end. In fact, all the examples and prophecies in Scripture show the contrary. The kingdom of the Devil with its seven heads (the complete number of heads) and its ten horns (the law according to man) becomes more and more degenerate and corrupt as the end approaches.

12 *And the ten horns which thou hast seen are ten*

kings, which have not yet taken a kingdom, but shall take authority as kings one hour with the beast.

We are now at a time when the ten horns (the law manipulated by man) are attempting to take a kingdom. The beast that comes up out of the sea has its crowns on its horns instead of its heads (Revelation 13:1). It's loyal to the law, or rather, to man's distortion of God's law. At the present time, many are attempting to institute a new world order under man's concept of law. The so-called Pax Americana is one of the prime movers behind this. The ten toes of the statue in Nebuchadnezzar's dream – that will soon be hit by the stone cut without hands – are also linked to taking authority jointly with the beast for one hour, as kings. Such would-be kings include most, if not all, modern democracies.

13 *These have one mind and shall give their power and authority unto the beast.*

They give their power and authority over to the natural, carnal man (the beast). In actuality, it's the Devil to whom they cede their power, because it's Satan who's really behind this.

14 *These shall make war against the Lamb, and the Lamb shall overcome them; for he is Lord of lords and King of kings; and those that are with him are called and chosen and faithful.*

Never doubt who the ultimate winner will be.

15 *The waters which thou hast seen, where the whore sits, are peoples and multitudes and nations and tongues.*

16 *And the ten horns which thou didst see upon the beast shall hate the whore and shall make her desolate and naked and shall eat her flesh and burn her with fire.*

Many of the humanistic powers of today's world hate the whore, traditionally identified as the church at Rome. Pedophile priests and pastors are being brought to trial. The courts are leaving churches and clergy all over the world desolate and naked as huge multimillion-dollar judgments are levied against them. This and other scandals are destined to get worse as more and more corruption in the church is exposed. What happened at the archdiocese of Boston in 2002 is just the tip of the iceberg.

> 17 *For God has put in their hearts to fulfill his will and to agree and give their kingdoms unto the beast until the words of God shall be fulfilled.*

Humanism has taken over virtually all the kingdoms of the world. It allows and even encourages the beast, with his name of blasphemy on his heads and with crowns on his ten horns, to dominate everything. This will be the case until the words of God shall be fulfilled. Those words will only be fulfilled when God has a clean, corporate people that he will anoint in fullness.

> 18 *And the woman which thou hast seen is that great city, which reigns over the kings of the earth.*

By linking the woman with *that great city*, she is personified at the time of John as Babylon (Rome), which continues to this day to wield influence over the kings of the earth, both religious and secular. Even though she now has secular and religious daughters all over the planet.

Revelation 18

> 1 *And after these things I saw another angel come down from heaven, having great power, and the earth was illuminated with his glory.*

The earth continues to be illuminated with the glory and clarity of heaven shining forth through messengers, or angels, of

God, who cleanse the earth as the stranglehold of false religion is broken.

> 2 *And he cried mightily with a strong voice, saying, Babylon the great is fallen, is fallen, and is become the habitation of demons, and the hold of every unclean and hateful bird.*

Once the abomination of desolation was set up in the Holy Place, the presence of God departed. Then the Holy Place, typed as the earth in prophetic language, became *the habitation of demons and the hold of every unclean and hateful bird.* Demons are likened to unclean and hateful birds that feed on carrion. There are many people in "Babylon" who remain alive in the flesh even though their souls have died spiritually. Such people provide a feast for the demons, who do not hesitate to kill and feed on their own kind.

> 3 *For all the Gentiles have drunk of the wine of the wrath of her fornication, and the kings of the earth have committed fornication with her, and the merchants of the earth are waxed rich through the power of her delicacies.*

All those with unclean, uncircumcised hearts have drunk of the wine of the wrath of the woman's fornication. The consequences of her fornication eventually provoke the wrath of God. All those who have drunk of her *wine,* those who through fornication participated in her corrupt life, will soon receive the plagues of her judgment. The *kings of the earth* and the *merchants of the earth* are the modern-day equivalent of the buyers and sellers that Jesus cast out of the temple. They have turned untold numbers of churches, synagogues, mosques, and temples into dens of thieves. These *kings* and *merchants* ignored the fact that Jesus said his Father's house was to be a house of prayer for all nations.

4 And I heard another voice from the heaven, saying, Come out of her my people, that ye not be partakers of her sins, and that ye receive not her plagues.

Her plagues are the seven vials of the wrath of God. To escape these plagues, we must cease and desist not only from all corrupt religious activity but, just as importantly, from all corrupt political and economic activity. When Jesus comes back, we want to be found faithful at whatever responsibility he has given us, be it small or great. We desire to use the gifts and talents that he has placed in our hands for the good of the kingdom of God. This can only happen if we are led 24/7 by the Spirit of God.

5 For her sins have reached unto the heaven, and God has remembered her iniquities.

6 Reward her even as she rewarded you and pay her double according to her works; in the cup which she has given thee to drink, give her double.

The vials of the wrath of God will definitely give all purveyors of false religions a double dose of their own medicine.

7 As much as she has glorified herself and lived deliciously, give her that much torment and sorrow; for she says in her heart, I sit a queen, and am no widow, and shall see no sorrow.

8 Therefore, shall her plagues come in one day, death and mourning and famine; and she shall be utterly burned with fire; for strong is the Lord God who judges her.

She has lived a life of sensual pleasure. Because harm has never touched her, she is confident that it never will. But her plagues shall come on the day of the Lord. It's the ten horns that shall burn her with fire (Revelation 17:16).

> 9 *And the kings of the earth, who have committed fornication and lived deliciously with her, shall bewail her and lament for her when they shall see the smoke of her burning,*
>
> 10 *Standing afar off for the fear of her torment, saying, Alas, alas, that great city Babylon, that mighty city; for in one hour is thy judgment come!*
>
> 11 *And the merchants of the earth shall weep and mourn over her, for no one buys their merchandise anymore:*

When Babylon goes up in smoke, the deception of the enemy is finished. This doesn't say that the merchants of the earth run out of merchandise. It says that no one buys their merchandise any longer. They're no longer able to use their rites, rituals, books, seminars, guilt trips, etc. to sell their merchandise to anyone. The entire scam has been exposed and judged with fire. Their weeping and mourning shows where their hearts have lain all along. They don't grieve because Babylon is fallen. They grieve because *no one buys their merchandise anymore.* They were only in it for the money.

> 12 *The merchandise of gold and of silver and of precious stones and of pearls and of fine linen and of purple and of silk and of scarlet and of all thyine wood and of all manner of vessels of ivory and of all manner of vessels of most precious wood and of brass and of iron and of marble*
>
> 13 *and cinnamon and odours and ointments and frankincense and wine and oil and fine flour, and wheat, and beasts, and of sheep, and of horses, and of chariots and of bodies and souls of men.*

The merchants advertise their false wares as if they possess legitimate value. Each item mentioned in the verses above prophetically represents a quality that cannot or should not be bought or sold.

- Gold - the nature of God
- Silver - redemption
- Precious stones - character
- Pearls - lessons learned at great price
- Fine linen - righteousness of the saints
- Purple - royalty
- Silk - comfort
- Scarlet - pride
- Thyine wood (a wood resistant to insects and rot) - long life
- Vessels of ivory - fantasy
- Vessels of most precious wood - dead works
- Iron - works of law
- Marble - eternal remembrance to posterity
- Cinnamon - uprightness
- Odors - prayers
- Ointments - healings
- Frankincense - intercession
- Wine - life
- Oil - anointing
- Fine flour - spiritual nourishment
- Wheat (seed) - seminars on evangelism
- Beasts - how to cater to the flesh
- Sheep - the Lord's sheep
- Horses - the power of the flesh
- Chariots - religious machinery bought and sold by salesmen similar to used car dealers

Ultimately they buy and sell the bodies and souls of men, of all humanity.

> 14 *And the fruits of the desire of thy soul are departed from thee, and all the fat and excellent things are departed from thee, and thou shalt find them no more at all.*

The con game is up. Their deception has been exposed, and it's impossible for them to remain in business. Their comfortable, luxurious life is gone.

> 15 *The merchants of these things, who were made rich by her, shall stand afar off for the fear of her torment, weeping and wailing,*
>
> 16 *and saying, Alas, alas, that great city, that was clothed in fine linen and purple and scarlet and decked with gold and precious stones and pearls!*

Everything having to do with Babylon – all the how-to seminars, the spiritual directors, the prosperity gospel worshippers of the sun-god of this world, the commentators, the media, the confessionals, the counseling centers, the prayer hot lines, the radio and TV shows, the publishers, the designers and manufacturers of religious images, icons, and fluff – all the buyers and sellers of the temple are out of work forever.

> 17 *For in one hour so great riches is come to nought. And every shipmaster and all the company in ships and sailors and as many as trade by sea stood afar off*
>
> 18 *and cried out when they saw the smoke of her burning, saying, What city was like unto this great city!*

The crews of all the religious "ships" cruising around on the sea of lost humanity, which lay guilt trips and prey on poor lost souls, realize that the game is up when they see the smoke of her burning.

> 19 *And they cast dust on their heads and cried, weeping and wailing, saying, Alas, alas, that great city, in which all that had ships in the sea were made rich by reason of her riches! for in one hour is she made desolate.*

All those who used their God-given gifts and ministries for personal or corporate gain and who contributed to building any kingdom other than the kingdom of God are now in a world of hurt.

> 20 *Rejoice over her, thou heaven, and ye saints, apostles, and prophets, for God has judged your cause upon her.*

This colossal judgment is a direct result of all the prayers of the saints that were collected in vials before the heavenly throne over the millennia (Revelation 5:8). It's appropriate to rejoice, because justice has been served.

> 21 *And a mighty angel took up a stone like a great millstone and cast it into the sea, saying, Thus with impetus shall that great city Babylon be thrown down and shall be found no more at all.*

It reminds you of what Jesus said regarding anyone that would harm even one of his little ones, doesn't it? *But whosoever shall cause one of these little ones who believe in me to fall, it would be better for him that a millstone such as is turned by an ass be hanged about his neck and that he be sunk in the depth of the sea* (Matthew 18:6).

> *And whosoever shall be a stumbling block to one of these little ones that believe in me, it would be better for him if a millstone were hanged about his neck, and he were cast into the sea* (Mark 9:42).

> *Then he said unto the disciples, It is impossible*

> *that offenses will not come, but woe unto the one through whom they come! It would be better for him if a millstone turned by an ass were placed around his neck and he were cast into the sea than that he should cause one of these little ones to stumble* (Luke 17:1-2).

The scene of judgment continues as we return to Revelation 18.

> 22 *And the voice of harpers and musicians and of pipers and trumpeters, shall be heard no more at all in thee; and no craftsman, of whatever craft he is, shall be found any more at all in thee; and the sound of a millstone shall be heard no more at all in thee;*

In Babylon there will be no more choirs, no more worship bands, no more how-to seminars, no more priests or pastors grinding out messages on their "millstone" to feed their hungry congregations. In fact, if before they were thrown out of the presence of God into the sea, a millstone were hung around the neck of every false minister, pastor, or priest that has caused harm to any of the little ones that believe in Jesus, there would soon be a great shortage of millstones.

> 23 *and the light of a lamp shall shine no more at all in thee; and the voice of the bridegroom and of the bride shall be heard no more at all in thee: for thy merchants were the princes of the earth in whose witchcraft all the Gentiles have erred.*

The lamps of all the foolish virgins shall fail. There will be no more weddings in Babylon.

The merchants of Babylon, who were the princes of the earth (of the religious realm on earth), instead of fomenting the gospel and salvation, they spread witchcraft and caused all the Gentiles to err! This might be why so many people out in the world hate religion and refuse to go to church meetings.

> 24 *And in her was found the blood of the prophets and of saints and of all that were slain upon the earth.*

Note that this does not say that the blood of the prophets and of the saints and of all that were slain upon the *sea* (of lost humanity) was found in her. This is not about the blood of those who were slain by the pagans or the communists. This is about those that were slain in the *earth*, in the Holy Place, which is symbolic of synagogues, churches, mosques, etc., ordained by man according to the dictates of false prophets. Untold millions have been tortured, imprisoned, burned at the stake, or beheaded. Even more have had their reputations smeared and their character assassinated. Babylon wants everyone to think that these horrible things only happened a long time ago in the dark ages. The truth is that not only do such things continue to this day, but their frequency is actually increasing.

Let us pray

> *Heavenly Father,*
>
> *We ask that we may be able to understand the vision from your perspective so that when this world begins to come down, when the things of men come down, we will not be among those who are filled with fear and terror. May we be among those who lift up their heads, knowing that their redemption is near.*
>
> *May we be sensitive to your Spirit so that we may be led continually by your Spirit and be kept far away from any deception. Amen.*

Chapter 20

The Marriage of the Lamb

Revelation 19

1 *And after these things I heard a great voice of a great company in the heaven, saying, Halelu-JAH; Salvation and glory and honour and power unto the Lord our God;*

2 *for true and righteous are his judgments; for he has judged the great whore, who corrupted the earth with her fornication, and has avenged the blood of his slaves at her hand.*

Slaves have an owner. God's slaves belong to him.

3 *And again they said, Halelu-JAH. And her smoke rose up for ever and ever.*

4 *And the twenty-four elders and the four animals fell upon their faces and worshipped God that was seated upon the throne, saying, Amen! Halelu-JAH!*

5 *And a voice came out of the throne, saying, Praise our God, all ye his slaves and ye that fear him, both small and great.*

Servants get paid and can resign. Slaves are purchased and have an owner. God not only bought us but paid a very great price for us.

> 6 *And I heard as it were the voice of a great company and as the voice of many waters and as the voice of many thunderings, saying, Halelu-JAH; for the Lord God almighty reigns.*

JAH is the shortened version of the sacred name of God (written as a Tetragrammaton in Hebrew as JHWH or YHWH), which is considered by the Jews to be too sacred to pronounce. Now the Halelu-JAH chorus thunders forth from God's heavenly people, who are clean and qualified to pronounce his holy name.

> 7 *Let us be glad and rejoice and give glory to him; for the marriage of the Lamb is come, and his bride has made herself ready.*

Throughout history, there have been many examples of clean individuals that God has used. But this is the first time God has had a clean, corporate expression of his people. There is no leaven in this lump. Truly, the bride has made herself ready.

> 8 *And to her was granted that she should be arrayed in fine linen, clean and bright: for the fine linen is the righteousness of the saints.*

The steps of a good man are ordered by the LORD (Psalm 37:23). Righteousness is a state of being. We cannot be righteous unless God works in and through us. This is the only way to be clothed with fine linen.

> 9 *And he said unto me, Write, Blessed are those who are called unto the marriage supper of the Lamb. And he said unto me, These are the true words of God.*

This is a call, or invitation, to feed upon the true words of God instead of the corrupt fare served by the religious institutions of man. It's an invitation that he freely extends to all who truly seek him, and one we should accept with the utmost gratitude.

> 10 *And I fell at his feet to worship him. And he said unto me, See thou do it not: I am thy fellowservant and with thy brethren that have the testimony of Jesus; worship God; for the testimony of Jesus is the spirit of prophecy.*

There are many who prophesy, yet don't have the testimony of Jesus. They aren't true prophets. Although sometimes, like Balaam, their prophecies can come true even when their hearts are false. Balaam sought personal gain with his God-given gift. He went down in history as a false prophet, even though he claimed to be very careful to only prophesy what God said. There are many modern-day Balaams. In the end, they will share his fate.

> 11 *And I saw the heaven open, and behold a white horse; and he that was seated upon him was called Faithful and True, and in righteousness he judges and makes war.*

When *the heaven open*[s], the Day of Reconciliation is fulfilled. The white horse indicates that God is able to use men and women who are clean, whose hearts have been circumcised. It symbolizes those who are clean and will let God use them to get what he wants, rather than those who try to use God to get what they want. The people of the white horse are the believers who are willing to carry the presence of God right into the thick of the battle.

There is no collateral damage in this war. *If anyone desires to hurt them, fire comes out of their mouth and devours their enemies; and if anyone desires to hurt them he must in this same manner be killed* (Revelation 11:5). What the enemies of God's witnesses (martyrs) attempt to do to God's people is what happens to them! This is a war fought in righteousness, and these are righteous judgments.

> 12 *And his eyes were as a flame of fire, and on his head were many crowns; and he had a name written, that no one has known, but he himself.*

One glance from those eyes may pierce to the very core those who are false. The beast has many heads and has degenerated into placing crowns upon his horns instead of his heads. Jesus' head is his Father, and he gives the Father all the crowns of salvation, glory, honor, and power.

What is this name that no one knows but he himself? *To him that overcomes I will give to eat of the hidden manna and will give him a small white stone and in the stone a new name written, which no one knows except the one that receives it* (Revelation 2:17). The hidden manna is the incorruptible Word of God, which is hidden in the life of Christ (symbolized by the ark of the covenant in the Holy of Holies). The white stone means a complete change of nature (name). The Word of God has all power and all authority

> 13 *And he was clothed with a garment dipped in blood; and his name is called The Word of God.*

The Lord Jesus is our redeemer. He is also the avenger of blood. In Hebrew, *redeemer* and *avenger of blood* are the same word. He took our sin upon himself and redeemed us so we might become the righteousness of God. Without the shedding of blood there is no remission. *When some of the blood thereof* [i.e., of the burnt offering] *is sprinkled upon any garment, thou shalt wash whatever it was sprinkled on in the holy place* (Leviticus 6:27). The Holy Place (the realm of Israel and the church) is precisely where the blood of the saints must be avenged. This is where his *garment dipped in blood* must be washed until Israel and the church are clean. Every trace of the blood – of the life of Adam – must be removed by the washing of water, by the Word of God (Ephesians 5:26-27; Titus 3:4-6).

> 14 *And the armies that are in the heaven followed him upon white horses, clothed in fine linen, white and clean.*

White horses mean that everyone in the armies of heaven has a clean, circumcised heart. Fine linen refers to the righteous acts of the saints as God works in and through them.

> 15 *And out of his mouth goes a sharp sword, that with it he should smite the Gentiles; and he shall rule them with a rod of iron; and he treads the winepress of the fierceness and wrath of Almighty God.*

Many of those who claim to be of the people of God are really Gentiles, because their hearts are not circumcised. *And he that overcomes and keeps my works unto the end, to him will I give power over the Gentiles; and he shall rule them with a rod of iron; as the vessels of a potter they shall be broken to shivers* (Revelation 2:26-27). The *Word of God* on the white horse will tread the winepress of the fierceness and wrath of Almighty God, so as to bring the consequences of the evil, ripe clusters of grapes of the life of Adam (the carnal, natural man) upon all the Gentiles (upon all the unconverted) located in the Holy Place. There are only two kinds of grapes that matter: those that symbolize the life of Adam and those that symbolize the life of Christ.

> 16 *And he has on his garment and on his thigh a name written, KING OF KINGS, AND LORD OF LORDS.*

All of those who have come to maturity in the life of Christ will participate with Jesus as joint heirs in Christ. His garment is his covering, and the Holy Spirit covers all those who walk in his righteousness. His thigh has to do with his ability to walk in righteousness. He is able to cover us and cause us to walk in righteousness with him because he is KING OF KINGS AND LORD OF LORDS. He has all authority everywhere. The name written on his garment and on his thigh means that all of his promises will be fulfilled.

> 17 *And I saw an angel standing in the sun; and he cried with a loud voice, saying to all the fowls that flew in the midst of heaven, Come and gather yourselves together unto the supper of the great God,*
>
> 18 *that ye may eat the flesh of kings and flesh of captains, and flesh of mighty men and flesh of horses and of those that sit on them and the flesh of everyone, free and bond, both small and great.*

The sun represents the system and kingdoms of this world. Everyone who continues to operate in the flesh – *everyone, free and bond, both small and great* – will be judged and given over as food for the fowls that feed on carrion.

This battle is between those led by the Spirit and those who operate in the flesh. Flesh and blood cannot inherit the kingdom of God (1 Corinthians 15:50). We have been warned in advance that if we live according to the flesh we shall die, but if through the Spirit we put to death the deeds of the flesh we shall live (Romans 8:13).

> 19 *And I saw the beast and the kings of the earth and their armies gathered together to make war against him that was seated upon the horse and against his army.*

The beast and the kings of the earth are moved with fury and rage. They desire to kill and overcome all of the people of God.

But Jesus, in the form of The Word of God, will judge them all, and their evil desires will come down upon their own heads.

> 20 *And the beast was taken and with it the false prophet that wrought miracles in its presence, with which he had deceived those that had taken the mark of the beast and had worshipped its image. These two were cast alive into the lake of fire burning with brimstone.*

The lake of fire burning with brimstone is the second death, from which there is no escape. This is eternal perdition, otherwise known as hell. The beast (representing the attempted deification of the natural man) and the false prophet (representing those who prophesy by unclean spirits instead of by the testimony of Jesus) are cast alive into the lake of fire. This is the end of their deception for all eternity.

> 21 *And the others were slain with the sword that proceeded out of the mouth of him that was seated upon the horse; and all the fowls were filled with their flesh.*

These others reaped what they sowed.

Revelation 20

> 1 *And I saw an angel come down from heaven, having the key of the bottomless pit and a great chain in his hand.*

Jesus has the keys of Hades and death (Revelation 1:18). In Hades we find the bottomless pit.

> 2 *And he laid hold on the dragon, the serpent of old, which is the Devil and Satan and bound him a thousand years.*

Satan is bound with the great chain of death for a thousand

years. However, *one day before the Lord is as a thousand years, and a thousand years are as one day* (2 Peter 3:8). Even though we have literally had six thousand years (six prophetic days) since Adam and Eve were cast out of the garden of Eden, we must be careful in the interpretation of this Scripture. Almost all the numbers in the book of Revelation are symbolic in one sense while they may be literal in another.

If a thousand years are as a day, this could be saying that Satan will be bound for one day, the day of the Lord. During the conquest of Canaan, Joshua prayed and asked that the sun stand still so the day would last until all of the enemies of the people of God could be defeated. God granted his prayer. On the day of the battle, Joshua's forces trapped some enemy kings in a cave. Because they were fully occupied with pursuing the fleeing enemy, they left the kings prisoner in the guarded cave until they had time to deal with them (Joshua 10:12-27). God may pursue a similar course of action when he binds Satan. This *thousand years* during which Satan is bound (a time span which is also linked to the day of the Lord) could simply be however long God decides for it to be.

> 3 *and cast him into the bottomless pit and shut him up and set a seal upon it, that he should deceive the Gentiles no more, until the thousand years should be fulfilled; and after it is necessary that he be loosed a little while.*

Why would God cause the Devil to be bound for a thousand years, or for one very special "day," and then turn around and loose him for a little while? Why is this necessary? What could he be thinking?

Up until now, God's witnesses or martyrs have been proven faithful under adversity when the Devil has attacked them with all manner of trials and tribulations. Most of the witnesses, however, have not been proven under prosperity, which will be the scenario when the devil is locked in the bottomless pit and his power to attack them is curtailed. Even King Solomon, with all his wisdom, miserably failed the test of prosperity. Throughout history, after a generation or two of prosperity, Israel and the church have had a penchant to slip rapidly into apostasy. It's much easier to be faithful and true to the LORD under adversity (when he is all we have) than under prosperity (when there are so many pleasant things to distract us from him). Those who will rule and reign with Christ for all eternity must be proven faithful in prosperity.

> 4 *And I saw thrones, and those who sat upon them, and judgment was given unto them; and I saw the souls of those that were beheaded for the witness of Jesus and for the word of God and who had not worshipped the beast neither its image neither had received its mark upon their foreheads or in their hands; and they shall live and reign with Christ the thousand years.*

Those who have been *beheaded for the witness of Jesus* are those who have come under the headship of Christ. Of course, some have been literally beheaded, as is happening with increasing frequency. But martyrdom comes in many forms, and one of its purposes is to define and refine our relationship with our Lord. The apostle Paul said that even if he were to give his body to be burned, if he didn't have the love of God then this type of martyrdom would profit him nothing (1 Corinthians 13:3). Those who have come under Christ's headship, however, will reign with him for a time.

> 5 *But the rest of the dead did not live again until the thousand years were finished. This is the first resurrection.*

6 Blessed and holy is he that has part in the first resurrection; on such the second death has no authority, but they shall be priests of God and of the Christ and shall reign with him a thousand years.

Those who qualify for the first resurrection will face the greatest test of their lives: a thousand years of prosperity, or however long God decides this period should last. Even King David succumbed to serious temptation that proved almost fatal when he decided to relax in his palace and enjoy his victories while sending others to the battle (2 Samuel 11:1-5). We see a preview of this when we observe some who are seemingly successful in ministry spend huge sums on their own comfort after only three, four, or five years of prosperity. It's enough to send cold shivers up and down our spine if we contemplate how such people would cope with a thousand years of virtually unlimited blessing while Satan and his demons are bound. We may joke that we would enjoy the opportunity to live in such luxury. But we should never forget that even with all his God-given wisdom and heritage, unchecked prosperity took King Solomon into total apostasy within approximately twenty years.

Notice that the period of time that those who take part in the first resurrection, who shall be priests of God and of the Christ, shall reign with Christ is limited to *a thousand years.* After this, Satan shall be loosed from his prison, followed by general judgment. If everything were in the bag for those of the first resurrection, the Scripture would have to say that they would reign for ever and ever. However, this pronouncement isn't made until after the final judgment.

7 And when the thousand years are expired, Satan shall be loosed out of his prison

8 and shall go out to deceive the Gentiles which are upon the four corners of the earth, Gog and Magog, to gather them together for battle; the number of whom is as the sand of the sea.

Gog and Magog is a link to Ezekiel 38. *Gog* means a high or lofty mountain and appears to be another name for Satan. *Magog* means the multitude of Gog. Magog is linked to the sand of the sea, which has to do with religious people who are of the earth and not holy. For example, both Abraham and Jacob were promised Gentile descendants as numerous as the sand of the sea. All those who have been distracted, blinded, and swept away from being totally faithful to God by the prosperity of the things of this earth will be separated from those who are faithful to their heavenly calling. This is why Satan shall be loosed from his prison and shall go out to deceive the Gentiles for a little while before being cast into perdition. His deceptions will, in a sense, be used by God to separate the wheat from the tares and the chaff.

9 *And they went up of the breadth of the earth and compassed the camp of the saints and the beloved city; and fire came down from God out of heaven and devoured them.*

10 *And the devil that deceived them was cast into the lake of fire and brimstone, where the beast and the false prophet are, and they shall be tormented day and night for ever and ever.*

This final judgment keeps with the righteousness of God. What the Devil and his multitude attempt to do to the saints and to the beloved city is exactly what happens to them instead.

11 *And I saw a great white throne and him that was seated upon it, from whose face the earth and the heaven fled away; and their place was not found.*

12 *And I saw the dead, great and small, stand before*

> *God; and the books were opened: and another book was opened; which is the book of life; and the dead were judged by those things which were written in the books, according to their works.*

We know that our own works cannot save us or anyone else. Therefore, at the final judgment, it is essential that evidence of Jesus' work be found in and through us. If Jesus, by the Holy Spirit, has accomplished a work in our hearts, if our hearts have been transformed by the power and life of God (by his grace), then the fruit (works) of the Holy Spirit will be readily manifest. Jesus said that ye shall know them by their fruits (Matthew 7:16-20).

> 13 *And the sea gave up the dead which were in it; and death and Hades delivered up the dead which were in them; and the judgment of each one was according to their works.*

After the third vial, it's impossible for anyone to keep their soul spiritually alive in the sea of lost humanity. Therefore, all that are in this realm are given over to final judgment. *Death and Hades* refers to the first death, which kills the body (or flesh) but not the soul. It's hell, the second death, that can destroy both body and soul (Matthew 10:28). All the souls imprisoned in Hades are resurrected and must stand before God in final judgment.

> 14 *And Hades and death were cast into the lake of fire. This is the second death.*

> 15 *And whosoever was not found written in the book of life was cast into the lake of fire.*

Let us pray

Heavenly Father,

We ask that you keep your hand upon us. Lord, if you call us, if you choose us, if we are among those who are faithful unto you, if we will be included in the first resurrection and reign with you for a thousand years, may your hand of correction never be removed from upon us so that we might remain faithful unto the end. Amen.

Chapter 21

A New Heaven and a New Earth

Revelation 21

> 1 *And I saw a new heaven and a new earth; for the first heaven and the first earth were passed away; and there was no more sea.*

Jesus said that heaven and earth will pass away but that his words will never pass away. Isaiah and Peter prophesied new heavens and a new earth in which dwell righteousness (Isaiah 65:17; 2 Peter 3:13). In the new creation, there is no sea of lost humanity. There is no one who is not living in covenant with God. There are no pagan devil worshippers, no atheists, and no more religious deception by Satan's agents passing themselves off as angels of light.

> 2 *And I, John, saw the holy city, the new Jerusalem, coming down out of the heaven, prepared of God as a bride adorned for her husband.*

Note that the New Jerusalem is coming out of the new heaven. Old things are passed away in the new heaven and the new earth. All of this happened before the presence of the one seated upon the throne. Now that the Devil and all his followers have been cast into the lake of fire, only the new creation is perceived.

> 3 *And I heard a great voice out of heaven saying, Behold the tabernacle of God with men, and he will dwell with them, and they shall be his people, and God himself shall be with them and be their God.*

This is the fullness of the Feast of Tabernacles.

> 4 *And God shall wipe away all tears from their eyes; and death shall be no more neither shall there be any more sorrow nor crying nor pain; for the former things are passed away.*

The enemies of our joy have been destroyed, and the last enemy to be destroyed is death itself (1 Corinthians 15:26; Revelation 20:14).

> 5 *And he that was seated upon the throne said, Behold, I make all things new. And he said unto me, Write: for these words are faithful and true.*

Who is seated upon the throne?

> 6 *And he said unto me, It is done. I AM the Alpha and the Omega, the beginning and the end. I will give unto him that is thirsty of the fountain of the water of life freely.*
>
> 7 *He that overcomes shall inherit all things; and I will be his God, and he shall be my son.*

Jesus spoke several times of the *water of life* or *living water* (John 4:10-11,14; 7:38). It's also referenced elsewhere in Revelation (7:17; 22:1; and 22:17). In addition, we know that Jesus Christ is the overcomer, and it's the plan of God the Father for many of us to share in his victory as part of the overcoming body of Christ.

> 8 *But the fearful and unbelieving and the*

abominable and murderers and fornicators and sorcerers and idolaters and all liars shall have their part in the lake which burns with fire and brimstone, which is the second death.

My father was teaching on this passage to his tenth grade Sunday School class one day when a girl raised her hand and nervously asked, "Mr. Stendal, this just refers to non-Christian liars, right?"

Satan is the father of lies. In Scripture, this is false witness or false testimony (Exodus 20:16). It's understandable that God will lower the boom on all those who give false witness against their neighbor, but why are the fearful on this list? Because the love of God casts out fear, so the presence of fear is an indicator of the absence of faith (1 John 4:18). All those who have the presence of God inside will be able to overcome their fears.

As to the rest of the list, Scripture links unbelief with disobedience. The abominable are those who do things that are incompatible with the presence of God. Murder is almost inextricably linked with uncontrolled anger and hate (Matthew 5:21-22). Fornicators are unclean, and nothing that is unclean will be in the new creation. Sorcerers are involved in witchcraft, which is rebellion against God. And those who break the Word of the Lord commit iniquity and idolatry (1 Samuel 15:23). Idolaters also run contrary to the direct command of God that we are to have no other gods before him (Exodus 20:3-4). As discussed earlier, there are many things in this world that can become idols.

9 *And there came unto me one of the seven angels who had the seven vials full of the seven last plagues and talked with me, saying, Come here, I will show thee the bride, the Lamb's wife.*

10 *And he carried me away in the spirit to a great*

and high mountain and showed me that great city, the holy Jerusalem, descending out of the heaven from and with God,

11 *having the clarity of God; and her light was like unto a most precious stone, even like a jasper stone, shining like crystal.*

The two realms that have been separated since the rebellion of Adam and Satan will be fully joined once again forever. There will literally be heaven on earth. The prayers of the saints that have been stored for millennia in the seven vials of God will be fulfilled, and the will of God will be done on earth even as it is done in heaven (Matthew 6:10).

12 *And it had a wall great and high, with twelve gates, and at the gates twelve angels, and names written thereon, which are the names of the twelve tribes of the sons of Israel:*

The names of the twelve tribes have been mentioned and explained in the context of those sealed in Revelation 7 (in Part 1 of this book). The tribes include all of the people of God from the old and new covenant, for a true Jew is whoever has a circumcised heart (Ephesians 2:11-13).

Twelve is a symbol of divine order, and it's the people of God who are the gates into the city. Jesus said that anyone who receives anyone he has sent, even one of his little ones, receives him (Matthew 18:4-5). Anyone who receives him receives his Father (Mark 9:37). This is the entrance into the city.

13 *On the east three gates; on the north three gates; on the south three gates; and on the west three gates.*

In the book of Numbers, the people of God are divided into four armies, with three tribes in each host. The people were ordered to camp around the tabernacle of the testimony of the presence of God with the host of Judah (with Issachar and Zebulun) to the east, the host of Dan (with Asher and Naphtali) to the north, the host of Reuben (with Simeon and Gad) to the south, and the host of Ephraim (with Manasseh and Benjamin) to the west (Numbers 2). In other words, anyone who approached the tabernacle of God in the wilderness would have to pass through the army of at least one of the twelve tribes. Similarly, anyone entering the city of God will pass through the people of God who form the gates to the city.

In the Law of Moses, the Levites were not numbered among the sons of Israel (Numbers 2:33). In Revelation chapter 7, however, there are twelve thousand sealed from among the tribe of Levi (unity) and none from the tribe of Dan (judgment). There are none from the tribe of Ephraim (double ash heap), but there are twelve thousand sealed from the tribe of Joseph (let God add). The one hundred and forty-four thousand who are sealed out of all twelve tribes are symbolic of all of the redeemed.

> 14 *And the wall of the city had twelve foundations, and in them the names of the twelve apostles of the Lamb.*

The wall of the city divides the clean from the unclean and the light from the darkness. The foundation, or basis upon which the wall is built, is the names of the twelve apostles. Apostles are those who are sent by Jesus Christ with full authority as his ambassadors. Those who overcome and are sent forth to represent Jesus Christ are each given a new name which describes their new nature (Revelation 2:17).

> 15 *And he that talked with me had a golden reed to measure the city and its gates and its wall.*

Now the *city*, the *gates* and the *wall* all measure up to the fullness of the righteousness of Jesus Christ. There will be no contaminated, unclean tribes or false apostles that misrepresent God or seek personal gain in the name of the Lord.

> 16 *And the city lies foursquare, and the length is as large as the breadth; and he measured the city with the reed, twelve thousand furlongs; and the length and the breadth and the height of it are equal.*

Twelve thousand furlongs means that everyone who makes up this city walks in the fullness of the perfection of divine order. The fact that it's foursquare and that the twelve thousand furlongs extend vertically as well as horizontally means that the dwellers of this city walk perfectly, according to divine order in the heavenly realm and upon the earth.

> 17 *And he measured its wall, a hundred and forty-four cubits, according to the measure of a man, that is, of the angel.*

The wall of one hundred and forty-four cubits (twelve times twelve) demonstrates the fullness of the effects and consequences of divine order, which is redemption.

> 18 *And the material of its wall was jasper; but the city was of pure gold, like unto clean glass.*

> 19 *And the foundations of the wall of the city were garnished with all manner of precious stones. The first foundation was jasper ...*

Jasper is only mentioned six or seven times in Scripture, which depends on your Bible translation. The light of the city is *like unto a most precious stone, even like a jasper stone, shining like crystal.* This crystal is able to split light into the seven colors of the rainbow, surrounding the city with the glory of God. The glory of God protects the city. Jasper was the fourth stone on the fourth, or last, row of the pectoral of judgment (breastplate) of the high priest (Exodus 28:20). The last tribe sealed in Revelation 7 is the tribe of Benjamin (meaning son of my right hand). This is symbolic of those who will sit at the right hand of the Father and reign and rule with Jesus Christ. The *pure gold like unto clean glass* represents the transparent righteousness of Christ.

> 19 *And the foundations of the wall of the city were garnished with all manner of precious stones. The first foundation was jasper; the second, sapphire, the third, a chalcedony; the fourth, emerald;*
>
> 20 *the fifth, sardonyx, the sixth, sardius; the seventh, chrysolite; the eighth, beryl; the ninth, topaz; the tenth chrysoprasus; the eleventh, jacinth; the twelfth, amethyst.*

In the Old Testament, there were twelve precious stones on the pectoral of the breastplate above the heart of the high priest. Jasper was the last stone on the last row. Now it's the first foundation. Truly the last has now become the first!

All the precious stones represent the fruit of the Holy Spirit, which is godly character, in the lives of the saints (1 Corinthians 3:11-14).

> 21 *And the twelve gates are twelve pearls; in each one, one; each gate was of one pearl; and the street of the city was pure gold, as shining glass.*

The pearl is mentioned in eight verses in the New Testament. Eight is the number of new beginnings. Pearls are formed in the sea by oysters that secrete layer upon layer of mother of pearl upon imperfections, or impurities, that penetrate their shell. The *tribes* of the people of God are formed, in like manner, as we live here in the world among the sea of imperfect humanity. This is one of the many ways God works all things together for good for those who love him and are called according to his purpose (Romans 8:28).

> 22 *And I saw no temple in her; for the Lord God Almighty is her temple, and the Lamb.*

The entire holy city of God is now the spiritual equivalent of the Holy of Holies.

> 23 *And the city had no need of the sun neither of the moon to shine in her, for the clarity of God has illuminated it, and the Lamb is its lamp.*

The Sun of Righteousness and the clarity of God is the light of the city. The light of the sun of this world and the waxing and waning of the light of this world's moon are no longer necessary.

> 24 *And the Gentiles that have been saved shall walk in the light of her; and the kings of the earth shall bring their glory and honour into her.*

Saved Gentiles may refer to individuals, families, tribes, or nations. There are now only two realms, the realm of the heavens and the realm of the earth, and the two converge in the holy city. Interestingly, kings of the earth still exist. They come to worship and bring their glory and honor into the city of God.

> 25 *And her gates shall never be shut by day; for there shall be no night there.*

No night or darkness will ever be there.

Even though the gates will never be shut, there are still gates. This means that there are those who come and go from the city. It also means that there is strict control over who and what is allowed to enter in. It's clear that there are those who will reign with Jesus Christ for all eternity and those who will be reigned over. There will be many positions and levels of responsibility inside and outside the holy city (1 Corinthians 15:40-42).

26 *And they shall bring the glory and the honour of the Gentiles into it.*

Who are *they*? Evidently, they are among those who are permitted to enter the city.

27 *And there shall in no wise enter into it anything unclean or that works abomination or makes a lie, but only those who are written in the Lamb's book of life.*

Is *your* name in that book?

Revelation 22

1 *And he showed me a pure river of water of life, clear as crystal, proceeding out of the throne of God and of the Lamb.*

The river of God is restored to fullness. In the beginning of the old creation, the river started from a single source then split into four branches that watered the entire garden of Eden (Genesis 2:10). Ezekiel prophesied that this river would flow again from the presence of God during what appears to be the millennial reign of Jesus Christ (Ezekiel 47:1-2). Now, entering eternity, there are very important changes.[9]

2 *In the midst of her plaza and on either side of the river was the tree of life, which brings forth twelve manner of fruits, yielding her fruit every month; and the leaves of the tree are for the healing of the Gentiles.*

The millennial river seen by Ezekiel flowed from the house of God. It watered the desert and healed the sea. Every fruitful tree grew upon its banks (Ezekiel 47:12). There is no mention of a desert and no longer any sea, yet provision is made for *the*

9 See *The River of God*, Russell Stendal, Aneko Press.

healing of the Gentiles. The garden of Eden had one tree of life. Now there are multiple trees of life!

> 3 *And there shall be no longer be any cursed thing; but the throne of God and of the Lamb shall be in her; and his slaves shall serve him;*

The curse shall be entirely broken. God's slaves belong to him. Jesus bought and redeemed us at a great price.

> 4 *and they shall see his face; and his name shall be in their foreheads.*

Those who belong to God shall see his face. His name (nature) shall be in their foreheads. They shall have the mind of Christ.

> 5 *And there shall be no night there; and they need no lamp neither light of the sun; for the Lord God shall give them light; and they shall reign for ever and ever.*

There shall be no night and no need for light from a lamp or light from the sun wherever the river of God flows. God will provide all the light needed. Jesus said that rivers of the water of life would flow from the innermost part of our being. The river of God will flow in fullness wherever his true people are. They shall reign for ever and ever, instead of for a thousand years. This is eternity.

> 6 *And he said unto me, These words are faithful and true; and the Lord God of the holy prophets has sent his angel to show unto his slaves the things which are necessary that they be done quickly.*

This book of Revelation is for those who belong to God. There are things that need to be done – and *done quickly* – by all who understand this message.

> 7 *Behold, I come quickly; blessed is he that keeps the words of the prophecy of this book.*

Here the word *quickly* is used in the archaic sense of *suddenly*. This means that even though there might be a delay of many years between when this was written and when Jesus comes back, his return will be sudden when it finally happens.

> 8 *And I, John, saw these things and heard them. And when I had heard and seen, I fell down to worship before the feet of the angel who showed me these things.*
>
> 9 *Then he said unto me, See thou do it not: for I am thy fellowslave and with thy brethren the prophets and with those who keep the words of this book: worship God.*
>
> 10 *And he said unto me, do not seal the words of this prophecy of this book; for the time is at hand.*

This book has been unfolding on many different levels ever since it was written about 90 AD. It contains broad spiritual applications to every individual, important messages to the churches or congregations, historical application throughout the centuries, and, of course, an end-time grand finale.

> 11 *He that is unjust, let him be unjust still; and he who is filthy, let him be filthy still; and he that is righteous, let him be justified still; and let the saint be sanctified still.*

There are only two basic possibilities for all humanity: clean or unclean, righteous or unjust, wheat or tares. Each individual is progressing in one direction or the other.

> 12 *And, behold, I come quickly, and my reward is with me, to give each one according as his work shall be.*

When Jesus suddenly returns, he will bring his reward with him. Those who are found faithful will be rewarded. Those who have been misrepresenting him and those who have harmed any of his family will be dealt with (Isaiah 61:1-3).

> 13 *I AM the Alpha and the Omega, beginning and the end, the first and the last.*
>
> 14 *Blessed are those who do his commandments that their power and authority might be in the tree of life and they may enter in through the gates into the city.*

Those who do his commandments will be treated much differently from those who do not. It isn't possible to do his commandments unless we have his life.

> 15 *But outside are the dogs and the sorcerers and the fornicators and the murderers and the idolaters and whosoever loves and makes a lie.*

Here are broad categories of those who will never, ever be allowed to enter in through the gates into the city. It's only in the new man in Christ that any of us will be able to enter there. Dogs refer to those who are unclean and not converted (Gentiles) and not necessarily to our four-legged furry friends. After reading verse 21:8, which says in no uncertain terms that *the fearful and unbelieving and the abominable and murderers and fornicators and sorcerers and idolaters and all liars shall be cast into the lake of fire*, many may wonder why there is any question or possibility of such people attempting to enter the holy city after the final judgment. In the next section I have some final thoughts on all of this.

> 16 *I, Jesus, have sent my angel to testify unto you these things in the congregations. I AM the root and the offspring of David and the bright and morning star.*

This is a message or testimony addressed to those among the congregations of the people of God.[10]

> 17 *And the Spirit and the bride say, Come. And let him that hears say, Come. And let him that is thirsty come; and whosoever will, let him take of the water of life freely.*

Here are two clear witnesses: the Spirit and the bride. They both bear the same witness. The water of life is freely available and flows by the Spirit through each member of the bride to anyone who is thirsty and wishes to drink of it.

> 18 *For I testify unto everyone that hears the words of the prophecy of this book, If anyone shall add unto these things, God shall add unto him the plagues that are written in this book;*
>
> 19 *and if anyone shall take away from the words of the book of this prophecy, God shall take away his part out of the book of life and out of the holy city and from the things which are written in this book.*

The words of *the book of this prophecy* could actually apply to the entire Bible and most certainly include this book of Revelation. The end-time teachings, doctrines, and beliefs of many people – including some who are in positions of authority – include events and terminology that are not mentioned or included in Scripture. Others omit the warnings. Entire Bible translations have been watered down or doctored up according to the bias or doctrinal orientation of the translator(s). Let the reader beware.

> 20 *He who testifies these things saith, Surely I come quickly. Amen. Even so, come, Lord Jesus.*
>
> 21 *The grace of our Lord Jesus Christ be with you all. Amen.*

---

10 See *The Morning Star*, Russell Stendal, Aneko Press.

Let us pray

Heavenly Father, May your message and truth be clear to those who seek clarity. May the revelation of the life of the resurrected Jesus Christ, which is the true Apocalypse, shine into the depths of our souls and destroy any residue of the old fallen nature of Adam. Amen.

Final Thoughts

Upon reviewing this manuscript, several of my friends asked me some compelling questions. One in particular has to do with whether anyone will be given a "second chance." Here are my final thoughts:

The Limits of Our Knowledge.

We are not to *learn above that which is written* (1 Corinthians 4:6). Therefore, we must be careful not to extrapolate or infer beyond what the Holy Spirit reveals to us from what is clearly written in Scripture. The apostle Paul wanted to make sure that his teaching was centered on that which is written. He even said that he heard things in the third heaven that it is not lawful for a man to utter (2 Corinthians 12:4). I think that it's acceptable for us to speculate in private about genuine questions that come up, but we must keep our ministry within the bounds of what is clearly spelled out in Scripture.

The Criteria for the First Resurrection.

The bar is set rather high for the first resurrection.

> *And I saw thrones, and those who sat upon them, and judgment was given unto them; and I saw the*

> *souls of those that were beheaded for the witness of Jesus and for the word of God and who had not worshipped the beast neither its image neither had received his mark upon their foreheads or in their hands; and they shall live and reign with Christ the thousand years. But the rest of the dead did not live again until the thousand years were finished. This is the first resurrection* (Revelation 20:4-5).

I feel confident that this refers not only to those who have literally had their heads chopped off like John the Baptist but also to all those who truly have Jesus Christ as their head. This agrees perfectly with the description of those whose souls are found under the heavenly altar (Revelation 6:9). Those under the blood of Jesus Christ who gave up their own lives so that they may live the life of Christ (Romans 5:10).

Note that this clearly states that *the rest of the dead did not live again until the thousand years were finished* and that it's clearly labeled *the* ***first*** *resurrection.*

The *rest of the dead* means all those who have died but do not meet the criteria for the first resurrection.

I don't see anything in Scripture that indicates that so-called carnal Christians or those who are lost will be included in the first resurrection or be resurrected before *the thousand years* are finished. The judgment described in Revelation 11:18 seems to agree with this. It says, *And the Gentiles were angry, and thy wrath is come, and the time of the dead, that they should be judged, and that thou should give the reward unto thy slaves the prophets and to the saints and those that fear thy name.*

Some think this judgment happens prior to the *thousand years* and some think it coincides with Revelation 20:12.

I think it occurs prior to the *thousand years* and that the dead who are judged are those who take part in the first resurrection.

They are judged, for we shall give account of every idle word, and then rewarded. There is no mention of anyone being cast into the second death or lake of fire.

The *time of the dead, that they should be judged* could also refer to those who are biologically alive yet dead in trespasses and sin, who misrepresent God while they claim to be part of the people of God. Jesus will immediately deal with this at his return.

A Second Chance?

a) I do see, however, a possibility that might provide a "second chance." Nevertheless, since none of this is clearly spelled out in Scripture and it would require us to infer or extrapolate. Therefore, I cannot, in good conscience, preach or teach that anyone will be *guaranteed* a second opportunity. There are simply too many Scriptures that point out that we will all be held accountable for what we do in the time allotted to us to live upon the earth (Hebrews 9:27).

b) The possibility that I see does not come during the *thousand years* reign but immediately afterward. In fact, since Scripture also states that for the Lord a thousand years are as a day and a day as a thousand years, I am not even completely sure that Revelation 20 is speaking of a literal thousand years. It could be referring to a special day, such as when Joshua prayed for the sun to stand still. The day of the Lord could last however long the Lord decides. Still, based on the six thousand years of past history, a strong case can be made for a literal thousand years.

> It is *when the thousand years are expired and Satan shall be loosed out of his prison and shall go out to deceive the Gentiles which are upon the four corners of the earth, Gog and Magog, to gather them*

> *together to battle; the number of whom is as the sand of the sea. And they went up on the breadth of the earth and compassed the camp of the saints and the beloved city; and fire came down from God out of heaven and devoured them. And the Devil that deceived them was cast into the lake of fire* (Revelation 20:7-10).

I believe Gog is another term for Satan and Magog is the people of Gog.

If this is the exact same time when Hades gives up her dead and ***if*** those who were locked up in Hades still have the ability to choose, then it seems to me that there could be the possibility that some of the dead who are bodily resurrected in the general resurrection prior to final judgment could make the choice at that time not to join Satan in his battle against the camp of the saints and the beloved city (Revelation 20:13). This would put them on a different footing at the time of final judgment that immediately follows. In fact, this could even be part of the final judgment.

Along the same line of thought, this might explain why, after his death, Scripture records that Jesus Christ went and *preached unto the imprisoned spirits, which in the time past were disobedient* (1 Peter 3:19-20).

There are also many possibilities regarding how the final judgment will actually play out regarding each individual case. **Any possibility, however, that I can see of anyone having a "second chance" after death hinges on their somehow making it past the final judgment without getting cast into the lake of fire**. In order to do this, at some previous point their name has to have been written in the Lamb's book of life or the book of the life of the Lamb (Revelation 13:8). There is also the possibility of names being *blotted out of the book of the living* (Psalm 69:28).

c) What are the minimum requirements for being included in the book of life? (Philippians 4:3).

God keeps books on everyone according to their works. Salvation is by grace and through faith, yet judgment is according to works (Ephesians 2:8-9; Revelation 20:13). Our works cannot save us, nor can they save anyone else. There must be evidence of the work of God in us and through us. This could be as simple as yielding to our conscience. Only God knows each heart.

Solomon seems to have barely made it. He came to the conclusion, after a great deal of perversion and abomination, that the whole purpose of man is to fear God and keep his commandments (Ecclesiastes 12:13). Judah had a sordid past. Yet he qualified in God's book when he said, in effect, "Take me and let my brother go" (Genesis 44:33). Jesus said that anyone who receives even a little child in his name receives him. He also told his disciples that anyone who gives even a cup of water will receive a reward. All kinds of very interesting things have been written down in God's books, and all the books will be opened on the judgment day.

Scripture refers to a book of righteousness as well as to a number of other books (Joshua 10:13; 2 Samuel 1:18). *Righteousness* is the same word in Hebrew as *justice.* On the judgment day, *the judge shall sit down and the books shall be opened* (Daniel 7:10).

The judge is Jesus Christ. He has a double right to pass judgment, not only because he created everyone and everything in the first place, but because he died to redeem everyone (Colossians 1:16; 1 Corinthians 15:22). Therefore, every one of his creatures belongs to him, and he may do as he pleases with each one.

> *And I saw the dead, great and small, stand before God; and the books were opened: and another book was opened; which is the book of life; and the dead were judged by those things which were written in the books according to their works* (Revelation 20:12).

God said, *I will have mercy on whom I will have mercy and will show clemency on whom I will show clemency* (Exodus 33:19). Jesus said, *Blessed are the merciful, for they shall obtain mercy* and *I will have mercy and not sacrifice* (Matthew 5:7; 9:13).

But again I remind you, Scripture does not hold out any possibility of anyone entering the eternity of the new heavens and the new earth without their name having been previously written in the Lamb's book of life.

Final Judgment

If chapters 40 to 47 of Ezekiel are a picture of what happens during the *thousand years*, and I believe this to be the case, this is when God sets into place and commissions a *house* to his exact specifications, which is his holy nation, and fills it with his presence. This is the fulfillment of the earnest of the inheritance poured out at Pentecost. This causes the river of God to flow from the throne, out of both sides of the house, toward the east country, through the *desert*, and into the sea. *Every living soul, which swims wherever these two rivers shall come, shall live.* Eventually, the river of God brings life to the sea of lost humanity until all that is left are some salt marshes (Ezekiel 47:11).

By the time the *thousand years* are expired, the general resurrection occurs, and the final judgment takes place. John relates, *And I saw a new heaven and a new earth, for the first heaven and the first earth were passed away, and there was no more sea* (Revelation 21:1). No more lost humanity. Yet the realm of the earth and the realm of the heavens remain.

If we peg this to the prophetic plan of the Temple, the outer court with its brazen sea represents the fallen members of humanity who are not born again or circumcised in their heart (Gentiles). The Holy Place represents the *earth*, that is, the people of God who have been *born into the priesthood* but haven't come to maturity (perfection) in Christ. This is also known as the priesthood of all believers. A veil separates the Holy Place from the direct heavenly presence of God in the Holy of Holies that may only be entered by the high priest, who is now Jesus Christ. Our only access to this realm is in the life of Christ.

The temple described by Ezekiel has no veil. It has no separate Holy Place. It only has inside (the heavenly Holy of Holies) and outside (the earth that is being cleansed). There is also the remote *sea*. The members of the mature body of Christ, the sons of Zadok (righteousness), have access inside. The priests that caused Israel to sin are cut off from the presence of God and must minister outside. The river of God flows and makes inroads on the *sea* until at the end of the *thousand years* when only some *salt marshes* are left.

Regarding the reference in Ezekiel about the *dry bones*, it also says that *these are the bones of the house of Israel* (Ezekiel 37:11). Israel is the name of God. Israel is the name given to Jacob after he was converted in a face-to-face encounter with God. It indicates a change of nature. These dry bones are not associated with the name Jacob, much less with the Gentiles who are not in covenant with God.

The *dry bones* of the house of Israel represent those who are written in the Lamb's book of life but who feel sterile and have no real hope or even possibility of being the nation God desires. It's also true that flesh and blood cannot inherit the kingdom of God (1 Corinthians 15:50). These bones have no flesh, it has been dealt with, and no blood, because they have given up their own lives. For the life of the flesh is in the blood. Therefore, they are the perfect candidates for God to breathe life into by the Spirit. This is not just the resurrection of some individual people. It's the resurrection of a godly nation. This is the first resurrection. This is the nation that shall be born in a day (Isaiah 66:8).

After two days he shall give us life: in the third day he will resurrect us, and we shall live in his sight (Hosea 6:2). Two prophetic thousand-year days have passed since Jesus Christ was here the first time. Now, in the third day, he will resurrect us. This, I believe, speaks of the first resurrection and the millennium.

After the final judgment of Revelation 20:11-15, there is no longer any *sea*. Period. The entire *holy city* is now the same realm as the Holy of Holies. *But the fearful and unbelieving and the abominable and murderers and fornicators and sorcerers and idolaters and all liars shall have their part in the lake which burns with fire which is the second death* (Revelation 21:8).

The Holy City.

In Revelation 21, there are those who live inside the holy city and those who are referred to as *the Gentiles that have been saved* who *shall walk in the light of her* (the light of the holy city) *and the kings of the earth* who *shall bring their glory and honour into her* (Revelation 21:24). This seems to imply that there are some who live in the holy city and some who live in the new earth, in which the curse has been lifted, outside the holy city.

Those who live in the holy city have access to the heavenly realm and the earthly realm. In fact, the holy city is where the two realms intersect. The holy city is 1,200 furlongs foursquare. Its length and breadth and height are the same (Revelation 21). This measurement means that the inhabitants of the city walk in perfect divine order in the realm of the earth and in the realm of the heavens. There are also those mentioned above who appear to be limited to the realm of the earth, who shall walk in the light of her and bring their glory and honor into her. This seems to be confirmed by the following verse:

> *And there shall in no wise enter into it anything unclean or that works abomination or makes a lie, but only those who are written in the Lamb's book of life* (Revelation 21:27).

This issue seems to come up again in Revelation 22:14-15 when it says, *Blessed are those who do his commandments that their power and authority might be in the tree of life and they may enter in through the gates into the city. But outside are the dogs and the fornicators and the murderers and the idolaters and whosoever loves and makes a lie.* Why does it say that they are outside instead of specifying that they have been cast into the lake of fire? The lake of fire is definitely outside, but there appears to be some ambiguity.

The question is: Does this mean it's possible for there to be some whose names are written in the Lamb's book of life yet who, for one reason or another, at the judgment have been consigned to live outside the holy city in the realm of the earth, where they have the possibility to *walk in the light* of the holy city and *bring their glory and honor into her* as God continues to deal with them? Something similar to this happened to Joseph's brothers when they were allowed to live in the land of Goshen, and not at the royal palace (Genesis 45:7).

If those consigned to the realm of the earth got through the judgment by the skin of their teeth and then choose not to walk in the light of the city, and refuse to bring their honor and glory to the city, it appears that they would continue to be excluded from the city and could even get themselves cast into the lake of fire. This would just about have to be the case if God gave any borderline cases a "second chance." There is scriptural precedent for this (Matthew 18:23-35).

Sounding the Warning.

a) For those of us who are clearly called into ministry and set as watchmen, we are told that we have the responsibility to sound the warning. Otherwise, we will be responsible for the blood of those we are supposed to warn (Ezekiel 33:6).

It's clear from Scripture that God is trying to see how many can be saved, and that it's not his desire for people to be lost. Yet, it is also very clear that many will be lost and cast into the lake of fire.

> *Enter ye in at the narrow gate, for the way that leads to destruction is wide and spacious, and those who follow it are many; because narrow is the gate, and confined is the way which leads unto life, and there are few that find it* (Matthew 7:13-14).

There is no indication in Scripture that God ever takes man's free will away. If he were to do so, there could be no true love. There is no indication that man is ever forced to love God or to love his neighbor. It's true that many are overcome by sin and live in slavery to the world and the Devil. Yet, there is provision and opportunity in God's plan of redemption for sinful, fallen man to seek Jesus, who is the way, the truth, and the light, and respond to the call and to the love of God. For the redeemed, *where that Spirit of the Lord is, there is liberty* (2 Corinthians 3:17). The legion of demons which possessed the man of the tombs in the country of the Gadarenes could not prevent him from running after Jesus and worshipping him. And Jesus delivered him (Mark 5:1-16).

b) From Romans 1 it's clear that even those who haven't heard the Gospel are held responsible if they don't acknowledge their creator and if they aren't thankful to him. In fact, if they do this, it might just be enough for them to get written up in God's book.

c) Given all the confusion caused by so many people who preach a false gospel and have never been commissioned by God, I believe that at the final judgment all factors will be taken into account and no one will be able to argue with God's final verdict regarding each and every person who has ever lived.

Saved so as by Fire.

Let's take another look at the Scripture regarding those who are saved *so as by fire*, even if their work shall be burned up.

> *For no one can lay another foundation than that laid, which is Jesus the Christ.*
>
> *Now if anyone builds upon this foundation gold, silver, precious stones, wood, hay, stubble, the work of each one shall be made manifest, for the day shall declare it because it shall be revealed by fire; the work of each one, whatever sort it is, the fire shall put it to test.*
>
> *If the work of anyone abides which he has built thereupon, he shall receive a reward. If anyone's work shall be burned, he shall suffer loss, but he himself shall be saved, yet so as by fire* (1 Corinthians 3:11-15).

This is all based upon building upon the right foundation, which is Jesus Christ. Therefore, this Scripture does not promise that anyone who is *not* building on the right foundation can *be saved, yet so as by fire.*

In the highest sense, Jesus is the way, the truth, and the light. Anyone genuinely seeking the truth or standing for truth is really seeking him or standing for him. I would go as far as to say that anyone building upon the truth could really be building upon the foundation of Jesus Christ. Everyone has a God-given conscience that starts off sensitive to the truth. This functions, to some extent, even in societies that know little or nothing about the Gospel. God clearly holds everyone responsible, *because his eternal power and divinity, are clearly understood by the creation of the world and by the things that are made so that there is no excuse* regarding basic knowledge and defense of the truth (Romans 1:18-20).

What *day shall declare it*? In the highest sense, it's the day of the Lord ending with the judgment day. And yes, of course, the work we do in this present age will also be revealed by fire for what it is. At the present time, the fire mostly has to do with trials and tribulations. Although some are also facing the test of prosperity, which the people of God, Israel, and the church have almost always spectacularly failed in the past.

What is the *work* that *abides*? The only thing that I can think of that can possibly make it through the fire of judgment is the godly fruit and character developed in our lives and in the lives of those we have helped and influenced by the power and anointing of the Holy Spirit. The work that abides has to be founded upon the truth. It's only as we are lined up with the truth and tempered with mercy, that we can rest from our own ideas and labors and be at peace as we work the righteousness of Christ. *Mercy and truth are met together; righteousness* [justice] *and peace have kissed each other* (Psalm 85:10-11).

Time and resources spent on earthly things will not qualify unless God instructed us to obtain them or gave them to us along with instructions on how to use them. Even then, they are only tools, or scaffolding, to help us reach out to others with the mercy, love, and grace of God flowing in and through us.

Among the people of God, it's rare to find those who are one hundred percent mobilized to invest in heavenly treasure as God leads them. Many, if not most, Christians seem to only reach a very small percentage of their potential in Christ.

There are few who are willing to *sell* all that they have, in order to purchase *one pearl of great price* (Matthew 13:45-46).

Instead, most give priority to seemingly great works or wonderful things that may really go down in the end as wood, hay, and stubble.

Undoubtedly, one of the great purposes of God in deciding to have a first resurrection and a day of the Lord is to *reveal by fire* for *one thousand years*. Under unprecedented prosperity, he will observe the ability of all the chosen candidates – carefully selected by him over the past six thousand years – to build eternal work upon the right foundation. Their works will be revealed before he allows them to be part of his government in the holy city, which will reign and rule over the new heavens and the new earth for ever and ever.

Then, after the thousand years are expired, he will loose Satan out of his prison. Anyone who is not on the right foundation will be completely deceived and swept away before the new heavens and the new earth are revealed (Matthew 7:24-27; Revelation 20:7-10).

It's also interesting to note that although the holy city is built of gold and precious stones, there is no mention of silver being used there or in the Holy of Holies. While it's true that silver is capable of passing through the fire, it is prone to tarnish. In Scripture it's linked not only to redemption but also to the realm of the Holy Place and of the *earth*. If someone's work, on the right foundation, turns out to be wood, hay, stubble, or even silver, it's not likely that that person will be allowed to live in the holy city, much less take part in God's eternal government to reign and rule with Christ. They will most likely be allowed to live in the new earth among those who are to walk in the light of the city and bring their glory and honor to the city (Revelation 21:24).

Many are liable to find, in the end, that they have been doing a lot of redemptive work in Jesus' name that, like silver, rapidly loses its shine and tarnishes in the face of the corruption around us. Works corresponding to *silver* do not equate with God's rest, because silver must be constantly shined and polished. There are many people in this category who only "shine" if someone is constantly on their case. Ultimately, all of this relates to matters of the heart, and this is a region only God can judge.

Afterword

Joel 1

> 1 *The word of the LORD that went to Joel the son of Pethuel.*

Joel means "the LORD is God." *Pethuel* means "God delivers."

> 2 *Here this, ye old men, and give ear, all ye inhabitants of the earth. Has this been in your days, or even in the days of your fathers?*

> 3 *Tell your sons of it, and let your sons tell their sons, and their sons another generation.*

This message is for all the inhabitants of the earth (Israel and the church). It is to be passed on to every generation.

> 4 *That which the palmerworm has left the locust has eaten; and that which the locust has left the cankerworm has eaten; and that which the cankerworm has left the caterpillar has eaten.*

> 5 *Awake, ye drunkards, and weep; and howl, all ye drinkers of wine, because of the new wine; for it is cut off from your mouth.*

Those who are drunk on the old wine, their own life, will be in much trouble as the day of the Lord dawns. They need the new wine, the new life – God's life.

> 6 *For a people has come up upon my land, strong, and without number, whose teeth are the teeth of a lion, and he has the molars of a great lion.* Compare this with the fifth trumpet in Revelation 9.
>
> 7 *He has laid my vine waste and barked my fig tree: he has made it clean bare and cast it away; its branches are made white.*
>
> 8 *Lament like a young woman girded with sackcloth for the husband of her youth.*
>
> 9 *The grain offering and the drink offering of the house of the LORD has perished; the priests, the LORD's ministers, mourn.*

For the grain offering (representing the work of the hands of the priests, the Lord's ministers), the third part of a hin of oil must be mingled with the grain, and a drink offering of one-third of a hin of wine is required. Those who cling to their old life are cut off from the oil (anointing) and the wine (new life) due to the invasion of the locusts (Revelation 9:7-8). Without oil or wine, God will reject them, and the work of their hands (Revelation 6:6). They have the same problem as the foolish virgins (Matthew 25:8).

Jesus told the Pharisees that *ye compass sea and land to make one proselyte, and when he is made, ye make him twofold more a son of hell than yourselves* (Matthew 23:15).

Joel 1

> 10 *The field was destroyed, the land mourns; for the wheat was destroyed; the new wine was dried up, the oil perished.*

> 11 *Be ye ashamed, O ye husbandmen; howl, O ye vinedressers, for the wheat and for the barley; because the harvest of the field is lost.*

The wheat represents the Passover, and the barley represents Pentecost. Those who continue to minister or participate in these realms without the life and the anointing of God will lose the harvest (Matthew 23:13).

> 12 *The vine has dried up, and the fig tree has perished; the pomegranate tree, the palm tree also, and the apple tree, even all the trees of the field, have withered: therefore joy has withered away from the sons of men.*

This is the same as when the third part of the trees is burnt up. The trees in the realm of Pentecost will all be burnt up because they do not have the seal of God in their forehead. Right now the wheat and the tares are still growing together in the field. Right now those who belong to God minister and participate alongside those who do not. In the day of the Lord the tares will be separated from the wheat, and the wheat will be separated from the chaff.

> 13 *Gird yourselves, and lament, ye priests: howl, ye ministers of the altar: come, lie all night in sackcloth, ye ministers of my God: for the present and the drink offering is taken away from the house of your God.*

Remember, in the New Covenant we are in the priesthood of all believers (1 Peter 2:5, 9). The company of the two witnesses prophesy during the entire time that is necessary to correct this situation (42 months or 1,260 days). The company of the two witnesses demonstrates that they are sober and vigilant. They are not drunk on their own lives. They are willing to lay down their lives for Christ and for the cause of the gospel.

Their purpose and message is to call Israel and the church to individual and corporate repentance.

> 14 *Sanctify a fast, call a solemn assembly, gather the elders and all the inhabitants of the earth into the house of the LORD your God and cry unto the LORD.*

A fast, in the most holy sense, means that we are not to feed our own lives (Isaiah 58). For the Lord desires his life to come forth in us. This is the only way to gather all the inhabitants of the earth into the Holy of Holies of the house of the Lord. We must come together in the fullness of his life, which is the only safe place (Psalm 91).

> 15 *Alas for the day! for the day of the LORD is at hand, and it shall come as a destruction from the Almighty.*
>
> 16 *Is not the food cut off before our eyes, the joy and the gladness from the house of our God?*
>
> 17 *The seed has rotted under their clods, the storehouses were laid desolate, the barns were destroyed for the wheat is withered.*

The seed is in the fruit. Those who have not come to maturity in Christ have no incorruptible seed to plant, and all the corruptible seed is being destroyed in the day of the Lord. Those who continue to plant immature seed (because we are the seed) will see it rot under the clods (as if someone were to plant wheat seed that was only in the milk stage), as their storehouses (the trappings of religious structure) are laid desolate and their barns (church buildings) are destroyed. Here in Colombia we have seen hundreds of church buildings and religious structures laid desolate or destroyed in the face of the army of "locusts."

> 18 *How the beasts groan! The herds of cattle are*

perplexed because they have no pasture; the flocks of sheep are condemned.

19 *O LORD, to thee will I cry for the fire has devoured the pastures of the wilderness, and the flame has burned all the trees of the field.*

The effect of the first trumpet is the burning of all the green grass. Those who have chosen to be "carnal" Christians are in a huge bind because their sources of spiritual nourishment have not only been burned up in the realm of the earth (the church), but they have also been burned up everywhere. Those who feed on New Age or Eastern Mysticism or on anything else will find that there will be no provision anywhere.

20 *The beasts of the field also cry unto thee for the rivers of waters are dried up, and the fire has devoured the meadows of the wilderness.*

Those who have been playing with false fire and false prophets do not even have "water" to drink after the effects of the third trumpet, when the star called "wormwood" crashes into the rivers and waters of the land of religion.

Joel 2

1 *Blow the shofar in Zion, and sound an alarm in my holy mountain; let all the inhabitants of the earth tremble for the day of the LORD comes, for it is near at hand;*

The trumpets are to sound an alarm to warn the people ahead of time. At the sound of the seventh trumpet, the mystery of God shall be finished (Revelation 10:7), and there shall be time no longer. We know this mystery pertains to Christ in you, the hope of glory (Colossians 1:26-28). To those who are not secure in Christ, this will be:

2 a day of darkness and of gloominess, a day of clouds and of shadow that spreads itself upon the mountains as the dawn: a people great and strong; there has not ever been the like, neither shall there be any more after him, even to the years of many generations.

3 A fire devours before him and behind him a flame burns: the earth is as the garden of Eden before him, and behind him a desolate wilderness; neither shall anyone escape him.

The day of the Lord is linked to the Day of Reconciliation (Atonement). Those who do not heed the message of the trumpets and do not repent from their own works and afflict their souls (turn their back on their own lives in repentance so they may come to maturity in Christ) will be cut off or destroyed. God is offering us the opportunity to return to the garden of Eden, while everything else in the land will become desolate wilderness. No one in the realm of Israel and the church will be able to escape this judgment.

4 His appearance is as the appearance of horses; and as horsemen, so shall they run.

5 Like the thunder of chariots they shall leap over the tops of mountains, like the noise of a flame of fire that devours the stubble, as a strong people set in battle array. Compare this to Revelation 9:7.

6 Before him the peoples shall fear: all faces shall go pale.

7 They shall run like mighty men; they shall climb the wall like men of war, and they shall march each one in his ways, and they shall not break ranks.

> 8 *No one shall crowd his companion; they shall walk each one in his path: and even falling upon the sword, they shall not be wounded.*
>
> 9 *They shall go through the city; they shall run upon the wall; they shall climb up upon the houses; they shall enter in at the windows like a thief.*

Jesus warned that those who do not watch will not know in what hour he shall come upon them – that he will come as a thief (Revelation 3:3). Paul and Peter also gave the same warning (1 Thessalonians 5:2; 2 Peter 3:10).

> 10 *The earth shall quake before him; the heavens shall tremble: the sun and the moon shall go dark; and the stars shall withdraw their shining:*
>
> 11 *and the LORD shall utter his voice before his army: for many are his camps and strong, that execute his word; for the day of the LORD is great, and very terrible; and who can abide it?*

All the events described by the trumpets of Revelation take place under the direct command of the Lord, as everything that can be shaken on earth and in heaven quakes and trembles. Some carnal Christians have accepted the false assumption that if they figure out a secret way into heaven, they will be safe. For those who cling to their own corrupt lives, the heavens will be a more dangerous place than the earth! God is not just cleansing the earth; he is also cleansing the heavens. All that is corrupt and unclean in the heavens will be cast down to the earth, so it can be exposed, dealt with, destroyed, or locked up. No safe refuge will exist for anyone other than the secret place of the most high (Psalm 91; Jeremiah 23:22). We must be hidden in Christ.

> 12 *Therefore also now, saith the LORD, turn unto*

> *me with all your heart and with fasting and with weeping, and with mourning:*
>
> 13 *and rend your heart, and not your garments, and turn unto the LORD your God for he is gracious and compassionate, slow to anger and great in mercy, and he does repent of chastisement.*
>
> 14 *Who knows if he will return and repent and leave a blessing behind him even a present and a drink offering unto the LORD your God?*

Who knows if he will return and extend a blessing and a present? A present is the work of his hands, and only his work can save us. A drink offering is the wine of his life. Malachi 4:6 ends on a similar note speaking of the end-time ministry of Elijah (Elijah means God himself): *and he shall convert the heart of the fathers to the sons, and the heart of the sons to the fathers, lest I come and smite the earth with destruction.* The Jews were stubborn and refused to repent as a nation at the first coming of Jesus Christ at the end of the age of law. The destruction of their land was swift and fierce.

We hope that the second coming at the end of the church age of grace will be different. It depends on whether or not the message of the trumpets of God is received by all of God's people. Scattered individual repentance will not be enough to forestall this judgment upon the institutions of the church. Corporate repentance is required.

> 15 *Blow the shofar in Zion, sanctify a fast, call a solemn assembly:*
>
> 16 *gather the people, sanctify the meeting, assemble the elders, gather the children and those that suck breasts; let the bridegroom go forth of his chamber and the bride out of her closet.*

> 17 *Let the priests, the ministers of the LORD, weep between the porch and the altar, and let them say, Forgive thy people, O LORD, and do not give thine heritage to reproach that the Gentiles should rule over her: why should they say among the peoples, Where is their God?*

Even in the natural realm, many powerful forces are stirring that do not like the west. They do not like Israel. They do not like the United States. It is high time for repentance – as individuals, in our congregations, and in our nations.

> 18 *Then the LORD will be jealous for his earth and forgive his people.*
>
> 19 *Yea, the LORD will answer and say unto his people, Behold, I will send you bread and new wine and oil, and ye shall be satisfied therewith: and I will no longer make you a reproach among the Gentiles:*
>
> 20 *But I will remove far off from you he of the north wind and will drive him into a land barren and desolate; his face shall be toward the east sea, and his end unto the western sea, and he shall exhale his foul odour, and he shall decompose, because he has lifted himself up.* This is a parallel passage with Daniel 12.
>
> 21 *Fear not, O land; be glad and rejoice: for the LORD has done great things.*
>
> 22 *Be not afraid, ye animals of the field; for the pastures of the wilderness shall become green again, for the trees shall bear their fruit, the fig tree and the vine shall give their fruits.*
>
> 23 *Ye also, sons of Zion, be glad and rejoice in the*

LORD your God for he has given you the former rain according to righteousness, and he will cause to come down for you the rain, the former rain, and the latter rain as in the beginning.

God will have a mature people that he can plant in the earth and multiply. This time no tares will be sown among the wheat, because Satan will be locked up for one thousand years in the bottomless pit (Revelation 20:1-3).

24 *And the floors shall be full of wheat, and the vats shall overflow with wine and oil.*

25 *And I will restore to you the years that the caterpillar has eaten, the locust, and the cankerworm, and the palmerworm, my great army which I sent among you.*

26 *And ye shall eat in plenty and be satisfied, and praise the name of the LORD your God that has dealt wondrously with you; and my people shall never again be ashamed.*

27 *And ye shall know that I am in the midst of Israel and that I am the LORD your God, and there is none other; and my people shall never be ashamed.*

This prophecy has not yet been fulfilled. When it is fulfilled, the need for God's witnesses to wear sackcloth will not exist.

28 *And it shall come to pass after this that I will pour out my Spirit upon all flesh; and your sons and your daughters shall prophesy, your old men shall dream dreams, your young men shall see visions:*

29 *and even upon the slaves and upon the handmaids in those days will I pour out my spirit.*

> 30 *And I will show wonders in the heaven and in the earth, blood, and fire, and pillars of smoke.*
>
> 31 *The sun shall be turned into darkness and the moon into blood before the great and the terrible day of the LORD comes.*
>
> 32 *And it shall come to pass that whoever shall call on the name of the LORD shall escape: for in Mount Zion and in Jerusalem shall be salvation, as the LORD has said, and in those who are left, to whom the LORD shall have called.*

Peter quoted this Scripture in his message on the porch of the temple on the day of Pentecost. The Holy Spirit, however, made a slight change in the text in order to fit the situation. Instead of saying, *I will pour out my Spirit upon all flesh* under the anointing of the Holy Spirit, Peter said, *I will pour out* ***of*** *my Spirit upon all flesh* (Acts 2:17 emphasis added).

Pentecost is the feast of firstfruits, in which the earnest or down payment of the Spirit was poured out. Pentecost is not the fullness of our inheritance in Christ. This has been reserved for now. The fullness of the Spirit will not be poured out on those who are unclean or immature. This is why the day of the Lord will commence with such a total cleansing of the earth.

Only after God's people are clean and pure will he judge the world (the realm of the sea).

Joel 3

> 1 *For, behold, in those days and in that time when I shall cause the captivity of Judah and Jerusalem to end,*

God will use the day of the Lord to bring this about, and the time is now. In order for *the captivity of Judah and Jerusalem to end*, the people of God must be cleansed. God will place his seal on the foreheads of those who are his, and everyone else in the "earth" will either be brought to repentance or purged. Then he will deal with those who dwell in the "sea."

> 2 *I will gather together all the Gentiles, and will cause them to descend into the valley of Jehoshaphat, and there I will enter into judgment with them because of my people and of my heritage Israel, whom they scattered among the nations, and parted my land.*

Jehoshaphat means "whom the LORD judges." Natural Israel was scattered among the nations, and their land was divided. Christians were scattered among denominations, and the great truths and heritage of the faith have been divvied up among many. Just look at how many entities elbow one another for custody of sacred sites in natural Jerusalem. Everything concerning doctrine, truth, and heritage of the people of God rightfully belongs to God. Soon he will gather all the Gentiles (all those with uncircumcised hearts) into the valley of *Jehoshaphat* and sort everything out.

Appendix A

Ephesians 4

8 *Therefore he saith, When he ascended up on high, he led captivity captive and gave gifts unto to men.*

9 *(Now he that ascended, what is it but that he also descended first into the lower parts of the earth?*

10 *He that descended is the same also that ascended up far above all the heavens, that he might fulfill all things.)*

The verses above are definitely in the key manuscripts of the Received Text (*Textus Receptus*) and undoubtedly even form the basis for that part of the Apostles' Creed which states that Jesus *descended into hell.* The problem is that Bible translators mistook Hades for hell or they used *hell* to describe both the first death and the second death, which is misleading. Jesus descended into Hades (the first death), not into hell (the lake of fire or second death).

The reason that Ephesians 4:8 is in what appears to be italics in some editions of the KJV and NKJV is because it is a direct quote of Psalm 68:18 – *Thou hast ascended on high, thou hast led captivity captive, thou hast received gifts for men, yea, for the rebellious also that the LORD may dwell among them.*

In the original editions of the KJV (and most other Reformation Bibles), **italics** are only used to denote English words or phrases the translators added to complete what they felt was implied or required in order to convey the original meaning of the Hebrew or Greek text.

These strict criteria were modified in many of the modern editions of the KJV and most editions of the NKJV so that they use **oblique type** when they identify a passage in the New Testament as being a direct quote of an Old Testament passage. This introduces confusion because it's almost impossible for the uninitiated to parse the slight difference between italics and oblique type. This is unfortunate, bordering on deceptive, because people may begin to doubt the authenticity of key passages of Scripture.

Appendix B

There are thirty-two references to *the day of the LORD* in the *Jubilee Bible* (and dozens of additional references that refer to *the day* or *that day*). Here they are in context and in numerical order:

1. Isaiah 2

> 10 *Enter into the rock, and hide thee in the dust from the terrible presence of the LORD and from the glory of his majesty.*
>
> 11 *The lofty looks of man shall be humbled, and the haughtiness of men shall be bowed down, and the LORD alone shall be exalted in that day.*
>
> 12 *For the day of the LORD of the hosts shall be upon every one that is proud and lofty and upon every one that is lifted up; and he shall be brought low:*
>
> 13 *And upon all the cedars of Lebanon that are high and lifted up and upon all the oaks of Bashan,*
>
> 14 *and upon all the high mountains and upon all the hills that are lifted up,*

15 *and upon every high tower, and upon every fenced wall,*

16 *and upon all the ships of Tarshish and upon all pleasant pictures.*

17 *And the loftiness of man shall be bowed down, and the haughtiness of men shall be made low; and the LORD alone shall be exalted in that day.*

18 *And he shall utterly abolish the idols.*

19 *And they shall go into the holes of the rocks and into the caves of the earth, because of the terrible presence of the LORD and because of the glory of his majesty when he shall arise to smite the earth.* Compare this to Revelation 6:15.

20 *In that day man shall cast his idols of silver and his idols of gold (which they made each one for himself to worship) into the caves of the moles and of the bats,*

21 *to go into the clefts of the rocks and into the caverns of the cliffs from before the fearful presence of the LORD and from the glory of his majesty, when he shall arise to smite the earth.*

22 *Cease from man, whose breath is in his nostrils; for of what is he to be accounted of?*

2. Isaiah 13

2 *Lift ye up a banner as an example upon the high mountain, exalt the voice unto them, raise the hand, that they may enter in by gates of princes.*

3 *I have commanded my sanctified ones; I have also*

called my mighty ones for my anger that they might rejoice with my glory.

4 *The noise of a multitude in the mountains like as of a great people; a tumultuous noise of kingdoms, of Gentiles gathered together: the LORD of the hosts orders the host of the battle.*

5 *They come from a far land, from the end of the heavens, even the LORD, and the instruments of his indignation, to destroy the whole earth.*

6 *Howl; for the day of the LORD is at hand; it shall come as destruction from the Almighty.*

7 *Therefore all hands shall be faint, and every heart of man shall melt:*

8 *And they shall be filled with terror; anguish and pain shall take hold of them; they shall be in pain as a woman that travails: they shall be amazed one at another; their faces shall be as flames.*

3. Isaiah 13

9 *Behold, the day of the LORD comes, cruel and with wrath and fierce anger, to lay the earth desolate; and he shall destroy the sinners thereof out of it.*

10 *For this reason the stars of the heavens and the lights thereof shall not shine: the sun shall be darkened in his going forth, and the moon shall not give forth her light.*

11 *And I will visit evil upon the world and iniquity upon the wicked, and I will cause the arrogancy of*

the proud to cease and will lay low the haughtiness of the strong.

12 *I will make the noble man more precious than fine gold and man more than the gold of Ophir.*

13 *Because I will shake the heavens, and the earth shall be moved out of her place, in the indignation of the LORD of the hosts and in the day of his fierce anger.*

4. Isaiah 34

1 *Come near, ye Gentiles, to hear; and hearken, ye peoples; let the earth hear, and all that is therein, the world and all things that come forth of it.*

Remember that in prophetic language, in the highest sense, *Gentiles* refers to those who do not have circumcised hearts (Romans 2:28-29).

2 *For the indignation of the LORD is upon all the Gentiles, and his fury upon the entire army of them; he shall destroy them and deliver them to the slaughter.*

3 *Their slain shall be cast out, and their stink shall come up out of their carcasses, and the mountains shall be melted with their blood.*

4 *And all the host of heavens shall be dissolved, and the heavens shall be rolled together as a scroll; and all their host shall fall down as the leaf falls off from the vine and as the leaf falls from the fig tree.* This coincides with Revelation 6:14.

5 *For in the heavens my sword shall become drunk; behold, it shall come down in judgment*

> *upon Idumea or Edom and upon the people of my anathema.*

Anathema is linked to abomination (Deuteronomy 7:26; Daniel 11:31; 12:11; Matthew 24:15; Mark 13:14). Anyone in the Holy Place who has not been born into the line of the High Priest (the priesthood of all born-again believers) is an unclean abomination before the Lord. This is anathema. *Any anathema of men which is devoted shall not be ransomed, but shall surely be put to death* (Leviticus 27:29). This is what will happen to any tares (sons of the Evil One) growing in the Holy Place (the realm of the earth, the church) on the day of the Lord (Matthew 13:36-43).

Edom means "red" and refers to those who do their own thing and make their own kingdoms. Those who have been using God to get what they want will be separated from those who have surrendered to God and are doing his will by the power of the Holy Spirit.

> 6 *The sword of the LORD is filled with blood; it is made fat with fatness and with the blood of lambs and goats with the fat of the kidneys of rams, for the LORD has a sacrifice in Bozrah and a great slaughter in the land of Idumea.*

> 7 *And the unicorns shall fall with them, and the bulls with the calves; and their land shall become drunk with blood, and their dust shall be greased with fatness.*

Unicorn means "one horn," and in Scripture it means the rhinoceros. Spiritually it refers to someone who has blindly given themselves over to projecting the power of the Enemy.

> 8 *For it shall be the day of the LORD's vengeance and the year of recompenses for the controversy of Zion.*

5. Isaiah 58

> 13 *If thou turn away thy foot from the sabbath, from doing thy will on my holy day; and call the sabbath the delightful, holy, glorious day of the LORD; and shalt honour him by not doing thine own ways, nor seeking thine own will, nor speaking thine own words:*

The prophetic day of the Lord starts at the beginning of the seventh millennium. At this time God requires us to only do his will – to do his work, his way. We must cease and desist from our own ways and our own will and our own words.

> 14 *Then shalt thou delight thyself in the LORD; and I will cause thee to ride upon the high places of the earth and cause thee to eat of the heritage of Jacob thy father: for the mouth of the LORD has spoken it.*

6. Lamentations 2

> 22 *Thou hast called as to a day of solemnity my terrors from everywhere, so that in the day of the LORD's anger no one escaped nor remained: those that I have swaddled and brought up my enemy has consumed.*

Every work will be tried by fire. Those who are religious proselytes will be separated from among the true sons of God. In some places, most people will be consumed. In Jeremiah's day, God would have spared Jerusalem for the sake of one righteous man, but there were none (Romans 3:10). Now, there is only one. Therefore, we must be found in Christ. *For ye are dead and your life is hid with the Christ in God* (Colossians 3:3).

7. Ezekiel 13

1 *And the word of the LORD came unto me, saying,*

2 *Son of man, prophesy against the prophets of Israel the prophesy and say unto those that prophesy out of their own hearts, Hear ye the word of the LORD:*

3 *thus hath the Lord GOD said: Woe unto the foolish prophets that follow their own spirit and have seen nothing!*

4 *O Israel, thy prophets are like the foxes in the deserts.*

5 *Ye have not gone up into the gaps, neither made up the hedge for the house of Israel to stand in the battle in the day of the LORD.*

6 *They have seen vanity and lying divination, saying, The LORD saith: and the LORD has not sent them, and they have made others to wait for the word to be confirmed.*

7 *Have ye not seen a vain vision and have ye not spoken a lying divination, whereas ye say, The LORD hath said it; albeit I have not spoken?*

8 *Therefore thus hath the Lord GOD said: Because ye have spoken vanity, and seen lies; therefore, behold, I am against you, said the Lord GOD.*

9 *And my hand shall be against the prophets that see vanity and that divine lies: they shall not be in the assembly of my people, neither shall they be written in the book of the house of Israel, neither shall they return to the land of Israel; and ye shall know that I am the Lord GOD.*

It would be bad enough for someone to be caught doing their own works on the day of the Lord. Infinitely worse, however, would be for someone to be prophesying lies and vanity while claiming that this is the word of the Lord.

8. Ezekiel 30

> 2 *Son of man, prophesy and say, Thus hath the Lord GOD said: Howl ye, Woe of the day!*
>
> 3 *For the day is near, even the day of the LORD is near, a cloudy day; it shall be the time of the Gentiles.*

The following four references from Joel 1 and 2 have been covered in context in the Afterword.

9. Joel 1

> 15 *Alas for the day! for the day of the LORD is at hand, and it shall come as a destruction from the Almighty.*

10. Joel 2

> 1 *Blow the shofar in Zion, and sound an alarm in my holy mountain; let all the inhabitants of the earth tremble for the day of the LORD comes, for it is near at hand;*

11. Joel 2

> 11 *and the LORD shall utter his voice before his army: for many are his camps and strong, that execute his word; for the day of the LORD is great, and very terrible; and who can abide it?*

12. Joel 2

31 *The sun shall be turned into darkness and the moon into blood before the great and terrible day of the LORD comes.*

32 *And it shall come to pass that whoever shall call on the name of the LORD shall escape: for in Mount Zion and in Jerusalem shall be salvation, as the LORD has said, and in those who are left, to whom the LORD shall have called.*

13. Joel 3

14 *Multitudes, multitudes in the valley of decision for the day of the LORD is near in the valley of decision.*

15 *The sun and the moon shall be darkened, and the stars shall withdraw their shining.*

16 *The LORD also shall roar out of Zion and utter his voice from Jerusalem; and the heavens and the earth shall shake; but the LORD will be the hope of his people and the strength of the sons of Israel.*

17 *So shall ye know that I am the LORD your God, that I inhabit Zion, the mountain of my holiness: then shall Jerusalem be holy, and no stranger shall pass through her any more.*

14. Amos 5

14 *Seek that which is good, and not that which is evil that ye may live; and so the LORD, the God of the hosts, shall be with you, as ye have spoken.*

15 *Hate the evil and love the good, and establish*

judgment in the gate; it may be that the LORD God of the hosts will be gracious unto the remnant of Joseph.

In Revelation 7, the tribe of Joseph (which means "God shall add") is included in the list of the tribes from which there are some who have the seal of God in their foreheads. Over the past two millennia, God has grafted many Gentiles into the good olive tree of Israel, because a true Jew is not a true Jew merely according to external appearance; likewise, the true people of God are all who are in Christ and have circumcised hearts (Colossians 2:11).

16 *Therefore the LORD, the God of the hosts, the Lord, said this: Wailing shall be in all streets, and they shall say in all the highways, Alas! alas! and they shall call the husbandman to mourning and such as are skilful of lamentation to wailing.*

17 *And in all vineyards shall be wailing, for I will pass through the midst of thee, saith the LORD.*

18 *Woe unto you that desire the day of the LORD! to what end is it for you?*

15. Amos 5

18 *the day of the LORD shall be darkness, and not light.*

19 *As if a man fled from a lion, and a bear met him; or went into the house, and leaned his hand on the wall and a serpent bit him.*

16. Amos 5

20 *Shall not the day of the LORD be darkness, and not light? even very dark, and no brightness in it?*

21 *I hate, I despise your solemnities, and I will not savour your assemblies.*

22 *Though ye offer me your burnt offerings and your presents, I will not accept them; neither will I regard the peace offerings of your fat beasts.*

23 *Take away from me the noise of thy songs; for I will not hear the melody of thy instruments.*

24 *But let judgment run down as waters, and righteousness as a mighty stream.*

17. Obadiah 1

15 *For the day of the LORD is near upon all the Gentiles as thou hast done, it shall be done unto thee; thy reward shall return upon thine own head.*

16 *For as ye have drunk upon my holy mountain, so shall all the Gentiles drink continually; they shall drink, and they shall swallow down, and they shall be as though they had not been.*

17 *But in Mount Zion shall be deliverance, and it shall be holiness; and the house of Jacob shall possess their possessions.*

18 *And the house of Jacob shall be a fire, and the house of Joseph a flame, and the house of Esau for stubble, and they shall kindle in them and devour them; and there shall not be any remaining of the house of Esau; for the LORD hath spoken it.*

18. Zephaniah 1

> 7 *Be silent before the presence of the Lord GOD: for the day of the LORD is at hand: for the LORD has prepared a sacrifice, he has bid his guests.*

19. Zephaniah 1

> 8 *And it shall come to pass in the day of the LORD's sacrifice that I will make a visitation upon the princes and upon the king's sons and upon all such as are clothed with strange apparel.*

Compare this verse to the parable that Jesus gave of the wedding feast (Matthew 22:1-14) in which a man who did not have on a wedding garment was bound hand and foot and cast into the darkness outside.

The proper attire for this occasion is a white robe of fine linen, which Scripture clearly states is the righteousness of the saints (Revelation 19:8). We cannot do righteous deeds unless we are led, directed, and empowered by the Holy Spirit.

> 9 *In the same day I will also make a visitation upon all those that leap over the door, who fill their masters' houses with robbery and deceit.*
>
> 10 *And it shall come to pass in that day, saith the LORD that there shall be the noise of a cry from the fish gate and a howling from the school and a great destruction from the hills.*
>
> 11 *Howl, ye inhabitants of Maktesh, for all the merchant people are cut down; all those that brought ye silver are cut off.*

Maktesh means "a depression." All of those with ill-gotten gains are going to be in a lot of pain when all their earthly treasures go up in smoke. A cry will emanate from the fish gate because of those who have allowed the unconverted into the church. A howling will proceed from the schools of religion as the destruction from the hills descends on them. All those making merchandise of the things of the Lord will be cut off.

> 12 *And it shall come to pass at that time, that I will search Jerusalem with lamps and make a visitation upon the men that are settled on their lees, that say in their heart, The LORD will not do good, neither will he do evil.*
>
> 13 *Therefore their goods shall become a spoil, and their houses a desolation: they shall build houses, but not inhabit them; and they shall plant vineyards, but not drink the wine thereof.*

20. Zephaniah 1

> 14 *The great day of the LORD is near, it is near, and hastens greatly,*

21. Zephaniah 1

> 14 *the bitter voice of the day of the LORD; the mighty man shall cry there.*
>
> 15 *That day is a day of wrath, a day of trouble and distress, a day of wasteness and desolation, a day of darkness and gloominess, a day of clouds and thick darkness.*
>
> 16 *A day of the shofar and alarm upon the strong cities, and upon the high towers.*
>
> 17 *And I will bring distress upon men that they shall walk like blind men because they have sinned against the LORD, and their blood shall be poured*

out as dust and their flesh as the dung. Notice how the day of the Lord is linked to the trumpets (shofar).

22. Zephaniah 1

> 18 *Neither their silver nor their gold shall be able to deliver them in the day of the LORD's wrath, but the whole earth shall be devoured by the fire of his jealousy; for he shall make even a speedy riddance of all those that dwell in the earth.*

It is the dwellers or inhabitants of the earth (linked to the Holy Place of the realm of Israel and the church) who are in the direct line of fire as the day of the Lord begins. They suddenly realize this, as soon as the heavens are rolled up like a scroll, and they perceive the presence and throne of God and the wrath of the Lamb (Revelation 6:14-17).

23. Zephaniah 2

> 1 *Search yourselves and one another, O unfriendly people;*
>
> 2 *before the decree is executed, before the day passes as the chaff, before the fierce anger of the LORD comes upon you, before the day of the LORD's anger comes upon you.*

Those who are not flowing in the love of God had better search themselves and one another now before the decree is executed. Charity, the love of God, covers a multitude of sins (1 Peter 4:8; James 5:20). Jesus sent a stern warning about this to the congregation at Ephesus (Revelation 2:4-5).

24. Zephaniah 2

> 3 *Seek ye the LORD, all ye humble of the earth, who have wrought his judgment; seek righteousness, seek humility: it may be ye shall be kept in the day of the LORD's anger.*

The day of the Lord is a serious matter even for those who consider themselves to be among the righteous. Now is the time for all of us to do some soul-searching, to heed the admonition, and to make our calling and election sure (2 Peter 2:1-12). Righteous Noah found grace in the eyes of the Lord and was saved with his family in a wild, rollercoaster ride among mammoth waves when the waters covered the earth for 150 days. That had to have produced much soul-searching among the eight persons and animals that were saved while every other creature upon the face of the earth was destroyed (Genesis 7:21-24). Jesus said, *But as the days of Noah were, so shall also the coming of the Son of man be* (Matthew 24:37).

Righteous Lot was saved because God remembered the intercession of Abraham and sent two angels to drag semi-incredulous Lot and his wife and two daughters out of the city of Sodom. Even so, Lot's wife disobeyed the angels and looked back and was lost. Lot was so shell-shocked over the experience that he holed up in a cave in the mountains with his daughters (Genesis 19:18-30). Jude wrote about this later, linking the great day of judgment with what happened to Sodom and Gomorrah and the surrounding cities (Jude 6-7).

25. Zechariah 14

> 1 *Behold, the day of the LORD comes, and thy spoil shall be divided in the midst of thee.*
>
> 2 *For I will gather all the Gentiles against Jerusalem in battle, and the city shall be taken, and the houses*

rifled, and the women ravished; and half of the city shall go forth into captivity, but the remnant of the people shall not be cut off from the city.

3 *Then the LORD shall go forth and fight against those Gentiles as when he fought in the day of battle.*

If you desire a commentary on the entire book of Zechariah, read *The Correction Factor (Zechariah: A Key to Unlock the Book of Revelation)*, which sheds much light on the book of Revelation and on the day of the Lord.

26. Malachi 4

1 *For, behold, the day comes that shall burn as an oven; and all the proud, and all that do wickedly shall be stubble; and the day that comes shall burn them up, said the LORD of the hosts, that it shall leave them neither root nor branch.*

2 *But unto you that fear my name shall the Sun of righteousness be born, and in his wings he shall bring saving health; and ye shall go forth and jump like calves of the herd.*

3 *And ye shall tread down the wicked; for they shall be ashes under the soles of your feet in the day that I make, said the LORD of the hosts.*

This is clear. A great day is in store for those who are right with God.

4 *Remember ye the law of Moses my slave, which I commanded unto him in Horeb statutes and my rights over all Israel.*

God's people belong to him. Even when dealing with the

righteous, God can allow trials and tribulations, if it is for our good. This was difficult for Job to understand at first.

> 5 *Behold, I send you Elijah the prophet before the coming of the great and terrible day of the LORD:*

The name *Elijah* is a play on words; it means "God himself" or "my God." God himself will come forth in his people who are called and chosen and faithful. We have the earnest of the Spirit, but we have not yet tasted of the fullness of the seven Spirits of God that stand before the throne (Revelation 1:4).

> 6 *and he shall convert the heart of the fathers to the sons, and the heart of the sons to the fathers, lest I come and smite the earth with destruction.*

Several of these passages seem to offer hope that the total destruction of the earth can be avoided if there is contrition, repentance, conversion, and reconciliation among those who are in the earth (the realm of the church and Israel). This is definitely in keeping with the heart and character of God.

27. Acts 2

> 16 *But this is that which was spoken by the prophet Joel:*
>
> 17 *And it shall come to pass in the last days, saith God, I will pour out of my Spirit upon all flesh; and your sons and your daughters shall prophesy, and your young men shall see visions, and your old men shall dream dreams;*

The Holy Spirit made a slight modification of this quote out of the mouth of Peter on the day of Pentecost when he said, *I will pour out **of** my Spirit.* Joel had said, *I will pour out my Spirit.* Pentecost is the feast of the firstfruits; now, as we quickly approach the day of the Lord, it is the time of fullness. And the fullness of the Spirit will influence the fullness of the harvest.

> 18 *and for certain on my slaves and on my handmaids I will pour out in those days of my Spirit, and they shall prophesy;*
>
> 19 *and I will show wonders in heaven above, and signs in the earth beneath: blood, and fire, and vapour of smoke;*
>
> 20 *the sun shall be turned into darkness, and the moon into blood before that great and notable day of the Lord shall come;*
>
> 21 *and it shall come to pass that whosoever shall call on the name of the Lord shall be saved.*

28. 1 Corinthians 5

> 1 *It is reported commonly that there is fornication among you, and such fornication as is not so much as named among the Gentiles, that one should have his father's wife.*
>
> 2 *And ye are puffed up and have not rather mourned, that he that has done this deed might be taken away from among you.*
>
> 3 *For I verily, as absent in body, but present in spirit, have judged already, as though I were present, him that has so done this deed.*
>
> 4 *In the name of our Lord Jesus Christ, when ye are gathered together, and my spirit, with the power of our Lord Jesus Christ,*
>
> 5 *let such a one be delivered unto Satan for the*

destruction of the flesh, that the spirit may be saved in the day of the Lord Jesus.

God could be planning something like this on a massive scale with the events of the fifth trumpet (Revelation 9:1-12).

> 6 *Your glorying in not good. Know ye not that a little leaven leavens the whole lump?*
>
> 7 *Purge out therefore the old leaven, that ye may be a new lump, as ye are unleavened. For even Christ, our Passover, is sacrificed for us;*
>
> 8 *therefore let us celebrate the feast, not in the old leaven, neither in the leaven of malice and wickedness, but in the unleavened bread of sincerity and truth.*

Paul wrote the following after the abominable situation at Corinth had been resolved and the people in the church had been brought to repentance after they received his letter. He wrote a second letter asking that the person who had sinned be restored.

29. 2 Corinthians 1

> 12 *For our rejoicing is this, the testimony of our conscience, that in simplicity and godly sincerity, not with carnal wisdom, but by the grace of God, we have had our conversation in the world and more abundantly towards you.*
>
> 13 *For we write no other things unto you than what ye read or also know, and I trust ye shall know them even to the end*
>
> 14 *as also ye have known in part, that we are your*

rejoicing, even as ye also are ours in the day of the Lord Jesus.

30. 1 Thessalonians 5

1 *But of the times and the seasons, brethren, ye have no need that I write unto you.*

2 *For ye know well that the day of the Lord shall come as a thief in the night.*

3 *For when they shall say, Peace and safety; then sudden destruction shall come upon them, as travail upon a woman with child; and they shall not escape.*

4 *But ye, brethren, are not in darkness, that that day should take you as a thief.*

5 *Ye are all the sons of light, and the sons of the day; we are not of the night, nor of darkness.*

We are in a time now when many are saying, "Peace and safety." Those who are in the dark will be caught and destroyed. Those who are in the light will be well aware of the time and the season. This Scripture and Matthew 24:26-27 and others deal repeated blows to the concept of a *secret* rapture.

31. 2 Peter 3

8 *But, beloved, be not ignorant of this one thing, that one day before the Lord is as a thousand years, and a thousand years are as one day.*

9 *The Lord is not late concerning his promise, as some count lateness, but is patient with us, not willing that any should perish, but that all should come to repentance.*

> 10 *But the day of the Lord will come as a thief in the night, in which the heavens shall pass away with a great noise, and the elements, burning, shall be dissolved, and the earth and the works that are in it shall be burned up.*

When the heavens pass away with a great noise, it will be hard to miss this, no matter how asleep the people are. We all need to consider whether we are investing in earthly things that will be burned up on the day of the Lord or if we are investing in heavenly treasure. The only way to make good investments of our time and resources is if we allow the Lord to lead us every step of the way.

> 11 *Seeing then that all these things shall be dissolved, what manner of persons ought ye to be in all holy conversation and godliness,*
>
> 12 *waiting for and desiring earnestly for the coming day of God, in which the heavens being on fire shall be dissolved, and the elements shall melt with fervent heat?*

Scripture defines these *elements* as the elements of this world that held us in slavery before we knew Jesus Christ (Galatians 4:3, 9). These elements pertain to the trappings of religion and those who use such things to govern others (Colossians 2:8-23).

> 13 *Nevertheless we, according to his promises, wait for new heavens and a new earth, in which dwells righteousness.*
>
> 14 *Therefore, beloved, seeing that ye hope for such things, be diligent that ye may be found of him in peace, without spot and blameless.*

Regardless of whether you agree with the treatise set forth in this volume or not, it would behoove us all to make sure that we are *found of him in peace, without spot and blameless.*

32. Revelation 1

> 10 *I was in the Spirit in the day of the Lord and heard behind me a great voice as of a trumpet,*

This is the final reference to the day of the Lord in Scripture, and again it is indelibly linked to the sound of the trumpet and the voice of God.

Appendix C

Trajectory of the word ***arrebatar*** (the Spanish word for ***rapture***) in the *Jubilee Bible* working from the early Reformation translation of Casiodoro de Reina published 1569 (emphasis added to all the following verses).

1. Genesis 31 (Jacob contends with Laban)

39 *That which was* ***torn*** *of beasts I did not bring unto thee; I bore the sin; thou didst require of my hand that which was stolen, whether by day or by night.*

2. Genesis 49

27 *Benjamin,* ***ravening*** *wolf: in the morning he shall devour the prey, and in the evening he shall divide the spoil.*

3. Exodus 22

13 *If it is* ***torn*** *in pieces, then let him bring witness, and he shall not make good that which was* ***torn****.*

4. Exodus 22

31 *And ye shall be holy men unto me; neither shall ye eat any flesh that is* ***torn*** *of beasts in the field; ye shall cast it to the dogs.*

5. Leviticus 7

24 *And the fat of the beast that died of itself and the fat of that which is* ***torn*** *by beasts may be used in any other use, but ye shall not eat of it.*

6. Deuteronomy 33

20 *And to Gad he said, Blessed is he that caused Gad to be enlarged; he shall dwell as a lion and shall* ***tear*** *the arm with the crown of the head.*

7. Job 16

9 *His wrath has* ***torn*** *me and has been against me; he gnashed upon me with his teeth; my enemy sharpened his eyes upon me.*

8. Psalm 7

2 *Lest they* ***take*** *my soul, as a lion dismembers his prey when there is none to deliver.*

9. Jeremiah 5

6 *Therefore a lion out of the forest shall slay them, and a wolf of the desert shall destroy them and a tiger shall lie in wait over their cities; anyone that goes out from there shall be* ***torn in pieces*** *because*

their rebellions have been multiplied, and their backslidings are increased.

10. Ezekiel 22

25 *There is a conspiracy of her prophets in the midst thereof, like a roaring lion* ***ravening*** *the prey; they have devoured souls; they have taken treasures and honour; they have made her many widows in the midst thereof.*

11. Ezekiel 22

27 *Her princes in the midst thereof are like wolves* ***ravening*** *the prey, to shed blood, and to destroy souls, to follow their own greed.*

12. Hosea 5

14 *For I will be unto Ephraim as a lion and as a young lion to the house of Judah; I, even I, will* ***tear*** *and go away; I will take away, and there shall be no one left to escape.*

13. Hosea 6

1 *Come, and let us return unto the LORD; for he has* ***torn****, and he will heal us; he has smitten, and he will bind us up.*

14. Micah 5

8 *And the remnant of Jacob shall be among the Gentiles in the midst of many peoples as a lion among the beasts of the forest, as a young lion among the flocks of sheep, who, if he goes through*

*and treads down and **tears in pieces**, there are none that can escape.*

15. Nahum 2

12 *The lion **tore in pieces** enough for his whelps and strangled for his lionesses and filled his holes with prey and his dens with robbery.*

16. Matthew 11

12 *From the days of John the Baptist until now, life is given unto the kingdom of the heavens, and the valiant **take hold of it**.*

17. Matthew 13

18 *Hear ye therefore the parable of the sower.*

19 *When anyone hears the word of the kingdom and does not understand it, then the wicked one comes and **catches away** that which was sown in his heart. This is he who was planted beside the way.*

18. John 6

15 *Jesus therefore knowing that they would come and **take** him by force to make him king, he departed again into a mountain himself alone.*

19. John 10

12 *But the hireling, who is not a shepherd, whose own the sheep are not, sees the wolf coming and leaves the sheep and flees; and the wolf **catches** them and scatters the sheep.*

20. John 10

28 *and I give unto them eternal life; and they shall never perish, neither shall anyone* ***pluck*** *them out of my hand.*

21. John 10

29 *My Father, who gave them to me, is greater than all; and no one is able to* ***pluck*** *them out of my Father's hand.*

22. Acts 8

39 *And when they were come up out of the water, the Spirit of the Lord* ***caught away*** *Philip, so that the eunuch saw him no more, and he went on his way rejoicing.*

23. 2 Corinthians 12

2 *I know a man in Christ who fourteen years ago (whether in the body, I cannot tell; or whether out of the body, I cannot tell; God knows) was* ***caught up*** *to the third heaven.*

24. 2 Corinthians 12

3 *And I know such a man (whether in the body, or out of the body, I cannot tell; God knows)*

4 *who was* ***caught up*** *into paradise and heard unspeakable words, which it is not lawful for a man to utter.*

25. 1 Thessalonians 4

> 17 *then we who are alive and remain shall be* ***caught up*** *together with them in the clouds, to meet the Lord in the air, and so shall we ever be with the Lord.*

26. Jude

> 23 *And others save with fear,* ***pulling*** *them out of the fire, hating even the garment defiled by the flesh.*

27. Revelation 12

> 5 *And she brought forth a man child, who was to rule all the Gentiles with a rod of iron; and her child was* ***caught up*** *unto God and to his throne.*

Webster's Unabridged Dictionary still lists the primary meaning of the word *rapture* as "a seizing by violence." (Yet they call this meaning obsolete.)

Clearly the meaning of the word *rapture* has changed in modern times. The original meaning of the word, as defined by its use in Scripture, will apply equally well to the removing of the wicked from among the righteous or to being caught up to meet the Lord in the air, being torn right out of our flesh-and-blood existence. Paul calls this a mystery (1 Corinthians 15:50-51). John records that *in the day of the voice of the seventh angel when he shall begin to sound the trumpet, the mystery of God shall be finished, as he did evangelize unto his slaves the prophets* (Revelation 10:7).

Meet the Author

Russell Stendal, a former hostage of Colombian rebels, is a lifelong missionary to that same group in the jungles of Colombia. He is an influential friend to military and government leaders in Colombia, Cuba, Mexico, Venezuela, and the United States. Russell's ministry shares the gospel via twelve radio stations, hundreds of thousands of Bibles, books, and movies distributed through airplane parachute drops, and numerous speaking engagements for groups of leaders, prisoners, and individuals. Russell goes wherever the Lord leads, whether it's to speak with a president or to go deep into the jungle to help an individual in trouble. He has witnessed thousands commit their lives to Christ.

Connect with the Author:
Website: www.cpcsociety.ca
Newsletter Signup: www.anekopress.com/stendal-newsletter

Russell and his coworkers have built dozens of radio stations in Latin America that concentrate a clear message on remote and dangerous areas where persecution of Christians is rampant. More than 120,000 Galcom solar-powered radios have been deployed to those being discipled. Most of the programming is in Spanish, but they also transmit in almost a dozen native languages where a great move of God is presently taking place. Russell preaches through the Bible, a chapter or so per message. More than 1,000 messages have been recorded and aired repeatedly. The chapters of this book are samples of these messages preached on the radio in the Colombian war zone about ten years ago. The key website is www.fuerzadepaz.com. Pray for Russell and his team as they expand Spanish-language radio coverage into places like Cuba, Venezuela, Mexico, and Central America.

Plans are in the works for new stations broadcasting in English that will provide coverage into Africa (where there are over 300 million English speakers) and possibly even into Asia and the Middle East. The first stage, as the programming is refined, will be Internet radio. After that, we want to begin shortwave radio transmission and distribution of Galcom radios in Africa and elsewhere as God opens the doors. The new radios have digital audio Bibles on board, and the goal is to move in the direction of digital shortwave transmissions within the next few years.

Connect with Russell's Ministry

Website

www.cpcsociety.ca

Receive newsletter updates

http://goo.gl/amBsCD

Buy books

http://amzn.to/1nPLcNL

God's Plan for Spiritual Battle
Victory over Sin, the World, and the Devil
Russell M. Stendal

I love a good fight. When unjustly attacked, I have learned to seek the guidance and leadership of the Holy Spirit and retaliate by Overcoming Evil with Good. There is a huge difference between a Peacemaker and a Pacifist!

This Battle Plan for spiritual warfare, gleaned from the life and message of Jesus, especially the Sermon on the Mount and the Beatitudes, was on my heart even before I was kidnapped by terrorists and held hostage under extreme conditions in 1983. Since then, thousands of missionaries, pastors, and other Christians have been kidnapped, murdered, or forced to flee from their places of ministry in rural Colombia. Had these Christians known and understood this battle plan for spiritual warfare, they could have been victorious instead of prematurely suffering defeat.

Many who did choose to remain in the path of ever present danger have rallied around this message. A thriving underground church is multiplying in a huge area (about the size of North Korea) in the south and east of Columbia where Bibles, church buildings, formal ministry, and even house meetings have been prohibited for more than 25 years.

Severe persecution in rural Colombia has actually served to bring real Christians together in deepening Christian relationships, identify the true church, and cleanse believers from corruption. This has been possible because of the remnant that has been chosen to fight the good fight of faith.

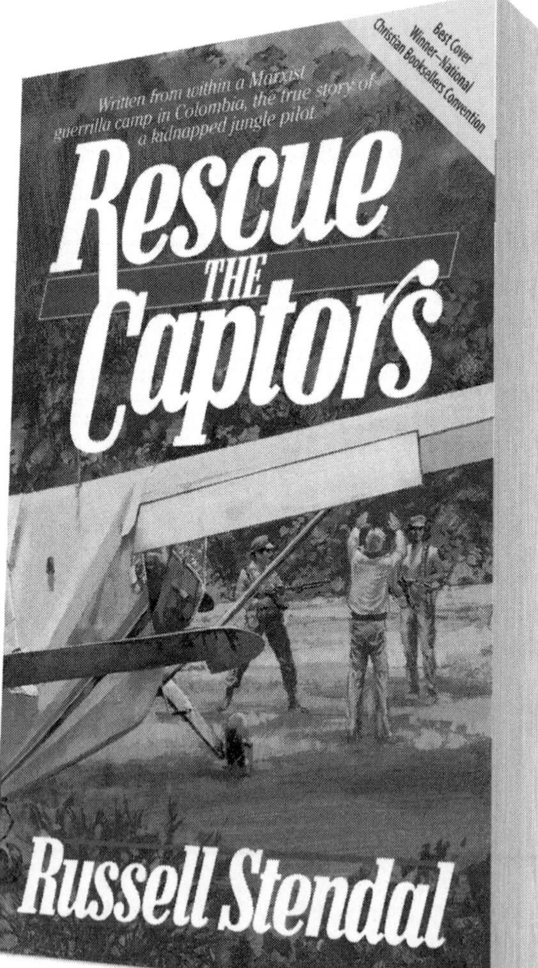
Best Cover
Winner—National
Christian Booksellers Convention
Written from within a Marxist
guerrilla camp in Colombia, the true story of
a kidnapped jungle pilot
Rescue
THE
Captors
Russell Stendal

Held at gunpoint deep in the jungle and with little else to occupy his time, Russell asked for some paper and began to write. He told the story of his life and kept a record of his experience in the guerrilla camp. His "book" became a bridge to the men who held him hostage and now serves as the basis for this incredible true story of how God's love penetrated a physical and ideological jungle.

I told my captors that they had two choices, either kill me, or let me go for whatever small amount my family could afford. One of the guerrillas turned and asked me if I was afraid to die. I replied that dying is obviously uncomfortable, but yes, I was prepared to die.

My captors tied me up and left the rope on day and night. They were seriously trying to completely break me psychologically and then brainwash me. Every day new things were done to alter me and work towards that goal. My captors started telling me scare stories. Some of these stories were about wild animals. They told me some of the wildest, hair-raising tales about lions and tigers that I have ever heard. These stories were designed both to intimidate me, reducing my ability to sleep, and to cause me to think twice before I decided to try to escape into the jungle again.

Available where books are sold

Made in the USA
Middletown, DE
28 August 2017